MASKS

By the same author

MASKS

Blackness, Race and the Imagination

ADAM LIVELY

Chatto & Windus
LONDON

First published 1998

2 4 6 8 10 9 7 5 3 1

First published in Great Britain in 1998 by
Chatto & Windus
Random House, 20 Vauxhall Bridge Road,
London SW1V 2SA

Random House Australia (Pty) Limited
20 Alfred Street, Milsons Point, Sydney,
New South Wales 2061, Australia

Random House New Zealand Limited
18 Poland Road, Glenfield,
Auckland 10, New Zealand

Random House South Africa (Pty) Limited
Endulini, 5A Jubilee Road, Parktown 2193, South Africa

Random House UK Limited Reg. No. 954009

**A CIP catalogue record for this book
is available from the British Library**

ISBN 0 7011 6244 9

Papers used by Random House UK Limited are natural,
recyclable products made from woods grown in sustainable forests.
The manufacturing processes conform to the environmental
regulations of the country of origin.

Typeset by Deltatype Limited, Birkenhead, Merseyside
Printed and bound in Great Britain by
Mackays of Chatham PLC

For my father

Contents

Contents

Introduction

On 12 October 1492 Christopher Columbus landed at Guanahani in the Bahamas. Over half a century earlier, in 1434, a Portuguese expedition had successfully rounded the long-feared Cape Bojador on the Atlantic coast of modern Morocco for the first time, thus laying open the sea route to sub-Saharan Africa. The cumulative impact of these events on the way that Europeans thought about themselves and the world around them was comparable to the shock at contacting intelligent life from another planet. For most people who participated in or knew about Europe's discoveries, everything they heard about these strange peoples confirmed an idea of European superiority and distinctive destiny. Yet even that formulation of superiority demanded a new structure of thought, a new way of assimilating puzzling questions and new realities. And for a few others, over time, these new horizons were to provide new perspectives on Europe itself – on its religion, its aesthetics, its social structures, its morality.

For Europeans of the fifteenth century, the Atlantic Ocean west of the Canaries and Azores was the outer space of its day. Indeed, Columbus's very mission to reach Asia by a westward route had a cosmological basis in the belief, drawn from the rediscovered writings of Ptolemy, that the world was a sphere suspended in the void. A century and a half after Columbus's voyage, America was still the great unknown. Cyrano de Bergerac's *Histoire comique des Etats et Empires de la Lune et du Soleil* was published in two parts in 1657 and 1662, and this early version of H. G. Wells begins with a landing in America, before the final ascent to the moon and sun is made. Extraterrestrial travel is projected imaginatively as an extension of the discoveries already being made in that New World beyond the empty ocean.

Sub-Saharan Africa, too, was an expanse of the unknown into which could be poured endless speculation. The anthropophagi and monstrous men envisaged in St Augustine's description of sub-Saharan Africa were not to be expelled until the Scotsman Mungo Park and other Europeans penetrated the interior of West Africa in the late eighteenth and early nineteenth centuries. It was not until Burton, Speke and Stanley made their expeditions into East and Central Africa in the nineteenth century that the legends dating from the writings of Ptolemy concerning the 'Mountains of the Moon' and the source of the Nile came to be confirmed. Even in the 1890s and 1900s, we find writers like Rider Haggard and John Buchan perpetuating fanciful myths such as the one of a white people, or at least a white ruler, at the heart of Africa. These were the *X Files* of their day.

The imagination can be an instigator of historical change; it was the speculation as to what might lie beyond the limits of the known that spurred Columbus to make that first voyage across the Atlantic. But the imagination can also be a way of coping with change, of assimilating it to what is already known. From the 'fantastic voyage' narratives of the seventeenth and eighteenth centuries, through the exotic imperial romances of the nineteenth, and up to the science fiction of the twentieth century, imaginative literature has been a means – like any mythology – of mediating between the domestic and that which lies at and beyond the limits of knowledge.

In 1441 a small ship under the command of Autan Goncalvez sailed from Portugal and, having rounded Cape Bojador, continued south until it put ashore on the seaboard of the Western Sahara. Goncalvez conceived the idea of pleasing his master, Prince Henry of Portugal, by capturing and bringing back examples of the local inhabitants. A party of men went ashore, and after coming across footprints among the sand dunes, 'they saw a naked man following a camel, with two assegais in his hand'. The man ran away, 'but Affonso Goterres wounded him with a javelin, and this put the

Moor in such fear that he threw down his arms like a beaten man'. Along with a 'Black Moress' discovered soon afterwards, he was captured and taken back to Portugal. About ten million more were to follow him, transported across the Atlantic to the sugar, cotton and tobacco plantations of the New World.

The Atlantic slave trade and European imperialism brought about a transformation of the Western world. They financed and provided markets for the Industrial Revolution. In America a bloody civil war was fought on the issue of slavery, without resolving the basic issue of racial inequality. It remains unresolved. In Europe the demographic backwash of Empire brought immigrants to the major cities. That which had been merely exotic and alien was now domestic, living next door. And it is this close experience of radical differences – differences of culture, manners, physical appearance – that has had such a profound impact on Western culture. It would be impossible, for example, to imagine modern music or dance without the central role of the African-American as icon and instigator.

This experience of radical cultural difference has spawned a vast discourse of race, an ongoing cultural and scientific debate as to what, if anything, race signifies. One purpose of this book is to show how central that debate has been to modern thought and sensibilities. In the eighteenth and nineteenth centuries, race was crucial to the gradual erosion of the intellectual authority of Christianity. Biblical chronology, the truth of Genesis, human origins – all these were issues to which the existence of racial difference seemed to carry a key. When, in the mid-nineteenth century, Darwin and his followers began applying the theory of evolution to humans, it was to racial difference that they returned again and again for inspiration, evidence and example. More recently, the vogue for genetic determinism has shown that 'racial science' was not necessarily discredited for ever by the Nazis.

But racial discourse goes far beyond the discredited 'theories of race' arraigned like so many dusty exhibits in a Museum of Defunct Anthropology. From the 1770s onwards, slavery was a moral and political issue of burning importance, and discussion and depiction of slavery turned as often as not on race. Race was a central element in the stream of poetry, prose and plays spawned by the abolition movement, much of it inspired by a renascent evangelical Christianity. In Chapter 2, I attempt to identify the aesthetic that lay behind this imaginative abolitionist literature, and to show how it – like the new 'racial science' of anthropology – drew on representations of racial difference dating back to the Middle Ages and beyond. In the late nineteenth century, similarly, race was central to debates about Empire, and Chapter 4 is concerned to show how at the turn of the century an undercurrent of doubt and pessimism concerning the future of Europe's colonies – and indeed of Europe itself – found imaginative expression in gothic images of racial apocalypse, images that drew on an existing pool of associations.

The effect of this, I hope, is to challenge the idea that racial prejudice can be attributed solely to bad science. There is a certain tradition of liberal writing about race that encourages this view, that tells a history of 'racism' in terms of a single line back through the Nazis and the eugenics movement of the early part of this century to the 'racial scientists' of the eighteenth and nineteenth centuries. I have tried to avoid using the term 'racism', in the belief that racial attitudes are too complex, too nuanced, and too embedded in particular historical modes of expression, always to be reduced to a discrete ideology – akin to 'socialism' or 'fascism' – with its own intellectual and institutional history. Telling the history of racial attitudes in terms of goodies and baddies, of racists and anti-racists, is a way of ignoring plurality and ambiguity, of seeing the world in black and white. In that respect it is a part of the problem rather than a part of the solution.

In particular, I hope to show how the liberal tradition, by virtue of its origins in the anti-slavery movements of the eighteenth and nineteenth centuries, is by no means 'colour-blind'. Imaginative writers coming out of the liberal tradition – Richard Wright, James Baldwin, Norman Mailer, John Updike and others – use a language of racial depiction and signification that has its roots, ultimately, in that of the evangelical abolitionists. This historical weight can be seen clearly in, for example, Baldwin's love/hate relationship with the quintessential abolitionist novel *Uncle Tom's Cabin*. *Rabbit*

Redux, Updike's classic State-of-the-Union novel of the Sixties, self-consciously deploys antique racial attitudes to Grand Guignol effect.

Writers like these force to the surface the subliminal world-view of the liberal tradition. In political discourse race is fiercely repressed, and denied anxieties can only be expressed in the form of coded (but nevertheless understood) references to 'crime' or 'community'. Liberal theorists from John Locke to John Rawls have tended to use a language of pure legalism, basing political authority on rules of procedure designed to ensure equity and fairness between individuals. It is a way of looking at the world that tends to sweep history and culture to one side, to resist attempts to contextualise. Does it matter that Locke was a shareholder in the Royal African Company and thus, by proxy at least, a slave-owner? For his ideas, many liberals would argue, it does not.

Although some radicals called for a return to Africa, most black American literature of the eighteenth and nineteenth centuries was written from within, or in association with, the abolitionist movement. It charges whites with hypocrisy, with not applying their own standards to themselves, and exhorts its own people to a racial 'uplift' that would raise blacks by their bootstraps to a level of civilisation. (Booker T. Washington's autobiographical *Up from Slavery* (1901), with its advocacy of vigorous, uncomplaining self-help, was the culmination of this way of thinking.) But the extraordinarily rich popular culture of slaves in the American South – which has been painstakingly and brilliantly reconstructed by modern American historians such as Eugene Genovese, Lawrence Levine and Sterling Stuckey – displayed a very different aesthetic and a very different attitude towards whites.

This was an illiterate culture, a culture of song, dance and anecdotal folk tale, but it was no less capable for that of attacking and subverting white values. In the face of white surveillance, blacks' principal weapon in this cultural war was humour, and the indirection allowed by disguise or mask. One could not imagine anything less like a homily for racial self-improvement than the acidly funny, bleakly amoral 'Brer Rabbit' stories. And even in the expression of their Christianity, the slaves discovered, in the spirituals, a distinctive aesthetic and even a means of political expression. As Eugene Genovese has written: 'The black variant of Christianity laid the foundations of protonationalist consciousness and at the same time stretched a universalist offer of forgiveness and ultimate reconciliation to white America.'[1] This rich rural culture – the culture of spirituals, minstrelsy and blues songs – was to survive the Civil War and Reconstruction into the twentieth century. The mass migration of Southern blacks to Northern cities such as New York and Chicago in the years around the First World War, and the opening up of the South itself through improved transport and electrification, made it available to a wider, national audience. In the 1900s black intellectuals like W. E. B. Du Bois and James Weldon Johnson began drawing attention to this wonderful legacy, and for such figures of the Harlem Renaissance as Langston Hughes and Zora Neale Hurston the return to folk roots was a principal theme of their art.

The 1920s was the period when this culture exploded into mass consciousness, challenging an older and more decorous literary culture. In New York, already a city of enormous cultural variety, the expanding population of Harlem – 'Black Manhattan', in James Weldon Johnson's phrase – came into contact with the modern media of commercial publishing and radio. Harlem became a Mecca for black musicians, dancers, actors, writers. Trumpeter Cootie Williams, born in Alabama, recalled: 'When I used to say my prayers at night, I used to say "Dear Lord, please hurry up and let me grow up so I can get to New York."'[1] For Edward 'Duke' Ellington, who moved to New York permanently in 1923, the city was 'a dream of a song, a feeling of aliveness, a rush and flow of vitality that pulses like the giant heartbeat of humanity. The whole world revolves around New York...'[2] The result of this cultural ferment was the Harlem Renaissance, the first self-consciously 'black' artistic movement.

[1] Quoted in Sterling Stuckey, Slave Culture: Nationalist Theory and the Foundations of Black America (Oxford University Press, 1987), p. 30.
[2] Quoted in Burton W. Peretti, The Creation of Jazz: Music, Race and Culture in Urban America (University of Illinois Press, Urbana, 1992), p. 47.

However much participants in the Renaissance may have differed as to how to achieve this end, it was an artistic movement held together by the desire, at least, not to emulate white models but to discover its own values. And Harlem was not alone. In the Caribbean – in Spanish-speaking Cuba and French-speaking Haiti and Martinique – writers were seeking an identity, an authenticity, a *negrismo* or *négritude*, free of white taint. But the situation is complicated by the fact that – notably in the case of Cuba – many of these advocates of a black aesthetic were themselves white. Though it was political at its core, the Harlem Renaissance and the other black arts movements of the 1920s blurred at the edges into a more generalised modernist interest in the black not just for what he was – the culture, language, approach to life that he brought – but for what he (or sometimes she) was thought to represent. The 1920s saw the birth of the idea of blacks as the inside outsiders of modern life, the ones who are both forced to be a part of the machine and at the same time represent a radical alternative to it. And that alternative was the primitive, the ancient, the endlessly fertile. At the world-famous Cotton Club in Harlem, Duke Ellington played 'jungle music'. When Darius Milhaud came to compose a ballet on the subject of *La Création du monde* in 1923, it was to the idiom of American jazz, which he had heard at first hand in Harlem, that he turned to generate an atmosphere of atavism. On a wider canvas, Jean Toomer's *Cane* (1923), like a number of books by white writers of the time, sought in the folk culture of the rural South an authenticity and immediacy that they could not find in urban living. And for the image of the black as outsider one has to look no further than Eugene O'Neill's startlingly expressionistic play *The Emperor Jones*, premiered in 1920, which has its hero pursued through a jungle by the relentlessly machine-like, accelerating beat of drums. The phrase 'urban jungle' may not have had its origins in 1920s New York – Upton Sinclair's *The Jungle* (1906) was set in the immigrant slums of Chicago – but it captures perfectly the mood of the age.

A largely improvised music, jazz has always leant on wit, on the individual musician's dialogue with the audience and that audience's sense of convention and desire. Parody, snatches of formulaic material turned upside down, a sense of style – all these are part of the dialogue. It is ironic that jazz has been stereotyped as a music of spontaneity and authenticity, for in fact it is much more self-conscious and even – if it weren't also so good to dance to – cerebral than the nineteenth-century music of salon and concert hall, the music of Mendelssohn, say, or Brahms – which comes drenched in emotional sincerity. It is this quality of wit, of light rhythms and obliqueness, that attracted so many European composers of the first half of this century, from Debussy and Ravel to Shostakovich and Michael Tippett.

In his essay on Charlie Parker, Ralph Ellison describes the saxophonist as 'a mocking bird', the bird that imitates others. Jazz is a music of disguises, of masks. It is a music that takes the form of a Broadway show-tune and blows it apart from the inside, a music that conducts its polyphonic conversation with itself in riffs and tags. For the first half of this century, it was the music that symbolised above any other the modern, the urban. And it also represented youth, and potential rebellion. After the first flush of liberalism following the Revolution, jazz was banned in the Soviet bloc. This language of subversion and irony can be heard, too, in some of the best black American literature of the century, in Langston Hughes's throwaway blues lyrics, in Ralph Ellison's surreally comic *Invisible Man* and in the contemporary anarchic satire of Ishmael Reed. The African-American critic Henry Louis Gates, under the influence of post-structuralism, has evolved a theory that the 'blackness' of black literature consists precisely in this flexible aesthetic, this prizing of the ability to play to a particular situation. Like Ralph Ellison, he traces the use of parody and rhetorical dexterity to such popular games of ritualised mockery as 'the dozens'. He has even used this as an argument in court to defend a rap group accused of obscenity.

This fluidity of identity is the result of a situation in which black Americans were forced by white society to play a part, that of subservient Negro. Right back to the Brer Rabbit stories and the slave narratives, we see dissimulation prized as an essential tool of survival. There is clearly scope for tragedy here, the tears of a clown, rather than just comedy. Throughout the twentieth century we find the figure of the tragic black hero, the man (it is nearly always a man) forced to fulfil a destiny not of his choosing. Sometimes, as in James Baldwin's *Another Country* (1962) and John Clellon Holmes's classic Beat novel, *The Horn* (1958), the results owe much to the sentimentality of Christian and liberal traditions. But already in the 1920s Eugene O'Neill was applying an older, pagan conception of tragedy to the racial situation in America. Jim and Ella, the inter-racial couple whose desperate, Strindbergian relationship is the focus of *All God's Chillun Got Wings* (1924), are neither of them passive or innocent victims. They throw themselves into their downfall, exalting it and calling it love.

Later in the century, influenced by surrealism and existentialism, we find writers outside the United States looking to the black as the figure forced to act out some apocalyptic drama at the heart of modern society. For Aimé Césaire, the absolute degradation and humiliation of the Martinicans is prelude to a revolutionary liberation both political and aesthetic. When, in *What Is Literature?* (1947), Jean-Paul Sartre issued his dictum that it was no longer possible to write *engagé* poetry, he excepted blacks on the grounds that, because of the intimate totalitarianism of racial oppression, blacks were able to express themselves authentically in a way that was both subjective and engaged with their objective situation. Jean Genet was drawn to blacks (late in life he became a public supporter of the Black Panthers) because they seemed to him to be people, like the prisoners and criminals of his most famous books, who acted out a part, a destiny, repressed by mainstream society. *Les Nègres* (1958), like *All God's Chillun Got Wings*, makes prominent use of masks to emphasise the ritualistic, even sacrificial element of racial confrontation.

Most of Part Two is concerned with these manifestations of black presence at the heart of modernism. The characteristic tone of modernism – relativistic, ironic, pluralistic and perpetually questioning – is inconceivable without that presence. The last chapter is concerned with the representation of race in some post–Second World War American novels, for it is here that we can see this modernist, tragic or parodic vision of the black come into conflict with the sentimental vision that dates back through

Victorianism to the culture of abolitionism. In some, such as John Updike's *Rabbit Redux* (1971), with its mixture of gothic Grand Guignol and realism, the tension is felt within a single book. In others, such as Jewish writer Bernard Malamud's *The Tenants* (1971), the author's own experience as a member of an ethnically marginal group may have been instrumental in enabling him to throw the narrative wholesale, and to bleakly comic effect, into the business of role-playing and ritual.

If Part Two is about the contribution that blacks and the idea of blackness have played in modernism, Part One is concerned with the key role that questions of race played in creating the conditions – especially as regards the loss of Christianity's position of intellectual and cultural hegemony – that made modernism possible. To understand the origins of this black modernism, one must go back to the early eighteenth century, to a time when the first 'scientific' investigations of racial difference were being conducted.

Part One

1

The Invention of Race

The modern idea of race as a scientific or pseudo-scientific means of classifying the human population by physical type was invented in the eighteenth century. The 'racial science' of the late nineteenth and twentieth centuries incorporated a vulgar Darwinism, envisaging a struggle for survival between the races, but in essence it was based on the eighteenth-century taxonomists who extended the classification of the natural world, begun earlier by Georges-Louis Leclerc, comte de Buffon and Carl Linnaeus, to mankind itself. This naturalisation of mankind, the placing of mankind within a purely natural order of things, was a step with profound implications for religion. For if humans were to be regarded as just another animal, to be classified and subdivided like any other animal, then what is left of mankind's special relationship with God? This was the challenge that the eighteenth-century naturalists posed for Christianity.

We more usually associate that kind of challenge with the impact of Darwinism, but the ground for the mid-nineteenth-century debates over apes and angels was being broken earlier by those who sought to grade humans by purely natural, physical criteria. At its extreme, this classificatory project led to 'polygenism', the belief that the races had different origins and were thus, in effect, different species. Polygenism was an extremely radical position to take in the eighteenth century, because it clashed with a central tenet of biblical Christianity – the belief that all humans are descended from Adam and Eve. Some polygenists, like the late eighteenth-century apologist for slavery Edward Long, were motivated by a visceral hatred of Negroes and a desire to prove whites' essential superiority. Others – such as Voltaire, who opposed slavery – seem to have been drawn to polygenism precisely because it represents such a radical challenge to Christianity. Indeed, given the lack of a theory of evolution to explain how the variety of existing human types could have descended from a single pair, the polygenist position was, for its time, the more rational. But monogenism, bolstered by a revived evangelical Christianity in England and America in the late eighteenth and early nineteenth centuries, remained the prevailing view. Even in the American South, the polygenist views of Samuel Morton and his 'American School' of anthropology failed to gain popular support because of the association of polygenism with atheism. But if the monogenists had the Bible on their side, they were nevertheless forced to account for those physical differences between humans that were being catalogued. In their unconvincing attempts to do so can be seen starkly the unsettling questions that race posed for Christianity.

Of course, Europeans had long been aware of the varieties of human type. While the philosophical basis and implications of racial classification were new, the actual attributes ascribed to different groups were as often as not traditional. When it came to race, the new language of science and rationalism coexisted with ancient prejudices and folkloric fantasy. To a large extent, in inventing the idea of race, the naturalists of the eighteenth century were putting old wine into new bottles. To understand modern racialism, one has to go back to these earlier representations of racial difference.

Before the eighteenth century, it is more accurate to speak not of 'racialism', in the sense of a worked-through ideology, but of a primitive European colour prejudice that equated blackness with ugliness, evil, danger and sexual transgression. One only has to look up 'black' in the *Oxford English Dictionary* to see the range of such associations as they were established by the sixteenth century; the word is used as a synonym for, among other things, malignant, sinister, foul, dismal, etc. Most tellingly, 'black man' could mean either a Negro or the Devil. These figurative meanings of blackness are a recurring theme in the language of Shakespeare's *Othello*, used dramatically both to present and to subvert the well-established stage stereotype of the villainous Moor.

The presence of 'Moors' and the practice of 'blacking up' in the Elizabethan theatre are but part of a broader and older folk tradition that testifies to an African presence at the very roots of European culture. A central feature of the English mummers' play, which had its origins in village festivals marking the stages of the agricultural year, was the enactment by men with blackened faces of a ritual battle in which St George slays an infidel opponent. These elements of blacking up and ritual battle were originally shared with the morris (or 'Moorish') dance. In *The Morris Book* (1907), which did so much to revive interest in morris dancing in the twentieth century, Cecil Sharp acknowledges the 'Moorish' origin of this most English of rural traditions, while at the same time seeking to distance it from these origins and give it a kind of retrospective Anglo-Saxon pedigree: '[T]he weight of testimony must be held to show Morocco as the fount and origin, no matter if the genius of our own folk – so very far removed from anything native to Africa – has, in the process of the centuries, altered until it bears, in spirit, little resemblance to the parent stock.' Morris dancing, Sharp continues, 'is become as English as fisticuffs ... a perfect expression in rhythm and movement of the English character'.

In fact, as Cecil Sharp was aware, the English morris dance was only one manifestation of a much more cosmopolitan phenomenon, with versions of the 'morisca' being found throughout Europe (except for Scandinavia) and later in Central America and the Caribbean. The Portuguese *mouriscada*, the Dalmatian *moreska*, the German *Moriskentanz*, the Austrian *Perchten*, the Romanian *calusari*, and the Spanish *Moros y Christianos* (which is still performed in Mexico) shared the elements of plumed hats, breeches with bells and ribbons, and the carrying of battle emblems – sword, staff, trident or handkerchief. The blacking up of the dancers, which has died out in the surviving forms, may in fact originally have had its roots in the practice of smearing ash on the face for rituals, and the elements of battle mime may have originated in vegetation symbolism (a battle of the seasons). But it is clear that at least by the sixteenth century the dances had acquired strong racial and religious connotations, as reflected in their names.

Another popular form that would seem to have drawn on common associations of blackness is the masked Harlequin of the *commedia dell'arte*. The French Harlequin, or Italian Arlecchino, may have had its origins in the late Middle Ages as a devilish figure. In *Le Jeu de la Feuillée* (c. 1262) by Adam de la Halle, a Harlequin procession passes by at night with the noise of bells, 'leaving on stage Croquesnot, a devil with a shaggy headdress ... to conduct the fairy Morgue as a bride to his master Hellequin, *le gringeur prinche qui soit en faerie* [the grinning prince in fairyland]'. Historians have also drawn parallels between the figure of Harlequin and the phallaphores of the ancient world, performers who wore giant phalluses and 'besmeared their countenances with soot ... or covered their faces with papyrus bark ... to represent foreign slaves'. Some representations of Harlequin show him wearing a similar giant phallus. In the *commedia dell'arte* as it emerged in the mid-sixteenth century and was to dominate European popular theatre for the next two hundred years, the black-masked Harlequin is, along with Pulchinella, the principal *zanno* or buffoon character. In many respects he is the archetypal sly and lazy servant, though it was also a role that demanded acrobatic clowning. Marmontel, writing in the *Encyclopédie* in 1787, gives an outline of Harlequin's main characteristics, as well as pointing to the African influence that is reflected in the sometimes Negroid features of contemporary visual depictions:

> It is likely that an African slave was the original model for this role. His character is a mixture of ignorance, naïveté, high spirits, stupidity and grace. He is like a sketch of a man, a great child who has flashes of reason and intelligence and in all of whose capers and awkwardness there is something sharp and amusing. The ideal Harlequin has the suppleness, agility and grace of a young cat, along with a superficial coarseness that renders his actions more amusing; his role is that of lackey – patient, faithful, credulous, greedy, always in love, always getting into

scrapes either on his master's account or on his own, distressing and consoling himself with the readiness of a child, one whose sorrows are as amusing as his joys.

By the time Marmontel was writing, the *commedia dell'arte* was already in decline as a vital, popular form with the increasing predominance of written scripts and naturalistic settings. But it survived long enough into the nineteenth century to overlap with another popular theatrical form – the American minstrel show – that was to present a much more degraded and overtly Negroid buffoon figure. In 1836 we find an English harlequinade being performed under the title *Cowardy, Cowardy, Custard; or Harlequin Jim Crow and the Magic Mustard Pot.*

The minstrel show was to be the most popular theatrical form in nineteenth-century America. But for all its distinctively American qualities, it should be seen in the context of the older European traditions of racial parody, stereotyping and ritualised insult. In these traditions we find the origins of the modern ethnic joke. And the use of humour demonstrates the potency of the anxieties and fears involved. As with all humour, but especially with jokes about sex, death or race, the amount of laughter is proportional to the strength of the taboo, the blockage to expression, that is being broken. Jokes are a serious matter. In these popular European traditions, we find blackness asssociated with evil, with danger, and with gross or transgressive sexuality. How did these powerful anxieties find their sublimation in the black racial mask, in the morris dance and the minstrel show? Why was blackness so bad?

One fear whose power it is easy to forget in the age of the electric light bulb is that of the dark, of the immensity of night, of the unknown. By the sixteenth century it had become a standard literary trope to associate the darkness of Negroes with the darkness of night. In *Romeo and Juliet* Act I scene 5 Shakespeare gives this association a romantic sheen:

> It seems she hangs upon the cheek of night
> Like a rich jewel in an Ethiop's ear.

Edmund Burke, in his *A Philosophical Enquiry into the Origin of*

Our Ideas of the Sublime and the Beautiful (1756), equates darkness with the sublime (i.e., in the precise eighteenth-century use of the term, with that which induces the strongest emotions of terror) and lightness with beauty ('the colours of beautiful bodies must not be dusky or muddy, but clean and fair'). That Burke intended his views on colour to apply to human complexion is clear from the passage where he attempts to refute John Locke's argument that ideas associating darkness with terror are culturally acquired rather than innate. Burke produces the following as proof that 'darkness [is] terrible to its own nature':

> Mr. Cheselden has given us a very curious story of a boy, who had been born blind, and continued so until he was thirteen or fourteen years old; he was then couched for a cataract, by which operation he received his sight. Among many remarkable particulars that attended his first perceptions and judgments on visual objects, Cheselden tells us, that the first time the boy saw a black object, it gave him great uneasiness; and that some time after, upon accidentally seeing a negro woman, he was struck with great horror at the sight. The horror, in this case, can scarcely be supposed to arise from any association.

The implications of Burke's argument can be seen if we carry out the thought-experiment of imagining that the child who gains his sight is himself a Negro. If, as Burke wants to argue, the equation of dark colours with terror is 'an association which takes in all mankind', then either Negroes are excluded from humanity, or the Negro boy must feel a profound horror at his own body. One could not meet a starker example of colour prejudice 'universalised'.

Much more psychologically complex, and perhaps more important, than the association with the dangers of night, is the association with sin. And, particularly in the Protestant imagination, there is the allied association with dirt, with filth and excrement. 'The Devil', writes Luther, 'does not come in his filthy black colours, but slinks around like a snake, and dresses himself up as pretty as may be.' At other times Luther waxes positively lyrical on the connections between spiritual and physical uncleanliness:

> The members of the body must not wait till filth says and decrees whether the body is healthy or not. We are determined to learn this from the members themselves and not from the urine, excrement and filth. In the same way we shall not wait for the Pope and bishops in Council to say: This is right. For they are no part of the body, or clean and healthy members and veritable ordure, for they persecute the true Evangel, well knowing it to be the word of God. Therefore we can see they are but filth, stench and limbs of Satan.

Later, we shall see how engrained the association of blackness with sin was even for those who saw themselves as friends of the Negro.

Then there is the association of blackness with sexuality, and especially with the image of the phallus. Twentieth-century psychologists have pointed out that the symbol of the phallus is not necessarily primarily sexual in intent, but may express deeper ideas of order, boundaries and limits. This is how Darian Leader expresses it in his book *Why do women write more letters than they post?*:

> The phallus is not the organ or the symbol of fertility but the symbol of a register beyond the real side of the copulation. We can see this in the use of the phallus in classical cultures: rather than being placed in the bedroom or in the fields to promote fertility, they are found at crossroads and limit points, marking boundaries. It is thus linked less to growth and plenty than to symbolic limits.

Given this, it is easy to see how the image of the phallus might attach itself to an outsider group, a group marked out physically as different. Their sexuality marks out the limits of what is permissible. Sexuality itself becomes the desire for order and boundaries. The phallus is a symbol both of that order and of the anarchy and otherness that threaten to destroy it.

So the important point about the association of blackness with sexuality in the European mind is that it is a *transgressive* sexuality. Hence the continuing mixture of fascination and taboo that surrounds the sexuality of black people in the white mind. Hollywood still cannot bring itself to portray black people in sexual relationships with each other.

The importance of transgression for the association of blackness with sexuality can be seen most clearly in the myth of the Hamite curse, which was the most important of these folkloric, pre-modern representations of blackness. Well into the nineteenth century, in fact, one finds plenty of references to blacks as 'Hamitic', to the 'curse of Ham' and to Negroes as 'hewers of wood and drawers of water'. In Genesis 9, after the Flood, Noah gets drunk and falls asleep naked in his tent. The middle one of his three sons, Ham (or 'Cham') comes into the tent and sees his father:

> When Ham, father of Canaan, saw his father naked, he told his two brothers outside. So Shem and Japheth took a cloak, put it on their shoulders and walked backwards, and so covered their father's naked body; their faces were turned the other way, so that they did not see their father naked. When Noah woke from his drunken sleep, he learnt what his youngest son had done to him, and said:
> 'Cursed be Canaan,
> Slave of slaves,
> Shall he be to his brothers.' (Genesis 9: 22–5)

The most striking features of this strange passage – leaving aside the oddity that in the original it is Ham's son Canaan who is punished, rather than Ham himself – are the element of sexual transgression in Ham's crime and the fact that blackness is nowhere mentioned in the original as part of the 'curse' put on Canaan and his descendants. The Hamite curse was discussed by the Church Fathers such as St Jerome and St Augustine without any mention of Negroes. Indeed, Augustine gives the passage an entirely allegorical interpretation, with Noah's drunkenness sym-bolising the passion of Christ and Ham representing those who proclaim themselves Christian but bring dishonour on Christ by their actions.

Throughout the Middle Ages, the three orders of society were often explained with reference to descent from Noah's sons, Japheth being the father of the nobles, Shem the father of the clerks and Ham the father of the serfs. The origins of the idea – which was current into the nineteenth century – that blackness was a specific part of the Hamite curse are extremely obscure. There is some evidence that it may have had its roots in early Jewish writings. The Hebrew *Ham* has connotations of 'dark' and 'hot', and Talmudic and Midrashic sources contain suggestions that 'Ham was smitten in his skin' and that Noah told Ham 'your seed will be ugly and dark-skinned'. This Judaic myth of the curse of Ham gained wide currency among Christians in the sixteenth century, the century that saw both the first great explosion of European overseas exploration and a revival of interest in Jewish writings through humanist scholarship. In 1577, for example, in the writings of the Elizabethan adventurer George Best, we find the idea that blackness is part of the curse firmly established, along with other embellishments that emphasise the element of sexual transgression:

[Noah and his sons and their wives were white and] by course of nature should have begotten ... white children. But the envie of our great and continuall enemie the wicked Spirite is such, that as hee could not suffer our olde father Adam to live in the felicite and Angelike state wherein he was first created ... so againe, finding at this flood none but a father and three sons living, hee so caused one of them to disobey his fathers commandment, that after him all his posteritie should be accursed ... [Noah commanded his sons that] while they remained in the Arke, they should use continencie, and abstaine from carnall copulation with their wives: ... which good instructions and exhortations notwithstanding his wicked sonne Cham disobeyed ... [to punish which, God willed that] a sonne should bee born whose name was Chus [Canaan], who not onely it selfe, but all his posteritie after him should bee so blacke and lothsome, that it might remain a spectacle of disobedience to all the worlde. And of this blacke and cursed Chus came all those black Moores which are in Africa.

The first detailed modern discussion of the causes of Negroes' blackness comes in a remarkable and typically elegant essay by Sir Thomas Browne, part of his monumental collection *Pseudoxia Epidemica* or *Vulgar Errors* (first edition 1646). In 'Of the Blackness of Negroes' he begins by pointing out how little in general is understood of the causes of colour differences in nature, of why grass should be green and flowers blue or purple or yellow –

> And lastly, why some men, yea and they a mighty and considerable part of mankind, should first acquire and still retain the gloss and tincture of blackness? Which whoever strictly enquires, shall find no less of darkness in the cause, than in the effect itself; there arising unto examination no such satisfactory and unquarrelable reasons, as may confirm the causes generally received; which are but two in number. The heat and scorch of the sun; or the curse of God on Cham and his posterity.

Browne first refutes the Hamite curse on purely biblical, textual grounds, but then goes on to question the whole idea that blackness should necessarily be seen as ugly or a curse. The relativism and open-endedness of his argument that notions of beauty are inherently subjective was rare in its day, but were to grow even rarer as systems of racial classification and distinction hardened during the course of the eighteenth century:

> Whereas men affirm this colour [black] was a Curse, I cannot make out the propriety of that name, it neither seeming so to them, nor reasonable unto us; for they take so much content therein, that they esteem deformity by other colours, describing the Devil, and terrible objects, white ... For Beauty is determined by opinion, and seems to have no essence that holds one notion with all; that seeming beauteous unto one, which hath no favour with another; and that unto one every one, according as custom hath made it natural, or sympathy and conformity of minds shall make it seem more agreeable. Thus

flat noses seem comely unto the Moor, an Aquiline or hawked one unto the *Persian*, a large and prominent nose unto the Romane; but none of these is acceptable in our opinion.

The question of the causes and origins of the physical differences between races was one of great importance to thinkers of the late seventeenth and early eighteenth centuries. A hundred years later, such questions would be intimately bound up with questions of the Negro's mental and moral character, and with arguments concerning the ethics of slavery. But until the mid-eighteenth century, slavery as an institution was hardly even questioned. (Montesquieu's celebrated attack on it in *De l'esprit des lois* was not published until 1748.) The interest in the question of race was scientific and philosophical rather than overtly moral or political. At this earlier period it is still appropriate to talk of a kind of primitive colour prejudice rather than racialism – an attitude that drew on a deep-seated cultural and religious aversion to the colour black, without it being systematised into a belief that blackness signified an innate and irrevocable separation from the rest of mankind. In the *Athenian Oracle* of 1704 – an extremely popular series of 'Notes and Queries' on every conceivable topic of the day – we find the following answer given to the question 'whether Negroes shall rise ... at the Last Day?':

The Pinch of the Question only lies – whether *White* or *Black* is the *better Colour*? For the Negroes won't be persuaded but that their Jett is finer and more beautiful than our Alabaster. – If we Paint the Devil black, they are even with us, for they Paint him *white*, and no doubt are as much in the right on't as we; none amongst them, who are legitimate, being born white, but such as a kind of *Leprous Persons* ... But after all, unless we are very partial, there is something natural in't. Black is the Colour of Night, Frightful, Dark and Horrid; but white of the Day and Light, refreshing and lovely. Taking then this Blackness of the Negro to be an accidental Imperfection ... I conclude thence, that he shall not arise with that Complexion, but leave it behind him in the Darkness of the Grave, exchanging it for a brighter and better, at his return again into the World.

After venturing towards a relativist position, the writer veers back to the 'natural' negative associations of blackness. Colour, however, is an 'accidental' rather than 'essential' quality. The same distinction is made in answer to a later question in the *Athenian Oracle* as to whether the 'Soul of Woman [is] inferior to the Soul of Man'. All souls are equal – 'As for *Essential* difference, there can be none, for then they must be perfectly *distinct Creatures*' – and at the Resurrection 'there will be nothing of Sex'. The case of blackness, however, is significantly different. It is not that colour disappears or becomes irrelevant at death. It is, rather, that Negroes will become white.

Blake expresses the same idea in 'The Little Black Boy', one of his *Songs of Innocence* (1789):

> My mother bore me in the southern wild,
> And I am black, but O! my soul is white.

Blake has his little black boy imagine meeting a 'little English boy' in heaven. Although there is a hint that the English boy will also lose his colour ('When I from black and he from white cloud free, / And round the tent of God like lambs we joy'), the final image of the poem is of the black boy's identification with the white boy:

> And then I'll stand and stroke his silver hair,
> And be like him, and he will then love me.

Blake's poem is part of a Christian tradition, existing alongside that of the Hamite curse, that pictured the Negro's blackness as the 'accidental' cloak (albeit an ugly one, and one perhaps with its own connotations of sinfulness) for a white soul. Origen, for example, drew a distinction between the 'natural' blackness of the Ethiopian and a blackness of the soul, which is caused by moral neglect. Such a dichotomy could clearly be allied with the idea of baptism as a washing away of sins. Richard Crashaw, the English Catholic poet, does so in his 'On the Baptized Aethiopian' from *Steps to the Temple* (1646), referring also to an ancient proverb – 'To wash an Ethiopian white', meaning to attempt the impossible:

> Let it no longer be a forlorne hope

> To wash an Aethiope:
> He's washt, his gloomy skin a peaceful shade,
>   For his white soule is made:
> And now, I doubt not, the Eternall Dove,
>   A black-fac'd house will love.

If blackness was merely an accidental quality, rather than the outward, visible sign of an innate and irredeemable fault – as in the myth of the Hamite curse – then that blackness must have some 'accidental' cause of its own. This is the first of Sir Thomas Browne's 'causes generally received; ... The heat and scorch of the sun'. This environmentalist theory of the origin of blackness was, according to Browne, the one 'generally received by the Ancients'. According to Isidore of Seville (d. 636), 'Ethiopia is so called from the colour of its people, who are scorched by the nearness of the sun. The colour of the people betrays the sun's intensity, for there is never-ending heat there.' Ben Jonson's *The Masque of Blackness*, mounted at court in 1605 with sumptuous set designs by Inigo Jones, presents a highly stylised version of the environmentalist theory, its language relishing the opportunity for contrasts of light and darkness:

> Sound, sound aloud
> The welcome of the orient flood,
>   Into the West;
> Fair Niger, son to great Oceanus,
>   Now honour'd thus,
> With all his beauteous race:
> Who, though but black in face,
>   Yet are they bright,
>   And full of life and light.
>   To prove that beauty best,
> Which not the colour, but the feature
>   Assures unto the creature.

Following this opening song, the personification of the river Niger tells how the Negresses of this land ('my daughters ... the first form'd dames of earth') formerly believed 'That in their black, the perfect'st beauty grows'. Their hair never turned grey (a persistent myth concerning Negroes) and they were never afflicted by the paleness of death. But Niger's daughters had been shaken out of this confidence in their own beauty by 'Poor brain-sick men, styled poets here with you' who 'sung / The painted beauties other empires sprung'. Cursing the sun that has scorched them, they set out in search of a land where they can lose their blackness. They arrive at England, where

> Their beauties shall be scorch'd no more:
> This sun is temperate, and refines
> All things on which his radiance shines.

As in Crashaw's poem – and literally here, in the way that Jonson staged his piece – blackness is a mask, a superficial deformity that hides an inner purity and whiteness.

The idea that Negroes' blackness was caused by the scorching action of the sun may have been attractive for Jonson's poetic purposes, but for a man of science like Sir Thomas Browne, writing forty years later in the first flood of the Baconian revolution, it had serious flaws. Most obviously, Negroes transported to temperate climates did not, as Jonson had fancifully imagined, lose their colour. 'And so likewise,' Browne adds, 'fair or white people translated in hotter countries received not impressions amounting to this complexion, as hath been observed in many *Europeans* who have lived in the land of the *Negroes*.' If the sun were the cause of blackness, then all people living at the same latitude would share the same colouring; but this, Browne points out, is not the case, as one could see by comparing Negroes with Native Americans also living in the tropics.

Clearly, the quality of blackness was, at least in part, inherited. This had been recognised by some. As Leonardo remarks in his *Note-Books*: 'The black races in Ethiopia are not the product of the sun; for if black gets black with child in Scythia, the offspring is black; but if a black gets a white woman with child the offspring is grey. And this shows that the seed of the mother has power in the embryo equally with that of the father.' Sir Thomas Browne, following Aristotle, suggests that while the sperm of Negroes is white, that whiteness contains accidental qualities of blackness: '[T]he generation and sperm of Negroes ... [is] first and in its naturals white, but upon separation of parts, accidents before invisible become apparent; there arising a shadow or dark efflorescence in the outside; whereby not only their legitimate and timely births, but their abortions are also dusky, before they have felt the scorch and fervor of the sun.'

Given that blackness was, in Browne's words, 'maintained by generation', and given – as orthodox Christians necessarily had to believe – that all humanity was descended from Adam, that still left the question of how Negroes first acquired their blackness. Browne, having demolished the theories that blackness is caused by God's curse on Canaan or by the action of the sun, admits that 'how, and when this tincture first began is yet a Riddle, and positively to determine, it surpasseth my presumption'. He does, however, put forward a number of tentative suggestions. Some of these – such as that it is caused by drinking certain waters, or 'by the Power and Efficacy of imagination ... so in *Hippocrates* we read of one, that from an intent view of a Picture conceived a *Negro*' – are entirely fanciful. But at the very end he puts forward a suggestion that is striking to the modern reader: 'We may say that men became black in the same manner that some Foxes, Squirrels, Lions first turned of this complexion ... that some Choughs have come to have red Legs and Bills, that crows became pyed: All which mutations however they began, depend on durable foundations; and such as may continue for ever.'

Browne passes on without telling us how such 'mutations' might operate. It would be more than a hundred years before evolutionary theories began to be developed – in Diderot's *D'Alembert's Dream* (1769) and subsequently in the work of Jean-Baptiste Lamarck (1744–1829) and Erasmus Darwin (1731–1802). Without a theory of evolution, the environmentalist explanation, in terms of the operation of the sun or other external factors on successive individuals, seemed the only possible answer to the riddle of how Europeans and Africans could have descended from a common stock. It was a theory stubbornly held to throughout the eighteenth century despite a mass of evidence to the contrary. With the expansion of the slave trade, more and more Africans found themselves in temperate climates – and it was becoming clear that they and their children and grandchildren were perversely failing to turn white. To maintain the environmentalist theory in the face of such evidence – and to explain other differences such as facial features – ever more bizarre and fanciful pieces of folklore were required. Oliver Goldsmith's *History of the Earth and Animated Nature* (1774) – a work of popularisation that drew heavily on Buffon's monumental *Histoire naturelle* (successive editions from 1749 to 1804) – pushes credibility to the limit by stating blatantly the assumption that was implicit in all environmentalist theories, that man's 'natural' state is white and that blackness is a 'deformity' or 'monstrosity':

> The colour ... most natural to man, ought to be that which is most becoming; and it is found, that, in all regions, the children are born fair, or at least red, and that they grow more black, or tawny, as they advance in age. It should seem, consequently, that man is naturally white; since the same causes that darken the complexion in infants, may have originally operated, in slower degrees, in blackening whole nations.

Unable to choose between the effects of the environment operating on the individual and, by some process of evolution ('in slower degrees') over generations, Goldsmith plumps for both. The same confusion can be seen in his treatment of racial differences other than colour:

> Nations who have long considered some artificial deformity beautiful, who have industriously lessened the feet, or flattened the nose, by degrees, begin to receive the impression they are taught to assume: and Nature, in a course of ages, shapes itself to the constraint, and assumes hereditary deformity. We find nothing more common in births than for children to inherit sometimes even the accidental deformities of their parents. We have many instances of squinting in the father, which he received from fright, or habit, communicated to the offspring; and I myself have seen a child distinctly marked with a scar,

similar to the one the father had received in battle. In this manner accidental deformities may become natural ones; and by assiduity may be continued, and even encreased, through successive generations. From this, therefore, may have arisen the small eyes and long ears of the Tartars, and Chinese nations. From hence originally may have come the flat noses of the blacks, and the flat heads of the American Indians.

Where Goldsmith is unsure as to whether the Negro's nose is flattened by accident or design, Buffon is more explicit:

Negresses nearly always carry their babies on their back while they are working. Some travellers have maintained that it is for this reason that Negroes all have large bellies and flat noses; the mother, in shaking him up and down, bangs his nose against her back, and, to avoid these blows, the child leans back as far as possible, pushing his belly forward.

'That we have all sprung from one common parent,' concludes Goldsmith confidently, 'we are taught, both by reason and religion, to believe.' This was the foundation of the environmentalist theory, and the cause of its dominance in the eighteenth century. It appealed to the theoretical egalitarianism of the *philosophes*, but also, and more importantly, to one of the most fundamental tenets of Christianity: the unity of man. As the Apostle Paul wrote in his Epistle to the Galatians: 'There is neither Jew nor Greek, there is neither bond nor free, there is neither male nor female: for ye are all one in Christ Jesus' (3:28). We find this most basic of Christian doctrines expressed in Augustine's *City of God* (413–26), in the chapter where he discussed human 'monstrosities' – both individual deformities such as Siamese twins, and fabulous accounts from Pliny and other Greek writers of monstrous races of Cyclops, pygmies and hermaphrodites. Augustine denies that even if such stories are true, they disprove common origins:

In fact, it would be impossible to list all the human infants very unlike those who, without any doubt, were their parents. Now it cannot be denied that those derive ultimately from one man;

and therefore the same is true of all those races which are reported to have deviated as it were, by their divergence in bodily structure, from the normal course of nature followed by the majority, or practically the whole of mankind. If these races are included in the definition of 'human', that is, if they are rational and mortal animals, it must be admitted that they trace their lineage from that same one man, the first father of all mankind. This assumes, of course, the truth of the stories about the divergent features of those races, and their great difference from one another and from us . . . The accounts of some of these races may be completely worthless; but if such people exist, then either they are not human; or, if human, they are descended from Adam.

All men are descended from Adam, who was fashioned by God in His own image. And being made in his image, they have a unique place in His creation. God sent His own son into the world as a man. For Thomas Aquinas, man is positioned in the scale of creation midway between angel and animal:

[L]et us consider the distinction of corporeal and spiritual creatures: firstly the purely spiritual creature, which in Holy Scripture is called angel; secondly, the creature wholly corporeal; thirdly, the composite creature, corporeal and spiritual, which is man.

The humanism of the Renaissance had elevated man still further. In Giovanni Pico della Mirandola's *Oration on the Dignity of Man* (1486), man is liberated from the 'Chain of Being' that, for Aquinas, bound brute creation to God; he is 'a creature of undetermined nature', free to roam up and down the scale of creation at will:

You, [God says to man] who are confined by no limits, shall determine for yourself your own nature, in accordance with your own free will, in whose hand I have placed you. I have set you at the centre of the world, so that from there you may more easily survey whatever is in the world. We have made you neither heavenly nor earthly, neither mortal nor immortal, so that, more freely and more honourably the moulder and maker of yourself, you may fashion yourself in whatever form you shall prefer. You shall be able to descend among the lower forms of being, which are brute beasts; you shall be able to be reborn out of the judgement of your own soul into the higher beings, which are divine.

Like a twentieth-century existentialist, Pico della Mirandola sees each individual as his own creator and inventor: 'When man came into life, the Father endowed him with all kinds of seeds and with the germs of every way of life. Whatever seeds each man cultivates will grow and bear fruit in him.'

Mankind, by virtue of its unique relationship with God, is special and indivisible. It is this belief, the essence of Christian humanism, that was challenged by the placing of humans within a system of natural classification, and even more by the idea that 'mankind' might in fact be composed of several distinct species. When this was combined with a relativism born of the growing awareness of non-European, non-Christian societies, the result was to put the whole of traditional religion up for debate. As a case study of this, let us take one of those 'fantastic voyage' narratives, inspired by extra-European discovery, that were so popular in the seventeenth and early eighteenth centuries. This is from the opening of a novel published in about 1710, and I quote it at length because it touches on so many of the themes that swirled around the question of race at that period:

A Captain of a Ship, having brought some Negroes from *Africa*, made a Present of one of the handsomest to a Friend of his, a Man of Figure and Substance, but whimsical, and hard to be pleas'd. This Negro, after having liv'd several Years with so rigid a Master, and suffered a thousand Abuses from him, could bear it no longer, and resolv'd, whatever might be the Consequence, to take Revenge in a way the most dangerous that cou'd be. For this end, he went to the Apothecary that serv'd the Family, and under pretence that they were extremely pester'd with Rats, he desired two or three Penyworth of *Arsenic*. The Fellow was scarce got out of the Shop to do some Errands, when the

Apothecary sent to tell the Gentleman, that since his Black came for the Ratsbane, he had thought of an admirable Composition to destroy those Vermin, and that if he pleas'd he would immediately send him the Receipt. The Gentleman, who was naturally of an uneasy temper, being surprised at this Message, and the more because he very well remember'd that he had us'd his Domestic barbarously but the Day before, sent for him to know what he meant to do with that Poison, and swore by all that's sacred, he would murder him, if he gave him the least Cause to suspect him. It happen'd that the Valet was not then in the way, but as soon as he came home, a Sevant-maid, who dreaded that she shou'd see him broke upon the Wheel, gave him secret notice of what had pass'd. The Wretch was sadly affrighted; and being conscious that he had not Courage enough to stand the Test, he stole away, and without more ado hang'd himself. Mean time, his Master was out of all Patience because he did not see him; and after having order'd Messengers to go and find him out, at the Places to which he had sent him, a Footman came and surpris'd him with the News, that he found him hanging in the Corn-Loft.

The Noise of this tragical Action was quickly spread every where. The Gentleman being one of my Master's best Patients, he went to him immediately, and desired him for several Reasons to order it so, that he might have the Body. The Gentleman being a Person of no small influence, made no scruple to assure him he should have it, and the very same Day he perform'd his Promise. As soon as the Body was put into our Hands, we dissected it, in form. All the Parts of it were disposed like those of the Body of a white Man, at least, we observ'd no Difference; but what surpris'd us was, to find under the *Epidermis*, a very thin delicate Membrane, which my Master had never perceived in other Bodies, and which I had never heard of before. He immediately sent for a famous Physician of the Town, to whom he imparted this Discovery, but the Doctor did not seem so much surprised as I expected, for the same thing had happen'd to him upon the like Occasion. We concluded that this must be the true cause of the Blackness of this Race of Men, forasmuch as this Tunick stifles, and no doubt absorbs the Rays of Light; as on the contrary, a Leaf of Quicksilver plac'd behind *Venice* Glass, makes them reflect, and strikes them back towards the Place from whence they came. This gave occasion to a strong Debate concerning the Origin of the *Ethiopians*, which, when we consider this remarkable Difference, seems not to be the same with other Men. Upon this Principle I was going to draw Consequences which would have tended to no less than the intire Subversion of the System of the Sacred Author in Debate. But I was silenc'd by being told, That there were many things, which it was the Will of Heaven we should admire, but are forbid to dive into.

I was much delighted to hear this Doctor discourse upon the Construction and Operations of the humane Body ... Our Ideas or the Images of our Thoughts, [said the Doctor] are no more different from one another, than our Perceptions are; for tho' we admit of two sorts of them, distinguished by the Terms, Conception and Imagination, 'tis certain that *Touching* is the sole Cause of both the one and the other: 'Tis the only Source of all Human Knowledge, and also of our Reason, which, when all is said and done, is nothing more nor less than the Union or Disunion of Names, which, by common Consent, we have impos'd upon Substances, as they appear to our Comprehension to bear a Conformity to their Qualities, and not at all to their Existence. Other Creatures having Organs like to ours, have no doubt the same Perceptions, and 'tis only the Degree of more or less, that can constitute the Difference. The Beasts therefore have Reason; and tho' they don't shew it, 'tis only for want, perhaps, of Speech to give Names, as we do to things which affect them by being put in motion; for, in other Matters, they are very capable of distinguishing —

Here our Physician was interrupted on a sudden, by a terrible Shriek from the Maidservant. The poor Girl, as she was bringing an Armful of Wood from the Corn-loft, had made a false Step, and fell from the Top of the Ladder to the Ground. We all ran out to her Assistance, and found that she had broke her right Leg. The Doctor, after having seen it dress'd the first time, went home, to my very great Concern; for, besides some Objections which I was ready to have offer'd, I should have been very glad to have heard the conclusion of so curious a Discourse; and was the more mortify'd afterwards, because I could never get another Opportunity to engage that ingenious Gentleman to talk with me upon the same Subject. (Simon Tyssot de Patot, *Les Voyages et Aventures de Jacques Massé* (1710). Translated into English as *The Travels and Adventures of James Massey* (1733))

Three European men stand over the dissected body of a Negro. The story of his death is significant for the way that it combines what were to become, as we shall see in the next chapter, the two most common eighteenth-century stereotypes of the African slave: the dangerous, cunning savage, bent on revenge against his captors; and the melancholy, suicidal victim. But what matters here is that the Negro is dead. The Europeans have secured his body and set about dissecting him in order to discover the cause of his blackness. Two issues arise from the dissection, but are then teasingly evaded: the origin of 'Ethiopians', and the question of whether language and reason are necessarily the prerogative solely of humans. In both cases, what is at stake is religious taboo.

The men standing around the dissecting table start debating 'the Origin of the *Ethiopians*' – which, the narrator observes, 'seems not to be the same with other Men'. He is about to draw heretical conclusions from this ('Consequences which would have tended to no less than the intire Subversion of the System of the Sacred Author') when he is warned off by his companions. There is clearly a code operating here, a system of veiled reference that the author expects his learned readership to understand. And equally clearly, the reference is to polygenism, the theory that Negroes and Europeans had separate origins.

In 1655, Isaac La Peyrère (1596–1676) published a revolutionary book, *Prae-Adamitae* (translated into English in the following year as *Man before Adam*), which claimed that men had existed before the creation of Adam, and hence that the Bible was not the history of the whole of mankind, but merely of one portion of it, the Jews. Other peoples, such as the American Indians or the Eskimos (on whom La Peyrère had made himself the leading European expert of his day) were the result of a separate and earlier creation. As secretary to the Prince of Condé in the 1640s, La Peyrère was a member of perhaps the most advanced and radical intellectual circle in Europe, a group that included Pierre Gassendi (teacher of Cyrano de Bergerac), Pascal, Grotius and the Englishman Thomas Hobbes, at that time in exile from the civil war in his homeland. La Peyrère's book was a direct challenge both to scripture and to the universalist pretensions of the Christian religion, and as such it was subject to a deluge of condemnation and pious refutation that was to last for the next 150 years. La Peyrère himself was imprisoned by the authorities and forced to recant. His heretical views – foreshadowed in the previous century by Paracelsus and Giordano Bruno – were based on critical exegesis of the Bible, on travellers' accounts of pagan societies, and above all on the pagan chronologies such as the Chinese, Mexican, Babylonian and Egyptian, which suggested that the world had existed long before 4004 BC, the date traditionally assigned by Christians to the Creation. La Peyrère himself considered the prehistoric, pre-Adamite world to have been of infinite duration.

For the next 150 years it was an extremely bold writer who would venture down La Peyrère's path. La Peyrère's younger contemporary, Spinoza, seems to have accepted the pre-Adamite theory without stating it openly. Voltaire, as so often, was bolder:

> We can be very good Christians without believing in centaurs, men without heads or with only one leg etc. But can we doubt that the interior structure of a negro may be different to that of a white, since the mucous netted membrane beneath the skin is white in the one, and black in the other? . . .
>
> The Albinos and Darians – the first originally of Africa, and the second of the middle of America – are as different from us as from the negroes. They are yellow, red, and grey races . . . All are equally men, but only as a fir, an oak, and a pear tree are equally trees; the pear tree comes not from the fir, nor the fir from the oak . . .
>
> The inclinations and characters of men differ as much as their

climates and governments ... There is none but a blind man, and even an obstinate blind man, who can deny the existence of all these different species. It is as great and remarkable as that of apes.

Other eighteenth-century authors, while recognising the force of the polygenist argument, were more circumspect about drawing conclusions. Lord Kames, a leading figure of the Scottish Enlightenment, pours scorn on environmentalism but ends up by deferring to biblical authority. His celebrated *Sketches of the History of Man* (1774) begins by dismissing Buffon's account of the origin of human races and his definition of a species in terms of an ability to interbreed. For Kames, species are identified by their obvious physical differences, by their characters and temperaments, and by their suitability for different climates and environments. By that definition, Kames is confident that there are different species of men, not simply variations on one common stock:

> Certain it is, that all men are not fitted equally for every climate. Is there not then reason to conclude, that as there are different climates, so there are different species of men fitted for these different climates ... It is thus ascertained beyond any rational doubt, that there are different races or kinds of men, and that these races or kinds are naturally fitted for different climates: whence we have reason to conclude, that originally each kind was placed in its proper climate ...

The obvious conclusion as far as religion is concerned, according to Kames, is 'That God created many pairs of the human race, differing from each other both externally and internally; that he fitted these pairs for different climates, and placed each pair in its proper climate; that the peculiarities of the original pairs were preserved entire in their descendants ...' But, a little wistfully, Kames points out that 'this opinion, however plausible, we are not permitted to adopt; being taught a different lesson by revelation, namely, that God created but a single pair of the human species. Though we cannot doubt of the authority of Moses, yet his account of the creation of man is not a little puzzling, as it seems to

36

contradict every one of the facts mentioned above.' Kames's solution to the problem – which, one senses, he himself found not entirely satisfactory – is that the scattering of mankind and the institution of the different races must have coincided with the creation of different languages when God destroyed the Tower of Babel: 'the confusion of Babel is the only known fact that can reconcile sacred and profane history.'[1]

Unlike his relation David Hume, Lord Kames was unwilling to extend the differences between white and black to a presumption of the innate mental inferiority of the latter:

> The colour of the Negroes ... affords a strong presumption of their being a different species from the Whites; and I once thought, that the presumption was supported by inferiority of understanding in the former. But it appears to me doubtful, upon second thoughts, whether this inferiority may not be occasioned by their condition.

But even as Kames was writing, there were others who were beginning to use the polygenist theory to 'prove' the inherent mental and moral inferiority of Negroes, and thus to justify the practice of slavery. Polygenism was beginning its rapid descent from being a speculative theory of rationalistic anti-Christian free thought to being a weapon in the armoury of politically motivated racial obsessives.

One of the earliest and most notorious examples of this is Edward Long's *History of Jamaica* (1774), which was an extended justification of slavery against the first stirrings of British abolitionist sentiment. An attitude of condescension, pity or contempt for non-European 'savages' was practically universal in the late

---

[1] The pre-Darwinian Lord Kames sees nature essentially as a static grid. The physical similarity between members of the same race is evidence, for him, of this original pattern or design: '[W]ere all men of the same species, there never could have existed, without a miracle, different kinds, such as exist at present ... [W]e find men of different kinds, the individuals of each kind remarkably uniform and differing no less remarkably from the individuals of every other kind. Uniformity without variation is the offspring of nature, never the chance.' Darwin's theory of evolution by natural selection would show that 'uniformity' is indeed the offspring of chance, and that chance and nature are not antithetical.

eighteenth century, but the specificity and burning intensity of Long's Negrophobia is striking. Its starting point is a feeling of physical revulsion, especially as regards 'their bestial or fetid smell'. He swiftly moves on to more general matters: '[T]hey are void of genius, and seem almost incapable of making any progress in civility or science. – They have no plan or system of morality among them. Their barbarity to their children debases their nature even below that of brutes. They have no moral sensations; no taste but for women, gormandizing, and drinking to excess; no wish but to be idle.' So it goes on. Perhaps not entirely coincidentally, Long heaps on to the Negro exactly those vices that were commonly attributed by contemporaries to the West Indian planter class of which he was a member. 'When we reflect on the nature of these men,' he sums up, 'and their dissimilarity to the rest of mankind, must we not conclude, that they are a different species of the same *genus*?'

Long goes on to argue that just as the universe is ordered in the form of a scale or chain ascending from inert matter to God, so there is a chain linking animals to the highest manifestation of humanity (the European). For Long, the crucial gaps in this chain are filled by Negroes and 'oran-outangs' (the term then commonly used for the great apes in general, including chimpanzees): 'Oran-outangs do not seem at all inferior in the intellectual faculties to many of the Negroe race; with some of whom, it is credible that they have the most intimate connexion and consanguinity. The amorous intercourse between them may be frequent; the Negroes themselves bear testimony that such intercourses actually happen; and it is certain that both races agree perfectly well in lasciviousness of disposition.' The conclusion is stark: '[A]n oran-outang . . . is a human being, *quoad* his form and organs; but of an inferior species, *quoad* his intellect; he has in form a much nearer resemblance to the Negroe race, than the latter bear to the white man . . .'

In the nineteenth century, polygenism formed the basis of the 'American School' of anthropology, whose Negrophobia was echoed in the ethos of the Anthropological Society of London, which was founded in 1860. The pseudo-science of the American

38

School was taken up by political defenders of Southern slavery
such as John C. Calhoun, but its obvious contradiction of biblical
Christianity limited its popular appeal in the American South.
Polygenism could only emerge in the nineteenth century when and
where the religious taboos against it had sufficiently weakened.
Even then, the forces against it were strong. Many anthropologists,
such as James Prichard, the leading British figure in the field in the
early and mid-nineteenth century, clung to monogenism despite its
obvious faults because, given his anti-slavery opinions, the implications of polygenism were too horrifying to contemplate. And then,
in the third quarter of the nineteenth century, the uncertain life of
the polygenist theory of human races was curtailed by the
Darwinian revolution, for Darwin seemed to provide an account of
divergence from a common stock that did not need to resort to
incredible environmental explanations.

These, then, are the 'Consequences' against which the narrator
of *Les Voyages et Aventures de Jacques Massé* is warned once he
begins to speculate on racial origins. One can gauge just how
heterodox polygenism was by the fact that Jacques Masse is
quickly warned off the subject, whereas other tenets of Christianity – the story of the Flood, the doctrine of the Trinity, even the
afterlife – are given a much more openly dismissive treatment later
in the book. Towards the end of the story, a Chinaman with whom
the narrator enters into a long dialogue comments of Christ that
'the very Miracles, which are ascribed to this Great Person, are not
to be understood literally, but in an improper and figurative sense,
as all the Parables of the Gospel are understood in'. And the Old
Testament is dismissed as 'a Compound of Emblems, Allegories,
Metaphors, Hyperboles, Types and Comparisons invented for the
Comfort and Instruction of the Children of God'.

The story of *Les Voyages et Aventures de Jacques Massé* casts a
sidelight on how, in the seventeenth and early eighteenth centuries,
speculations about racial differences and exotic cultures were
closely intertwined with religious scepticism. Published anonymously at some point between 1710 and 1720 (the exact date is
uncertain), it recounts the extraordinary voyage of its hero/
narrator to the 'Austral Land' south of the Equator, where after a

number of adventures the group of shipwrecked Europeans discover a utopian and highly ordered society. The land is divided geometrically into squares by a network of canals. Each of these 'cantons' contains a stipulated number of villages, each of which is constructed to a uniform and rational design. The society itself is pyramidal, with a king at the apex. But since it is entirely cut off from the outside world, without hostile neighbours, there is no military establishment. The king is subject to the same laws as his fellow citizens and there is no capital punishment. The first rulers of the Austral Land had claimed their legitimacy from their descent from the sun-god, but the society had become more enlightened since then, and the kings had lost any religious rights over their fellow citizens.

One curious detail about the people making up this utopian, rationalist society in the interior of the Austral Land is that they are white; they are contrasted with the men that the Europeans encounter between the coast and the interior, who are described in the English version of 1733 as 'black as Newcastle colliers'. This picture of a white-inhabited interior echoes the belief – which has persisted down the centuries as a small but significant footnote to European myths about Africa – that there was a race of whites living at the heart of the continent. The Middle Ages saw the myth of Prester John, the supposed white (or at least mulatto) Christian emperor of Ethiopia. Voltaire, in his *Essai sur les moeurs* (1757), cites the reports of early Portuguese travellers to the effect that a race of Albinos inhabit the interior of the African continent. Indeed, he places 'Albinos' next to 'Whites, Negroes ... Hottentots, Lapps, Chinese, Americans' as constituting the 'entirely different' races of mankind. Buffon also cites this race of white Africans, but for contrary purposes to Voltaire so far as the polygenist/monogenist debate was concerned. For Buffon, the existence of this white race at the heart of Africa is further proof of the environmentalist hypothesis – the interior being, according to him, higher, damper and less scorched by the sun.

And it is difficult not to perceive a connection between this myth of a white element at the heart of darkest Africa and the important and peculiar role that Africa plays in Swedenborgian mysticism. Emanuel Swedenborg (1688–1772) began his career as a scientist, but from the middle of the eighteenth century began writing prophetic spiritual works that were to have a lasting influence to the present day. According to Swedenborg, God had created not one true church, but a whole series. Each had been created by God in the place where man had the truest knowledge of Him, and each had thereafter declined from its original purity. The European Christian church was in decay, according to Swedenborg, and it had been shown to him that it was in Africa that God was to found the next true church. In the last decades of the eighteenth century, followers of Swedenborg were to the fore in projects to found a New Jerusalem in West Africa. The reason for God's singling out Africa, according to Swedenborg, was that Africans were more intuitive than Europeans:

> The African race is preeminently capable of receiving light of illustration, for it is their character to think interiorly, and so to receive truths, and to acknowledge them. Others, such as the Europeans, think only exteriorly, and receive truths in the memory; nor do they see them internally by virtue of any intellectual light.

Given the importance in this passage of the familiar Christian imagery of light/darkness, it is scarcely surprising to find Swedenborg expounding the conventional Christian view of the significance of the Negroes' colour and of their true 'whiteness': 'The Africans are among the blackest of all, and they love to be punished and harshly treated, and they come into heaven, and afterwards they say that they detest the blackness because they know that their souls are white and their bodies black.'

Just as the black skin of the Negro conceals an inner light, so a new celestial light will burst from the interior of Africa. Again and again Swedenborg comes back to the geographical specificity of his vision; it is only in the interior of Africa, not on the coasts, that the new church will arise:

> Thus it was shown in obscure vision how the celestial doctrine would proceed in Africa, namely, towards the interior parts all

the way to the middle. And that then it would go towards those who are at the sides by the Mediterranean, but not to the coasts; and then after a time it would bend backwards [*se reflecteret*] towards Egypt. By this the Angels were gladdened, that now an advent of the Lord anew was at hand, and that a new church with which they can be conjoined would be installed. The doctrine does not reach to the Africans dwelling at the coasts ...

As a scientist, Swedenborg would have been familiar with Buffon's *Histoire naturelle*, where the insistence on the existence of a white African race exactly parallels the insistence in Swedenborg's mystical revelations on the interior spirituality of Africa:

M. Bruce has made to me an observation of the utmost importance concerning the Negroes; which is that there are only Negroes on the coasts – that is to say the low-lying lands of Africa, and that in the interior of that part of the world, the men are white.

Finally in the strange tradition of projecting a white society into the heart of Africa, one could mention some imperial romances of the late Victorian and Edwardian period. In John Buchan's *Prester John* the connection with the earlier tradition is manifest. Rider Haggard's *King Solomon's Mines* imagines the remains of a non-Negro civilisation in the heart of Africa, while *She* portrays a tyrannical white princess.

Les Voyages et Aventures de Jacques Massé is clearly a fiction, though a modern reader, accustomed to expect some kind of artistic unity, would hesitate to call it a 'novel'. There is an extraordinary range of material contained in it, from ruminations on natural history, astronomy, geology and critical biblical exegesis to adventure stories and a self-contained melodrama of sexual intrigue. Judged by later aesthetic criteria, *Jacques Massé* is a mess. It has disappeared from the 'canon' and in modern times is mentioned only in specialised monographs. (André Le Breton, in his history of the eighteenth-century French novel, published in 1898, devotes four pages to it, noting especially some similarities to the later *Robinson Crusoe*.) But in the eighteenth century it would seem to have been popular and controversial. A second French edition was published in 1734, and English and German translations in 1733 and 1737. A steady succession of editions in different languages appeared throughout the rest of the century. In his *Lettres philosophiques*, Voltaire mentions as one of his influences 'l'auteur déguisé sous le nom de Jacques Macé'.

And who was 'l'auteur déguisé sous le nom de Jacques Macé'? Simon Tyssot de Patot was Professor of Mathematics at the Ecole Illustre in the Dutch town of Deventer. He had in fact been born in England, in 1655, but grew up in France before his Huguenot family moved to Holland (traditionally a refuge for English and French Protestants) in 1664. As an adult, Tyssot seems to have led a fascinating double life. Outwardly a conventional Calvinist professor, living within the rigid norms of provincial Dutch society, he was also the author of two anonymously published works of fiction that cast scandalous doubt on the very bases of Christian faith. It is true that Tyssot did give some open indications of freethinking tendencies; in 1723, expecting to be named Rector of the Ecole Illustre, Tyssot wrote as an acceptance speech a *Discourse on the Subject of Chronology*, which attempted to 'conciliate' between traditional biblical chronology and that of non-Christian societies – Egyptian, Persian, Chinese and Chaldean. The age of the world was a subject to which freethinkers constantly returned throughout the seventeenth and eighteenth centuries, and – as in the case of La Peyrère's writings – was one that was pivotal to the argument about racial origins. Significantly, perhaps, Tyssot was not given the rectorship, though his *Discourse* was published. But this open gesture towards religious scepticism and cultural relativism was nothing compared to the assault on Christianity launched in his anonymous works such as *Les Voyages et Aventures de Jacques Massé*. It seems that in the mid-1720s Tyssot was on the verge of being unmasked, for in 1727, at the age of seventy-two, he published his *Lettres choisies*, in which he gives an account of his life, owns up to the authorship of the novels and openly ridicules Christianity, deifying Reason in its place. Tyssot was promptly dismissed from his professorship and forced to leave Deventer in disgrace. He thereafter disappears into obscurity, though it is known that he died in 1738 at the extremely advanced age, for the eighteenth century, of eighty-three.

In terms of literary merit, Simon Tyssot de Patot may have been a foot-soldier of the Enlightenment compared to such Parnassian figures as Voltaire, Diderot and Montesquieu. But as an early Deist (i.e. putting forward the purely philosophical idea of a 'supreme creator' shorn of the 'superstitious' trappings of biblical Christianity) his strange life and works provide almost a parable of the way that free thought and scepticism struggled to come to birth from within the confines of Western, Christian traditions of thought. He was, in many respects, a Voltairean before Voltaire.

The 'fantastic voyage' genre to which Tyssot de Patot and Voltaire were drawn was a crucial form of expression for this scepticism. It was primarily a French tradition, encompassing most famously Cyrano de Bergerac's *Histoire comique des Etats et Empires de la Lune et du Soleil* (1657, 1662) and Gabriel Folgny's *La Terre Australe connue* (1676, later published under the title *Les Aventures de Jacques Sadeur*), but one of its later and most famous examples was by an Anglo-Irishman, Jonathan Swift – *Gulliver's Travels* (1726). One indication of the popularity of the genre is a collection of *voyages imaginaires* published in Paris between 1787 and 1789; incorporating many of the most famous 'fantastic voyages' – as well as more realistic narratives by foreign authors, such as Daniel Defoe's *Robinson Crusoe* (1719) and Laurence Sterne's *A Sentimental Journey* (1768) – the collection runs to an impressive thirty-six volumes. Certain classical models – such as the works of Lucian and Heliodorus – were significant in the genesis of fictional 'fantastic voyages', but far more important in terms of both forms and content were the narratives of actual voyages that proliferated with the great expansion of European exploration and colonisation from the sixteenth century onwards. While Defoe's *Robinson Crusoe* uses the trappings of the traveller's narrative to enhance the credibility of a realistic narrative – based, indeed, on a true story – Swift uses it to comic effect ('the author was so distinguished for his veracity, that it became a sort of proverb among his neighbours at Redriff, when any one affirmed a thing, to say that it was as true as if Mr. Gulliver had spoke it') as the frame for an evidently fabulous voyage.

Most early explorers and colonisers were probably not unlike the picture that Defoe cheerfully and uncritically paints in *Captain Singleton* (1720), his post-*Robinson Crusoe* yarn about a trip through equatorial Africa. Unquestioning of their own superiority and the inherent villainy of the natives, Singleton and his band of Europeans shoot and pillage their way across the continent with never a philosophical thought to cloud their minds. Defoe's vision of Hobbesian egotism in *Captain Singleton* may have been close to the reality of early European expansion, but there were some at home who were prepared to ponder the implications of the existence of non-European societies. Certainly, in the imaginative use of the travel narrative form, one frequently finds an implicit criticism of, or scepticism about, European society or religion – either through the implied contrast with an imagined utopia or (as in some chapters of *Gulliver's Travels*) through the projection of a dystopia.

Defoe's *Robinson Crusoe* is sometimes crudely characterised as no more than an expression of European imperialist arrogance. While there is certainly something of that in the book, particularly in the way Crusoe arrogates an empire for himself and demands the submission of Friday and the other non-Europeans he meets, much of the force of the reader's identification with Crusoe (on which, of course, has depended the enduring appeal of the book) derives from the doubts that Crusoe experiences. Crusoe's religious faith is unquestioning and traditional, even somewhat old-fashioned for the time; he sees around him innumerable portents and evidences of God's Providence. Yet at moments of crisis, such as the encounter with the cannibals, his experiences push him in the direction of a kind of cultural relativism:

> How do I know what God Himself urges in this particular case? It is certain these people either do not commit this as a crime; it is not against their own consciences reproving, or their light reproaching them. They do not know it to be be an offence, and then commit it in defiance of divine justice, as we do in almost

all the sins we commit. They think it no more a crime to kill a captive taken in war, than we do to kill an ox; nor to eat human flesh, than we do to eat mutton.

When I had considered this a little, it followed necessarily that I was certainly in the wrong in it, that these people were not murtherers in the sense that I had condemned them in my thoughts; any more than those Christians were murtherers who often put to death the prisoners taken in battle . . .

Defoe was not a writer given to abstract speculation – which is what, along with the enormous bulk and range of his writings, makes him so attractive to the historian as a barometer of his times. He was above all an observer. Others, particularly in France, were more ready to use the fictional voyage – and in particular the opportunities for cross-cultural comparison that it afforded – as a way of voicing dissident opinions. Tyssot de Patot puts his religious scepticism into the mouth of a Chinaman whom Jacques Massé meets in Goa, having been imprisoned by the Inquisition. Voltaire used the picaresque travel adventure as the form of his 'philosophical tales' (*Candide*, *Zadig*, *L'Ingénu*) criticising European institutions and ideas.

China and Islam were the most popular points of comparison for eighteenth-century *philosophes* eager to prove the contingency of European institutions and Christian beliefs. Both offered 'civilised' societies with their own long histories, their own values, their own cosmologies. Other peoples in Asia and the Pacific, or in Africa and the Americas, were designated 'primitive' or 'savage'. But for Rousseau, and for Diderot in the *Supplément au voyage de Bougainville*, even these primitives could be extolled as 'noble savages', a living, natural reprimand to the artificiality and perversion of European civilisation. And in the sentimental novel, as we shall see in Chapter 2, the African (or, which was the same thing, the slave) was seen as a repository of those virtues and authentic feelings smothered by the conventions and corruptions of society.

Polygenism, then, was closely allied to radical religious scepticism, while monogenism was clung to as a scientific gloss on scripture. But it would be misleading to overemphasise a simple monogenist/polygenist dichotomy. The eighteenth-century founders of the modern 'science' of anthropology – Linnaeus, Buffon, Blumenbach – were all monogenists, yet all, to varying degrees, emphasised mankind's division into a small number of races with fixed and clearly defined properties. Particularly in a context where – as can be seen above in the extracts from Lord Kames's *Sketches of the History of Man* – terms like 'race', 'species' and 'kind' were used loosely and interchangeably, the emphasis on present-day separation and division was as important as the argument about the ancient origins of those divisions. In addition, these monogenists could be as dogmatic in their assignment of mental and moral characteristics as any polygenist. (One should also note that there was no necessary correlation between views on monogenism and on slavery. The polygenist Voltaire was an outspoken opponent of slavery.) The Swedish botanist Carl Linnaeus, whose *Systema Naturae* (1735) for the first time included man within a complete classification of the natural world, offered the following division of mankind:

1. Wild man. Four-footed, mute, hairy.
2. *American.* Copper-coloured, choleric, erect. *Hair* black, straight, thick; *nostrils* wide; *face* harsh; beard scanty; obstinate, content, free. Paints himself with fine red lines. *Regulated* by customs.
3. *European.* Fair, sanguine, brawny. *Hair* yellow brown, flowing; *eyes* blue; *gentle*, acute, inventive. *Covered* with close vestments. *Governed* by laws.
4. *Asiatic.* Sooty, melancholy, rigid. *Hair* black; eyes dark; severe, haughty, covetous. *Covered* with loose garments. *Governed* by opinions.
5. *African.* Black, phlegmatic, relaxed. *Hair* black, frizzled; *skin* silky; *nose* flat; *lips* tumid; *crafty*, indolent, negligent. Anoints himself with grease. *Governed* by caprice.

Thus Linnaeus freely mixes physical description with highly subjective moral and aesthetic judgments. Buffon was sceptical about Linnaeus's rigid system for classifying nature, preferring to emphasise how differences were built up through small, incremental gradations. But he too saw physical characteristics and mental and moral faculties as closely allied in non-European man's slow degeneration from his white original. The German Johann Friedrich Blumenbach's 1795 fivefold division of mankind (*Caucasian*, *Mongolian*, *Ethiopian*, *American* and *Malay*) – which remained the basic classificatory system employed by the US Immigration Service up until the 1950s – was explicitly based on aesthetic criteria:

> *Caucasian variety.* I have taken the name of this variety from Mount Caucasus, both because its neighbourhood, and especially its southern slope, produces the most beautiful race of men, I mean the Georgian ... [T]hat stock displays ... the most beautiful form of the skull, from which, as from a mean and primaeval type, the others diverge by most easy gradations on both sides to the ultimate extremes (that is, on the one side the Mongolian, on the other the Ethiopian).

By the time Blumenbach was writing, racial differentiation was becoming more specific and 'scientific'. Blumenbach attempted to show that skull shape could be used as an index for racial classification. The Dutch painter Peter Camper devised an influential system to show various 'facial angles'. The European, he argued (like Blumenbach, he took his models from classical sculpture), had a prominent forehead and steep descent to the chin, whereas the African suffered from prognathism (prominent jaw and receding forehead). As Camper made clear, this was intended as an index not only of race, but of intelligence or bestiality: 'If I make the facial line lean forward, I have an antique head; if backward, the head of a Negro. If I still more incline it, I have the head of an ape; and if more still, that of a dog, and then that of an idiot.' Camper's system, which was subject to its own vagaries of measurement, was criticised by Blumenbach, but it had a considerable impact on French scientific thought in the nineteenth century. Craniometry was to be crucial for the American School of anthropology, and, more generally, phrenology (the study of the shape and size of the skull) held a central place in European thought in the nineteenth century.

The whole notion of 'racial science' based on precise, anthropometric measurement has been discredited since the Second World War, and not simply as a reaction to the dreadful historical events spawned by racial dogmas. Even without Auschwitz, the increased understanding of genetics would have undermined the notion of 'races' embodying fixed sets of determinate characteristics. Modern scientists find it more productive to talk a flexible language of 'population groups' and 'gene pools'. But it would be wrong simply to dismiss the anthropology of the late eighteenth and nineteenth centuries as 'bad science'. Its significance goes beyond that, both because of the support it gave to racial oppression in the real world, and because it was one aspect of a broader 'naturalisation' of European thought that occurred in the eighteenth century. This process of naturalisation was fundamental to the invention of the modern European idea of race.

All language is metaphorical, in that it describes particular things in terms of other things. Words are not themselves the things they describe. Yet the precision and fullness of our descriptions can give us the illusion of getting closer to what we are describing, of speaking the language that nature itself speaks. A yew is just another tree until we have called it a yew; a tree is just a big plant until we have called it a tree. But no matter how refined language becomes, there remains a distance between word and thing, and an important sense in which the descriptions are arbitrary rather than determined by the things they describe. No two yew trees are identical.

During the eighteenth century there was in Europe an attempt to take language closer to nature, to discover a 'fit' between words and the things they describe. Scientifically, this was done through classification, through increasing the number of words in order to approximate more nearly to the number of things in the world. The two pioneers of taxonomy in the eighteenth century, Linnaeus and Buffon, were deadly rivals and antagonists, but they shared a dream of reproducing in their classifications the very language of nature, of eradicating the metaphorical streak in language and 'pushing' it back on to some natural foundation. Linnaeus even envisaged the linguistic and typographical form of his classification of plants as being a kind of botanical calligram, with the ordering and division of the paragraphs mapping exactly the morphology of the plant itself. Where older 'histories' – Belton's *History of the Nature of Birds*, Duret's *Admirable History of Plants*, Aldrovandi's *History of Serpents and Dragons* – freely mixed empirical observation with mythological and ancient accounts, the newer 'natural histories' stripped away these accretions in order to disclose the structures supposedly inherent in the thing itself.

Linnaeus and Buffoon, as we have seen, included man in their classification of the natural world. But beyond that, as the eighteenth century progressed, every aspect of human activity – economics, morals, language, even religion itself – became susceptible to having its 'natural history' traced. Human society was a 'natural' phenomenon, in the sense of operating – in its economic life, to take a well-known and still controversial example – according to inherent regularities and laws that were independent of the will of any individual or group.

The 'naturalisation' of man in the eighteenth century raised the questions concerning man's relationship to nature, and to his own 'nature', that so preoccupy us at the end of the twentieth century. Are human beings subsumed in nature, or do they in some sense stand apart, controlling it? Is *Homo sapiens* 'just' another animal, albeit temporarily a successful one? What, ultimately, is 'human nature'? This last is perhaps the most important question of the modern world, the question underlying the great debates over evolution, over our treatment of the environment, and over the significance of such marks of 'natural' or genetic identity as race, gender and, possibly, sexuality. The 'politics of the body', that raises such passions at the end of the twentieth century, has its roots in the eighteenth.

This question of humanity's relationship with the animal kingdom, and with its own 'animal' nature, takes us back to Tyssot de Patot's *Voyages et Aventures de Jacques Massé*, and to that opening scene in which the three Europeans dissect the Negro. The association in the European mind between Negroes and monkeys (or more particularly, the great apes) has been one of the most persistent and pernicious elements of racial thinking since the first discovery by Europeans of the great apes in Africa in the seventeenth century. In 1699, about ten years before *Jacques Massé* was written, Dr Edward Tyson, an English physician, carried out a famous dissection of a chimpanzee. He showed for the first time that the chimpanzee was not (contrary to some fanciful travellers' tales) a pygmy race of man, but also that there were close anatomical similarities between apes and men. It is not improbable that Tyssot de Patot had in mind Tyson's book when he wrote the scene in which the Negro is dissected, for following the truncated discussion of racial origins, the Europeans find themselves addressing the question of man's animal nature.

If the influence of Tyson's dissection on Tyssot de Patot is conjectural, that of the English philosopher John Locke is clear. For Locke, human reason didn't belong to an abstract realm of Platonic ideas, or to some divine, God-given realm, but consisted rather in the association between different sense impressions. All human thought derived ultimately, through a chain of association, from the senses. Given this, and given the physical similarity between the sense organs of humans and those of animals such as the apes, Jacques Massé draws the conclusion that 'the Beasts therefore have Reason'.

By the later eighteenth century, intellectual radicals such as Rousseau, La Mettrie and Lord Kames's friend Lord Monboddo were suggesting that the traditional gulf between man and brute was bridged by the apes. Both Rousseau and Monboddo saw language as crucial. Language and reason formed the obvious demarcation between man and beast. Yet if, as John Locke and his even more sceptical followers like Hume had suggested, reason was based not on innate, abstract ideas, but on associations between sensations, and if, as Tyson had shown, there were strong similarities in the physical make-up (and hence sensations) of man and ape, was it inconceivable that apes could, if taught, express themselves like men? At the time such views were shocking, and later historians have raised a laugh at the expense of the 'eccentric' Scotsman Monboddo and his view that the gorilla was a kind of feral man. But recent developments – the work on sign language with chimpanzees; the discovery of the close similarities in the genetic make-up of man and ape; and the campaign by a number of leading philosophers and scientists for the great apes to be brought within the ambit of 'human rights' by having the legal status of 'persons' – however controversial, would seem to give at least some retrospective support to those in the past who have seen the ape as the bridge between man and the rest of nature.

Before Jacques Massé can get an answer to the question of whether language might be something we share with the beasts – after all, the subtext goes, we share it with the Negro – the men standing around the dissection table are interrupted. A number of purposes are served by the irruption of female, domestic reality – the serving-girl falling down the stairs – into the scene of male scientific speculation: it is comic, of course, and, like the earlier warning-off from the subject of the origins of races, it is a means of avoiding theologically explosive material. But beyond that, it serves to remind us that this is not a philosophical or physiological treatise – it is a work of fiction, a novel. The real, dramatic time of the narrative – that mundane time in which serving-girls fall down stairs – shatters the abstract time (one might almost say timelessness) in which the men's questions of physiology, philosophy and language revolve. Thus we are brought to another aspect of the naturalisation of thought in the eighteenth century – the emergence of the modern novel. Where Linnaeus and Buffon attempted to discover the true language of objective nature, the eighteenth-century novelists attempted to discover the language of man's subjectivity, his sensations and sentiments. In this field – just as when he is laid out cold on the scientist's dissection table – there was a tendency to see the Negro as being 'closer to nature', but this time in the sense of closer to the interior grounding of man's subjective nature, his authenticity.

Sources

Primary sources

Athenian Oracle, The (London, 1706–16), vol. II and Supplement (1710).

St Augustine, *City of God* (Penguin, Harmondsworth, 1972). See pp. 662–4 for his account of 'monstrous races' and statement of the common descent of mankind.

Blake, William, *Complete Writings* (Oxford University Press, London, 1966).

The Works of Sir Thomas Browne (London, 1846), vol. III, 'Of the Blackness of Negroes', pp. 263–75.

Buffon, Georges-Louis Leclerc, Comte de, *Histoire naturelle* (Paris, 1799–1800), vol. XX.

Burke, Edmund, *A Philosophical Enquiry into the Origin of Our Ideas of the Sublime and the Beautiful* (1756).

The Works of the Right Honourable Edmund Burke (London, 1826), vol. I.

The Works of the Late Profesor Camper on the Connexion between the Sciences of Anatomy and the Arts of Drawing, Painting, Statuary (London, 1794).

The Poems English Latin and Greek of Richard Crashaw (Clarendon Press, Oxford, 1927).

Defoe, Daniel, *The Life, Adventures and Pyracies of the Famous Captain Singleton* (Oxford University Press, London, 1969).

— *The Life and Strange Surprizing Adventures of Robinson Crusoe of York, Mariner* (Oxford University Press, London, 1972).

Goldsmith, Oliver, *An History of the Earth and Animated Nature* (London, 1774).

Jonson, Ben, *Complete Works*, vol. VII (Clarendon Press, Oxford, 1927).

Kames, Henry Home, Lord, *Sketches of the History of Man* (London, 1774).

Leonardo da Vinci's Note-Books (Duckworth & Co., London, 1906).

Long, Edward, *History of Jamaica* (London, 1774).

Marmontel, Jean-François, *Oeuvres complètes* (Paris, 1787), vol. V.

Pico della Mirandola, *Oration on the Dignity of Man*, in James Bruce Ross and Mary Martin McLaughlin (eds), *The Portable Renaissance Reader* (Penguin, Harmondsworth, 1977), pp. 476–9.

Monboddo, James Burnet, Lord, *Of the Origin and Progress of Language* (Edinburgh, 1774), vol. I.

Patot, Simon Tyssot de, *The Travels and Adventures of James Massey* (London, 1733).

Shakespeare, William, *Othello* (Methuen, London, 1958).

— *Romeo and Juliet* (Methuen, London, 1980).

Slotkin, J. S., *Readings in Early Anthropology* (London, 1965).

Tyson, Edward, *Orang-Outang, sive Homo Sylvestris: the anatomy of a pygmie compared with that of a monkey, an ape, and a man* (London, 1699).
Voltaire, *Essai sur les moeurs* and *Lettres philosophiques, Oeuvres complètes* (Paris, 1878–85), vols XI–XII and XX.

Secondary sources

Cohen, William B., *The French Encounter with Africans: White Response to Blacks, 1530–1880* (Indiana University Press, Bloomington, 1980).
Foucault, Michel, *The Order of Things: An Archaeology of the Human Sciences* (Vintage, New York, 1970).
Gates, Henry Louis, *Figures in Black: Words, Signs and the 'Racial' Self* (New York, 1982).
Gould, Stephen Jay, *The Mismeasure of Man* (Penguin, London, 1981).
Jones, Eldred, *Othello's Countrymen: The African in English Renaissance Drama* (Oxford University Press, London, 1965).
Jordan, Winthrop D., *White Over Black: American Attitudes Toward the Negro, 1550–1812* (University of North Carolina Press, Chapel Hill, 1968).
Lea, K. M., *Italian Popular Comedy: A Study in the Commedia dell'Arte, 1560–1620*, vol. I (OUP, Oxford, 1934).
Leader, Darian, *Why do women write more letters than they post?* (Faber, London, 1996).
Le Breton, André, *Le Roman au dix-huitième siècle* (Paris, 1898).
Mosse, George L., *Towards the Final Solution: A History of European Racism* (J. M. Dent, London, 1978).
Oreglia, Giacomo, *The Commedia dell'Arte* (Methuen, London, 1968).
Poliakov, Leon, *The Aryan Myth: A History of Racist and Nationalist Ideas in Europe* (Chatto & Windus, London, 1974).
Rosenberg, Aubrey, *Tyssot de Patot and his Work 1655–1738* (Martinus Nijhoff, The Hague, 1972).
Sand, Maurice, *The History of the Harlequinade*, vol. I (Martin Secker, London, 1915).
Sharp, Cecil J., and Herbert C. Macilwaine, *The Morris Book: A History of Morris Dancing* (Novello & Co., London, 1907).
Snowden, Frank M., *Blacks in Antiquity: Ethiopians in the Graeco-Roman Experience* (Harvard University Press, Cambridge, Mass., 1970).
Spink, J. S., *French Free-Thought from Gassendi to Voltaire* (Athlone Press, London, 1960).

2

Race and the Sentimental Imagination

God almighty has set before me two great objects, the suppression of the slave trade and the reformation of manners.
William Wilberforce in his diary, 1787

And we, father, can never guess from looking at a negro ... what
he may be when there is no white man to fear and hate, and where
he may reap whatever he has sown.
Harriet Martineau, *Demerara. A Tale* (1832)

The most insistent leitmotif running through white representations
of blackness since the eighteenth century is the idea that black
people are in some way closer to nature than whites. Seen
positively, they are more authentic and less emotionally inhibited
than Europeans. Seen negatively, they are closer to some inherent
evil, some heart of darkness, in human nature. Both views, the
optimistic and the pessimistic, share the notion that blackness is
truth-telling, that it reveals what human beings are really like when
stripped of the conventions of culture and civilisation.

The eighteenth-century anthropologists – echoed, as we shall
see, by Darwin and his followers – gave a literal rendition of this
theme of black naturalness. In a hierarchy of the human races,
Negroes are those which link us to the animal world. Others saw
in blackness an expression of authenticity, of connection with
natural feelings. This was the sentimental view of the African slave
promoted by the abolitionists, who – in a twist characteristic of

evangelical Christianity – exalted victimhood to a state of maso-
chistic nobility.

The popular culture of abolitionism – the plays, novels and
poetry on the subject of slavery that surrounded and supported the
political movement on both sides of the Atlantic – has been largely
left out of histories of racialism. Such works as Hannah Arendt's
The Origins of Totalitarianism (1951) and George L. Mosse's
Towards the Final Solution: A History of European Racism (1978)
are concerned primarily with tracing a history of racism back to the
eighteenth- and nineteenth-century classifiers. For this historio-
graphical tradition, racial attitudes derive ultimately from bad
science, from a dark side of the Enlightenment. In a way it is
surprising that the culture of abolitionism has been left out of the
equation, because the picture of the Negro that it painted has been
more influential on twentieth-century conceptions of blackness
than the esoteric researches of the head-measuring racial theorists.
The image of the black man as existential anti-hero, the bearer of
rebellion and authenticity, has its origins in the sentimental
aesthetic of abolitionism. White liberals are themselves written into
the complex, antique melodrama of racial attitudes, and to
understand the subconscious of modern white liberalism one must
go back to the culture of anti-slavery and its picture of the
suffering African.

Except for a few lone explorers such as Mungo Park – whose
Travels in the Interior Districts of Africa (1799) brought to Europe
the first modern information concerning the western Sudan and the
river Niger – the vast land-mass beyond the West African coastal
strip where European slavers pursued the trade remained *terra
incognita* until the second half of the nineteenth century, when the
African interior was 'opened up' to European economic exploitation, missionary activity and anthropological research. As the
Scottish writer James Montgomery put it in *The West Indies*, his
long poem 'written in honour of the Abolition of the African Slave
Trade, by the British Legislature, in 1807':

> From Nubian hills, that hail the dawning day
> To Guinea's coast, where evening fades away,

> Regions immense, unsearchable, unknown,
> Bask in the splendour of the solar zone.

But as we have already seen, eighteenth-century writers were happy to theorise about the nature of Africa and its inhabitants on the basis of ancient and fabulous accounts. Montgomery recognises Africa's status as a place of the imagination, a receptacle for fantasies and projections, when he goes on to describe it as

> A world of wonders – where creation seems
> No more the works of nature, but her dreams;
> Great, wild and beautiful, beyond control,
> She reigns in all the freedom of her soul.

In the late eighteenth and early nineteenth centuries, the single most dominant image of the Negro was that represented by Josiah Wedgwood's famous abolitionist medallion. The silhouetted figure of the kneeling slave – manacled hands raised in supplication, framed by the words 'Am I not a man and a brother?' – was an image that, like the CND peace symbol in modern times, came to be endlessly reproduced both in print and on artefacts such as cups, plates and brooches. The Negro, for Europeans, was by definition a slave, or at least a potential slave. To venture an opinion on the character, condition or potentialities of the Negro was inevitably to place oneself on one side or the other of one of the greatest political and moral issues of the day.

In revolutionary America, organised anti-slavery was limited to free blacks and to somewhat exclusive societies. The French Société des Amis des Noirs, formed in 1788, similarly lacked a popular base. It was in Britain that popular abolitionism was pioneered, based on a network of provincial 'corresponding committees', the widespread dissemination of propaganda and the mass petitioning of Parliament. Two vital ingredients of British abolitionism were its connections with religious dissent and with the wider move-ment for democratic constitutional reform. The Society for Effecting the Abolition of the Slave Trade was founded in April 1787 by the Quakers – who had already presented an abolitionist petition to Parliament in 1783 – with the support of evangelical members of the Church of England, notably Thomas Clarkson and William Wilberforce, Member of Parliament for the West Riding of Yorkshire. Wilberforce, a friend of the Prime Minister, William Pitt the Younger, was to lead the parliamentary campaign against the British slave trade, while Clarkson played a crucial organisational role in mobilising extra-parliamentary support and enabling abolitionism in the years 1788–92 to become popular without losing its 'respectability'. Clarkson was employed full-time by the society as a propagandist and organiser. In 1787 he made the first of his tours of provincial cities, forging links with reforming groups such as the Manchester Society for Constitutional Information and disseminating information about the slave trade. In the first fifteen months of its existence alone, the society produced over 15,000 copies of Clarkson's own pamphlet on the slave trade, as well as 1,500 copies of *An Historical Account of Guinea* by the American Quaker Anthony Benezet. Between 1787 and 1794 Clarkson made seven campaigning trips around Britain, covering some 35,000 miles.

We tend to take it for granted that the rapid creation of issues in the public mind is a product of twentieth-century electronic media, so that it comes as a surprise to discover just how quickly awareness of abolitionism spread during these years. And this awareness was reflected not just in political pamphlets and meetings, but in wider cultural forms. The late 1780s and early 1790s saw a spate of novels, plays and poetry that dealt with the slavery issue. In 1786 the surgeon-turned-novelist John Moore (1729–1802) published his popular *Zeluco*, the story of an evil and tyrannical Sicilian nobleman who becomes a slave owner in Cuba. Thomas Harwood's play *The Noble Slave* was staged in 1788, while 1790 saw two English translations, one dedicated to Wilberforce, of a lengthy and strongly Negrophile French novel by Joseph La Vallée, published in Paris the previous year as *Le Nègre comme il y a peu de Blancs*. Two years later Anna Maria Mackenzie published her melodramatic *Slavery; or the Times*. William Cowper's well-known poem 'The Negro's Complaint' appeared in 1788, Thomas Wilkinson's *An Appeal to England, on Behalf of the Abused Africans, A Poem* in 1789, a new edition of Thomas Day and John Bicknell's poem *The Dying Negro* (first published in 1773) in 1793 and Robert Southey's 'Poems concerning the Slave Trade' in 1794. Some of these works were written specifically as propaganda to further the abolitionist cause, while others were designed – with, one may conjecture, varying degrees of cynicism – to appeal to or exploit a popular interest.

The most striking instance of the latter – and the most impressive testimony to the swiftness with which abolitionism entered the public consciousness – was the opera *Inkle and Yarico*, first staged in London in August 1787 with music by Samuel Arnold to a libretto by the highly successful theatrical entrepreneur George Colman the younger. This piece – which was one of the most popular comic operas of its time, and remained so for at least fifty years – has been described as one of the first anti-slavery works for the theatre. In fact, though the libretto makes one or two bland passing gestures to anti-slavery sentiment, its primary purpose is to provide popular entertainment that mixes comedy and melodrama in an exotic setting. As an example of the tone of the play, and of the way in which topical references are slipped in, one might take the following passage of dialogue between Trudge, Inkle's servant, and Patty, a serving-woman. Trudge is describing his master's mistress, Yarico, who saved Inkle's life after a shipwreck. Inkle has brought her to Barbados and plans treacherously to sell her into slavery:

> *Patty.* Well; and tell me, Trudge; – she's pretty, you say – Is she fair or brown, or –
> *Trudge.* Um! she's a good comely copper.
> *Patty.* How! a tawny?
> *Trudge.* Yes, quite dark; but very elegant; like a Wedgwood teapot.
> *Patty.* Oh! the monster! the filthy fellow! Live with a black-a-moor!
> *Trudge.* Why, there's no great harm in't, I hope?
> *Patty.* Faugh! I wou'dn't let him kiss me for all the world: he'd make my face all smutty.
> *Trudge.* Zounds! you are mighty nice all of a sudden; but I'd

have you to know, Madam Patty, that black-a-moor ladies, as you call'em, are some of the very few whose complexions never rub off![1]

Colman's *Inkle and Yarico* is significant not as anti-slavery propaganda, but as a piece of popular entertainment that takes as a vehicle a theme of which its audience is assumed to have some knowledge. Although it is topical in this respect, and although the humour (much of it carried by the servant-class characters) appeals directly to its contemporary audience, the storyline of *Inkle and Yarico* was an old one. Colman's direct source seems to have been an essay by Richard Steele in the *Spectator* of March 1711, but the supposedly true story of Inkle and Yarico first appeared in Richard Ligon's *A True and Exact History of the Island of Barbadoes* (1657). In its original version Yarico is a beautiful Indian girl, but as the tale came to be repeated in different forms – it was translated into eight languages and inspired some forty separate works during the eighteenth century – its character changed. Yarico in many cases became a Negro virgin, and the slavery theme was brought to the fore. Colman further embellishes the tale by giving it a happy ending; Inkle, tricked out of the hand of Narcissa (daughter of the governor of Barbados, and his intended bride), sees the error of his ways and marries the faithful Yarico instead.

The fact that Colman based his libretto on a story almost 150 years old – a story that had practically acquired the status of folk tale – illustrates an important continuity in the way in which slavery was imagined by Europeans. The late eighteenth century may have seen an increase in the number of imaginative works dealing with slavery, in response to an increasing political concern with the issue, but the basic approach remained the same as it had been a hundred years earlier. As the historian David Brion Davis

[1] It is impossible to tell for sure whether or not the added resonance of Wedgwood's involvement in the abolitionist cause is fortuitous. I suspect not, given the sharpness of the dialogue throughout. In her introduction to this early nineteenth-century edition of the play, Mrs Inchbald gives Colman a rap on the knuckles for the frivolity of some passages in the libretto, but at the same time (and somewhat implausibly) praises it as 'a drama which might remove from Mr Wilberforce his aversion to theatrical exhibitions'.

has written, 'Europeans could conceptualize the meaning of enslavement only in the familiar terms that increasingly aroused a sensitive response from the middle class: the separation of young lovers; the heartless betrayal of an innocent girl; the unjust punishment of a faithful servant.'

These elements form the core of the Oroonoko story, the long-lived success of which exactly parallels that of *Inkle and Yarico*. Aphra Behn's short novel *Oroonoko, or the Royal Slave: A True History* was first published in 1688 and was based, the author claimed, on events that she herself had witnessed in Surinam. The story reached a wider public later with the stage adaptation by Thomas Southerne and John Hawkesworth. Southerne's version was performed every year for a century after 1696, while Behn's original novel was introduced into France in a translation by Antoine Laplace in 1745, and by the end of the century had been through seven editions. Research done into the catalogues of French private libraries over the period 1760–80 shows that *Oroonoko* was apparently among the nine most read English novels in France at the middle of the eighteenth century.

The subject matter of *Inkle and Yarico* and *Oroonoko* – innocence betrayed and star-crossed lovers – was also that of the slavery literature of the late eighteenth century. The enormous actual gulf between European and enslaved African was bridged in the imagination by projecting on to slavery conventional melodramatic scenarios. To the extent that the imaginative treatment of slaves and slavery changed, it was not because of any fresh observation of slavery (most of the authors concerned were entirely ignorant of, and uninterested in, actual, living slaves) but because the nature of the projections – the prevailing aesthetic attitudes and the feelings of guilt, hope and fear concerning the institution of slavery itself – had changed. To that extent, the European literature of the eighteenth and early nineteenth centuries – even the most fervently Negrophile and abolitionist – failed to bridge the gulf. The anti-slavery aesthetic spoke more of the reader and of his (or, very often, her) existence than it did of that of the slave, its ostensible subject. Herein, ultimately, lay the limits of sentiment.

A number of intellectual and cultural strands came together in the sentimental projections of the anti-slavery aesthetic. In the first place, there was the naturalisation of narrative that took place in the first half of the eighteenth century, the attempt to strip away an accretion of 'romance' in order to reveal the perceptions and emotions that constitute the 'true history' of individuals. The criterion by which a narrative was to be judged switched from the rhetorical to the epistemological, from the skill and elegance of exposition to the revelation of truth. The opening of Aphra Behn's *Oroonoko* sets out the kind of disclaimer (actually, of course, a kind of claim) that was to be repeated at the head of any number of eighteenth-century novels:

> I do not pretend in giving you the History of this *Royal Slave*, to entertain my Reader with the Adventures of a feign'd *Hero* . . . [I]t shall come simply into the World, recommended by its own proper Merits . . . there being enough of Reality to support it, and to render it diverting, without the Addition of Invention.

By about 1730 the *roman héroïque* had been supplanted in France by the *mémoire*, a fiction cast in autobiographical form and dealing with events of the recent past. In England, too, the journal or retrospective autobiography (*Robinson Crusoe* combines both forms) became the prevalent formal means by which the novelist could bring his story closer to the grain of individual experience. Samuel Richardson's *Clarissa* (1747–8), which enjoyed enormous popularity and influence on both sides of the Channel, was important in establishing the epistolary form as a way of bringing the narrative viewpoint closer still to the unfolding emotional drama. In his 'Eloge de Richardson' (1761) Diderot praises the English author for eschewing the futuristic and exotic and bringing literature down to the level of ordinary life.

> This author does not harrow us with descriptions of horrors, nor carry us on a magic carpet to distant countries; in his company we are not in danger of being devoured by savages, nor of frequenting hidden houses of ill-repute, neither does he

transport us to fairy-land. No, his stage is the real world in which we now live, the actions are true to nature, the actors live and breathe; they are the people we meet in society, and the incidents that befall them are such as might happen in any civilised country.

Diderot goes on to argue that though Richardson does take us on a journey, it is not a conventional one of travel narrative, but an inner journey, a journey to the dark recesses of the psyche where the passions are to be found. With an unforgettable image, Diderot reveals a racial aspect to this 'darkness':

> [Richardson] carries the torch to the back of the cave; he teaches us how to distinguish the subtle and dishonest motives which conceal themselves beneath other motives which are honest and which hasten to show themselves first. He blows on the sublime spectre that presents itself at the entrance to the cave; and the hideous Moor which it masks appears.

The association of the 'Moor' with sublime horror recalls Burke. But in addition, Diderot associates the black face and body stripped of its mask with the human psyche stripped of societal convention and pretence.

Had he lived to read it, Richardson would surely have been horrified at the gloss that Diderot puts on his novel. Far from wishing to demonstrate that morality was merely a tissue of convention masking a basic atavism, Richardson's avowed intention was to teach virtue by encouraging the reader to empathise with the tribulations of his heroine. 'My story', he wrote in a letter, 'is designed to strengthen the tender Mind, and to enable the worthy Heart to bear up against the Calamities of Life.' The reader learns virtue by way of sympathy and pity, by identifying with Clarissa's protracted sufferings at the hands of her malevolent family and her would-be seducer (and eventual rapist) Lovelace. Nor is virtue encouraged by the simple means of annexing to it immediate rewards: there is no happy ending for Clarissa, who dies a lengthy death. In Richardson's piously Christian scheme of things, Clarissa's reward belongs in another place.

Ten years after *Clarissa*, Adam Smith published his *Theory of Moral Sentiments* (1759), in which he builds an entire ethical theory on the propensity to identify with the sufferings of others, to put oneself in another's shoes:

How selfish soever man may be supposed, there are evidently some principles in his nature, which interest him in the fortune of others, and render their happiness necessary to him, though he derives nothing from it except the pleasure of seeing it. Of this kind is pity or compassion, the emotion which we feel for the misery of others, when we either see it, or are made to conceive it in a lively manner ... Though our brother is on the rack, as long as we ourselves are at our ease, our senses will never inform us of what he suffers. They never did, and never can, carry us beyond our own person, and it is by the imagination only that we can form any conception of what are his sensations ... By the imagination we place ourselves in his situation, we conceive ourselves enduring the same torments, we enter as it were into his body, and become in some measure the same person with him, and thence form some idea of his sensations, and even feel something which, though weaker in degree, is not altogether unlike them.

Smith's vision of a harmony between private desires and desirable public outcomes – which has obvious parallels with his later economic theory – was a development of the theory of 'benevolence' made famous by the third Earl of Shaftesbury (1671–1713). Shaftesbury was a pupil of Locke, but rejected his teacher's radical views on innate ideas. For Shaftesbury, the idea of the mind as a *tabula rasa*, a creature of sensation, was unpalatably materialist. Instead, he posited an innate moral sense – something between reason and intuition – that if unimpeded would lead people to benevolence and humanity towards others, rather than to the kind of aggressive egoism that according to Hobbes was the ground-zero of human nature. By the last quarter of the eighteenth century moral philosophy had moved on from Shaftesbury, but the idea of innate benevolence, of a 'sensibility' that combined the aesthetic, the moral, the emotional and even the physical, had entered the ground water of English literary culture. Shaftesbury himself had been influenced by Platonism, but in its new guise of 'sensibility' the idea of benevolence now laid more stress on intuition than rationality:

> Sweet SENSIBILITY! thou keen delight!
> Unprompted moral! sudden sense of right!
> Perception exquisite! fair virtue's seed!
> Thou quick precursor of the lib'ral deed!
> Thou hasty conscience! reason's blushing morn!
> Instinctive kindness e'er reflection's born!
> Prompt sense of equity! . . .
> To those who know thee not no words can paint,
> And those who know thee, know all words are faint.
>   (Hannah More, 'Sensibility')

For Hannah More, author of many pious and improving stories and poems – including a number on slavery – sensibility is not merely an intuition; it is a bodily faculty by whose sympathetic operation 'the feeling heart / Shapes its own wound, and points itself the dart'. The way in which she describes it echoes the language one finds again and again in the sentimental literature of the late eighteenth century, a physiological language of vibrating, pleasurably humming nerves:

> Nor is the trembling temper more awake
> To every wound calamity can make,
> Than is the finely-fashioned nerve alive
> To every transport pleasure has to give.

More was a member of the Clapham Sect, that group of influential evangelical Anglicans that also included Wilberforce. Although evangelical Christians accepted the notion of benevolence, they also pictured the soul as being mired in sin. Only personal redemption through Christ's love could save the sinner. The existential process of being redeemed from sin is frequently described as one of being freed from a metaphorical slavery:

> Long my imprisoned spirit lay

Fast bound in sin and nature's night;
Thine eye diffused a quickening ray –
I woke, the dungeon flamed with light;
My chains fell off, my heart was free . . .

An important reason for the leading role played by evangelicals in the abolition movement was surely that they saw externalised in the institution of slavery the battle between the dark bondage of sin and the light of Christian liberty that was carried on in each individual soul. The association was to achieve its fullest expression, as we shall see, in the most famous of all sentimental novels dealing with the 'peculiar institution'. *Uncle Tom's Cabin* is a novel about slavery, but it is above all a novel about sin and salvation, about heaven and hell.

Many particular historical examples could be brought forward to illustrate the interconnections between these aesthetic, philosophical and religious components of the anti-slavery aesthetic. In his *The Just Limitation of Slavery in the Laws of God* (1778) we find the evangelical abolitionist Granville Sharp evoking through a biblical example that act of imaginative projection and sympathetic identification that underlay both novelistic sentimentalism and Adam Smith's moral philosophy:

[The Israelites] were reminded of their Bondage in Egypt: for so the almighty *Deliverer* from *Slavery* warned his people to limit and moderate the *bondage*, which the Law permitted, by the remembrance of *their own former bondage* in a foreign land, and by a remembrance also of his great mercy in *delivering them* from that *bondage*: and he expressly referred them to their own *feelings*, as they themselves had experienced the intolerable yoke of Egyptian Tyranny!

Then there is the spiritual and intellectual biography of the Reverend John Newton (1725–1807). Newton's *Thoughts on the African Slave Trade* (1788) was one of the most influential pieces of propaganda published by the newly formed Committee for the Abolition of the Slave Trade, its authority and authenticity deriving largely from the fact that Newton drew upon his own experiences as a participant in the trade. In 1750, following an adolescence largely spent at sea, Newton was appointed commander of a slave ship and subsequently made three voyages to West Africa. In his *Authentic Narrative* (1764) he told the remarkable story of his conversion to evangelicism, laying stress (not without an element of retrospective irony) on the part played by a particular experience of his teenage years in mapping out his subsequent path to redemption:

> I became acquainted with Lord Shaftesbury. I saw the second volume of his Characteristics in a petty shop at Middleburgh in Holland. The title allured me to buy it, and the style and manner gave me great pleasure in reading, especially the second piece, which his lordship, with great propriety, has entitled, a Rhapsody ... thus, with fine words and fair speeches, my simple heart was beguiled. This book was always in my hand; I read it, till I could very nearly repeat the Rhapsody verbatim from beginning to end. No immediate effect followed, but it operated like a slow poison, and prepared the way for all that followed ... I so much admired the pictures of virtue and benevolence as drawn by Lord Shaftesbury.

And in his *Thoughts*, Newton uses the language of sentiment and sensibility to put the argument – often made by abolitionists – that the slave trade had 'dreadful effects ... upon the minds of those who were engaged in it':

> I know of no method of getting money, not even that of robbing for it upon the highway, which has so direct a tendency to efface the moral sense, to rob the heart of every gentle and humane disposition, and to harden it, like steel, against all impressions of sensibility.

By the time his *Thoughts* were published, Newton was already one of the most revered evangelical ministers of his day, a special adviser and confidant not only to Wilberforce, but also to literary figures such as Hannah More and the poet William Cowper. According to More, he could not spend half an hour in conversation without bringing up the subject of the African slave trade and his own former part in it.

The starting-point for the abolitionist attitude to the Negro was pity. 'Alas!' says Blandford, the Englishman who befriends the royal slave Oroonoko in Southerne's stage version of the story, 'I pity you.' And Oroonoko, for his part, is grateful for that pity: 'Do pity me: / Pity's a-kin to love; and every thought / Of that soft kind is welcome to my soul.' The basic story of the three-volume abolitionist novel by Joseph La Vallée, translated into English in 1790 under the title *The Negro as there are Few White Men*, parallels the Oroonoko tale, except for its happy ending: Itanoko, an African prince, is tricked aboard a slave ship and snatched away from his family and his childhood sweetheart. After many tribulations, the royal slave is reunited with his sweetheart, who by coincidence has been brought as a slave to the same colony, and the happy couple achieve their freedom. Sympathy is evoked by the simple means of an extremely flattering portrait of the hero's noble character alongside lurid descriptions of the cruelties he suffers. As the English translator (who dedicated his version to Wilberforce) comments in the Preface: 'I flatter myself that perusal of these sheets will rankle with remorses the guilty breast, and steal a sigh – perhaps a tear – from the sensibility of honest souls . . .'

In this respect, the literary treatment of the slave accorded with the wider sentimental enthusiasm for victims – first and foremost seduced and abandoned women, but also imprisoned debtors, children, etc. By the 1790s, sentimentalism was coming under sustained critical attack, and it is scarcely surprising to find the pity held out to the slave being seen cynically as merely the extension of a self-serving literary fad:

> [T]he poor African is . . . fair game for every minstrel that has tuned his lyre to the sweet chords of pity and condolence; whether he *builds immortal verse* upon his loss of liberty, or weaves his melancholy fate into the pathos of a novel, in either case he finds a mine of sentiment, digs up enthusiasm from its richest vein, and gratifies at once his spleen and his ambition. (Richard Cumberland, Introduction to *Henry* (1795))

Ironically, one of the sternest contemporary critiques of sentimentalism comes from the pen of Henry Mackenzie, whose own novel *The Man of Feeling* (1771) – 'not merely vulgar,' in the words of Aldous Huxley, 'but positively ludicrous ... vulgar to the point of ridiculousness' – has entered the canon as representing the nadir of the genre. In an article published in 1785 – long after he had given up writing novels himself – he questions whether all the tears and pity of sentimental novels are not just so much self-indulgence:

> In the enthusiasm of sentiment there is much the same danger as in the enthusiasm of religion, of substituting certain impulses and feelings of what may be called a visionary kind, in the place of real practical duties ... In morals, as in religion, there are not wanting instances of refined sentimentalists, who are contented with talking of virtues which they never practise, who pay in words what they owe in actions ... This separation of conscience from feeling is a depravity of the most pernicious sort ...

Mackenzie had followed up his *Man of Feeling* with a 'woman of feeling' novel, *Julia de Roubigné* (1777), and there is a brief but significant episode in the book that deals with slavery. The role that it plays in the creaking mechanism of Mackenzie's plot illustrates exactly the point he was later to make that in dealing with emotive subjects like slavery, sentimentalists were more concerned with the refinement of their own sensibility than with any practical outcome. Julia de Roubigné's father has fallen into debt and is helped out by the dull but worthy Montauban, who falls in love with Julia. Mistakenly thinking that her true love, Savillon, has married another while abroad, she submits to marrying Montauban. On learning of her mistake, she agrees to a farewell meeting with Savillon. Montauban, misinterpreting this meeting, is seized with jealousy and poisons her. As she is dying, Julia tells him of her innocence and, maddened by remorse, Montauban poisons himself.

Savillon's fateful absence involves a trip to stay with his uncle, a planter in one of the West Indian colonies. On arriving on the island, he feels a fastidious distaste for the moral climate of the place:

I fear I am unfit for the task [of becoming a successful planter]: I must unlearn feelings in which I have been long accustomed to delight: I must accommodate sentiment to conveniency, pride to interest, and sometimes even virtue itself to fashion.

In particular, Savillon is shocked by the cruel treatment of the slaves, though he takes comfort in an engagingly naïve reflection: 'I cannot easily imagine, that, in any latitude, the bosom is shut to those pleasures which result from the exercise of goodness.' He persuades his uncle to allow him to experiment with a gentler form of management, under which the slaves will work voluntarily rather than under the compulsion of the whip. Savillon persuades Yamba (a prince, of course) to be his overseer and explains his plans to one of the ordinary slaves, who shows appropriate gratitude:

'Yamba shall be my friend, and help me to raise sugars for the good of us all: you shall have no other overseer but Yamba, and shall work no more than he bids you.' The negro fell at my feet and kissed them; samba stood silent, and I saw a tear on his cheek.

Savillon's scheme is, of course, a success. The slaves flock to that part of the plantation on which he has been allowed to conduct his experiment, and the compulsion of kindness proves more profitable than that of the whip. Savillon makes a brief speech against the prevailing plantation system ('a theatre of rapine, of slavery, and of murder!') and again marks out his own moral high ground: 'Forgive the warmth of this apostrophe! Here it would not be understood; even my uncle, whose heart is far from a hard one, would smile at my romance, and tell me things must be so.' 'The master of slaves', he concludes, 'has seldom the soul of a man.' And then we return to the machinations of the main plot, never to touch the subject of slavery again. The episode on the plantation is a detail, its sole purpose to constitute another brick in the edifice of Savillon's nobility of character.

Mackenzie may have liked portraying sentimentalist idealists, but he himself was nobody's fool, becoming in time a pillar of Scotland's notoriously corrupt political establishment. 'A hard-headed, practical man,' one contemporary described him, 'as full of practical wisdom as most of his fictitious characters are devoid of it.' As if to bear out his later comments on the gap between sentimental affect and practical effect, in a pamphlet written in the 1790s Henry Mackenzie welcomes the defeat of parliamentary bills to abolish the slave trade and dismisses his earlier novelistic abolitionism as 'the momentary ebullition of romantic humanity'.

If kindness to the suffering slave was a useful index of noble sentiment, the converse was also the case: cruelty to slaves reflected above all on the moral depravity of the master. A crude but enthusiastic treatment of this theme is to be found in John Moore's popular novel *Zeluco. Various Views of Human Nature, Taken from Life and Manners, Foreign and Domestic* (1786). The subtitle hints at the story's rambling quality; on the opening page – the tone teetering between the titillating come-on and weary contemplation of the task ahead – Moore identifies the only connecting thread of his fictitious biography:

> Tracing the windings of vice . . . and delineating the disgusting features of villainy, are unpleasant tasks: and some people cannot bear to contemplate such a picture. It is fair, therefore, to warn readers of this turn of mind not to peruse the story of Zeluco.

On page 2 our young villain strangles his pet sparrow, and the rest of his career follows naturally from this: he tyrannises everyone around him, tricks rich widows into marriage, murders his own child and drives its mother mad. In the end he is satisfactorily dispatched with a stiletto in the guts. Early in the novel, after a brief and dishonourable career in the Sicilian army, Zeluco becomes a planter and slave-owner in Cuba, a 'situation in which the understanding cannot improve, and the disposition is the most likely to degeneration'. Zeluco's career as a slave-owner is a crucial turning-point on his road to moral ruin:

How many men have, for a great part of their lives, supported
the character of well-disposed good-natured people; and on
going from Europe to the West Indies, and becoming proprie-
tors of slaves, have gradually grown ill-tempered, capricious,
haughty and cruel. Even Zeluco, though of a capricious, violent
and selfish disposition, was not naturally cruel; this last grew on
him in consequence of unlimited power.

Zeluco orders the whipping to death of the gentle slave Hammo, a
prototype of Uncle Tom, and generally gives full vent to his
villainy. A dialogue between Zeluco and a humane physician
rehearses the familiar arguments for and against slavery, but the
clincher for Moore – and, briefly, for Zeluco himself – is the
consideration that it is 'infinitely more pleasing to be considered as
the distributor of happiness, than the inflictor of pain'.

For Mackenzie and Moore, slavery is a mirror in which is
reflected the simple outlines of their heroes and villains. Slavery as
an institution is of less interest than the sensibility (or lack of it) of
the observer. For Moore, Zeluco's slaves are without an independent history or *raison d'être*; they are merely 'those unfortunate
creatures whom Providence, for reasons we cannot penetrate,
subjected to his power'. So much for the slave trade.

By the 1790s, we find sympathy for the slave – or lack of it –
being used as an index not just of sensibility but of social class.
Hannah More is clear on the point that sensibility is not
democratically distributed:

> Let not the vulgar read this pensive strain,
> Their jests the tender anguish would profane...
> They never know, in all their coarser bliss,
> The sacred rapture of a pain like this:
> Then take, ye happy vulgar, take your part
> Of sordid joy, which never touch'd the heart.

We have already seen how in *Inkle and Yarico* jokes about race
and colour are given to lower-class characters. And in this context
it is worth noting how from the 'royal slave' Oroonoko to Yarico
– who comes equipped with her own serving-woman – it is a

practically unbending rule in eighteenth-century imaginative literature on slavery to describe any named African character as 'a
prince' or 'of royal blood', as though such social distinction were a
necessary make-weight to justify their presence in the narrative. It
is in part this attribution of 'nobility' in a specific sense that makes
for the continuity in representations of the Negro across a period,
from the mid-seventeenth to the early nineteenth century, when
literature in general moved from aristocratic, heroic characterisations to more bourgeois, democratic forms.

Nowhere do we find sympathy for the slave being allied with
social class as clearly as in Anna Maria Mackenzie's novel *Slavery;
or the Times* (1792), which is almost universally ignored in
secondary literature – one recent history of women's writing on
slavery blandly and rather inaccurately dismisses it as 'racist' – but
which provides an important example of how a sentimental
Negrophile aesthetic had become detached from its abolitionist
moorings. The book, based loosely on the true case of a Prince
Naimbana (whose story was written up in a contemporary tract,
possibly by John Newton), tells the story of an African prince,
Adolphus, who is sent by his father to England to be educated. The
novel, written in the form of letters, adopts all the overheated
conventions of the sentimental novel, as 'the noble Adolphus'
moves weepingly through scenes intended to highlight his own
selflessness and the brutality that surrounds him. That Adolphus is
a cut above his fellow Africans is constantly emphasised. As he
himself writes, bizarrely mixing 'rights of man' philosophy with
pure snobbery:

> I cannot forget that Adolphus is a *prince*, that Sambo and Omra
> are but his father's subjects. How should they then think as I
> do? I know that they are my fellow-creatures, claiming all the
> rights of humanity; but do not, good sir, do not suppose that
> they are my equals, in strength of mind, self-denial or descent.

Much of the plot of *Slavery* concerns the attempts of the
villainous Mr and Mrs Abrams to get their hands on the
inheritance of Adolphus's English sweetheart, Mary St Leger.
What overt 'racism' there is in the book is put into the mouths of

this couple, and is strongly associated in the reader's mind with their crude characterisation as vulgar parvenus, insensible to finer feelings. Mrs Abrams's malapropisms give her tirade against Adolphus a distinct social slant:

> [T]his scrubby negro, this *cannable*, this *selvidge*, chuses to insult me – sir, if he was a christian, or even a Jew, one would not mind it so much. But when the *parlemint*-house is all up in arms about 'em, when even all Mr Will-by-force can say stands for nothing, though he pretends they're free born like us, is such a puppy as *this* to chatter?

Adolphus's reaction is one of withering sang-froid:

> This vulgar nonsense was received with silent contempt by Adolphus, who now discovered, in his opposition to such coarse behaviour, the degradation of his own dignity . . .

Throughout the book, Adolphus and his African companions find that it is 'the lower class of people' who make 'ungenerous observations on their persons, dress, and manners'. *Slavery*'s social conservatism reaches its absurd apotheosis in the final scenes, when Mary's father is kidnapped by the revolutionary French national guard, who are working in cahoots with the Abrames. Adolphus – himself fervently opposed to the revolution – rescues his sweetheart's father, and the book ends with eulogies of 'the quiet regulations of a protestant monarchical government'. (As one of the Frenchmen concedes: 'The liberty we contend for blossoms sweetly in your nation.') Zimza, Adolphus's father, delivers a speech on slavery – apportioning blame even-handedly to Europeans and Africans, calling for amelioration rather than abolition and warning of the dangers of African vengeance. Discreetly, Anna Maria Mackenzie brings down the curtain before the denouement one would surely expect of such a narrative – a union between Adolphus and the fair Mary.

Anna Maria Mackenzie's *Slavery* looks forward to the day when 'the savage perfections of Africa are tempered by the soft polish of refined manners'. Conversely, the selfless integrity of Adolphus is used to highlight European decadence and corruption. The use of exotic or 'primitive' viewpoints to ridicule European *moeurs* had a long history by 1792.[1] What was different about sentimentalist authors like Mackenzie and La Vallée is that the role of such characters is no longer to introduce a note of free-thinking relativism, but rather to show characters who were closer to some universally shared benevolent nature. The Africans have a kind of moral authenticity ('Who could mortify the grandeur of an untaught soul, impelled alone by its native feelings? Who could check a liberality so amiable? How can the haughty masters of these wretched people account for such sublime affection...') because civilised society has yet to impose on them the shackles of sin and corruption.

To this mixture of Rousseau and Wesley is added the belief that moral truth is discovered beneath the whip, just as sensibility is exemplified by the ability to suffer along with the suffering of others. There is a strong physicality to the notion of sympathy as we find it in the sentimental novelists. The reader observes the slave-victim's nerves quivering beneath the lash, and her own nerves tremble in harmony. She dissolves or 'melts' in tears, just as Adolphus does at the many scenes of 'oppressed goodness' that he encounters.

The Marquis de Sade was publishing his novels at exactly this time, and a number of critics – Leslie Fiedler, for example, in *Love and Death in the American Novel* – have interpreted the gothic literature of sado-masochism as being but an alternative manifestation of sentimentalism. Indeed, the descriptions of the horrors of the slave trade in abolitionist literature have at times an almost pornographic attention to detail. Few readers' nerves would be unaffected by lines like these, from Stansfield's *The Guinea Voyage*:

> In painful rows with studious art comprest,
> Smoking they lie, and breathe the humid pest:

[1] In 1764 Gabriel Mailhol published *Le Philosophe Nègre*, a Voltairean philosophical tale in which the central Candide figure is a slave. Not that all the ridicule here is aimed at the Europeans; the very title carries an implicit paradox.

Moisten'd with gore, on the hard platform ground,
The bare-rub'd joint soon bursts the painful bound;
Sinks in th'obdurate plank with racking force,
And ploughs – dire task, its agonizing course! ...
Then flies the scourge, sparing nor sex nor age,
Stripe follows stripe, in boundless, brutal rage.
Then the vile engines in the hateful cause
Are plied relentless; in the straining jaws
The wrenching instruments with barbarous force
Give the detested food th'unwilling course.

Kindness and cruelty – this is the simple scale by which the relation of European and Negro is judged. The European is their distributor, the Negro their beneficiary or victim. Negroes as portrayed in sentimental literature are not quite passive, but certainly reactive; their actions are determined by those of the whites, assisted only by the prompting of a universal and benevolent inner 'nature'. In *The Negro as there are Few White Men*, Itanoko says of the Africans' response to the European's arrival in their land: 'Both in receiving and repulsing them, we followed the instinct of nature. We surely had not their knowledge, but a more tender heart...' The Negro lives in the moment, his actions stimulated by immediate experience. As J. Dubois-Fontanelle wrote in 1775 in his *Anecdotes Africaines*, a compilation of contemporary lore about the continent:

> For the most part, Africans live from day to day ... They think neither about the past nor the future; and just as their ancestors had little interest in leaving records for them, they are no more disposed to leave them for posterity.

It was an extremely rare writer in the eighteenth century who would attribute to Africa any independent culture or history worth speaking of. A notable exception was the French abolitionist Henri Grégoire, whose *De la littérature des nègres* (1808) was the first book to point out to Europeans the cultural achievements of individual blacks. But Maupertius was, in the context of his time, an eccentric. Much more typical even of Negrophile writers is the cultureless, Edenic portrait of Africa sketched by La Vallée in *The Negro as there are Few White Men*:

> [D]rawing the bow, course, swimming, wrestling, hunting, thus fleet the uniform days of the Negro's youth. Heaven would undoubtedly not suffer arts and sciences to be bestowed on us, we learn but what can be useful; we see no further than the wants of nature.

And a contemporary traveller's account, quoted as a footnote to Day and Bicknell's abolitionist poem *The Dying Negro*, sees West Africa through the same lens:

> Which way soever I turned my eyes on this spot, I beheld a perfect image of pure nature, an agreeable solitude bounded on every side by charming landscapes; the rural situation of cottages in the midst of trees; the ease and indolence of the Negroes, reclined under the shade of their spreading foliage; the simplicity of their dress and manners; the whole revived in my mind the idea of our first parents, and I seemed to contemplate the world in its primitive state.

Africans are closer to nature, both in the sense of the environment from which they come and in the sense of being, in modern parlance, more 'in touch with their feelings'. In Mackenzie's *Slavery* Adolphus apologises for the effusiveness of one of his letters with the comment that 'it was written without reflection, but it was dictated by my heart'. And Louisa Hamilton, confidante of his sweetheart Mary, describes 'our noble Adolphus' thus:

> His heart knows no guile. His passions wear no mask. His intercourse with our world has not sullied the purity of a mind which reflects, with added brilliancy, the virtues set before it. All is open and sincere in his conduct; I will venture to say all is equally so in his heart.

We have seen how the ancient associations of blackness with sexual transgression and excess were translated into the pseudo-scientific anthropology of the eighteenth century. The genteel, sentimental imaginative literature of the anti-slavery movement tends to steer clear of interpreting the Negro's physicality in overtly sexual terms.[1] The slave's physicality asserts itself through suffering; his body appears beneath the whip. The erotic content is reduced to a residual, sublimated sado-masochism. The slave's actions are dictated by this economy of violence, and consist of expressions of either gratitude or a desire for vengeance. This polarity of, on the one hand, effusive gratitude (with its corollary, forgiveness) and, on the other, violent retribution, forms an obsessional leitmotif of the eighteenth-century imaginative literature on slavery. Indeed, it is barely an exaggeration to say that just as whites are described exclusively in terms of their kindness or cruelty, every single action or speech of an African in this literature can be read in terms of where it can be placed on this scale from heartfelt thanks to brutal vengeance.

Dozens of examples could be produced from the works already cited of slaves kneeling in thanks or supplication, like the figure in Wedgwood's medallion, or responding to cruelty with schemes of bloody revolt. But two works not yet discussed demonstrate more fully this theme. Jacques-Henri Bernardin de Saint-Pierre is best known as the author of *Paul et Virginie* (1788), the Rousseauesque (he was a disciple of the great man, and wrote a memoir of him) tale of Edenic romance – set on the Indian Ocean island of Mauritius – that remained a best-seller throughout the nineteenth century. (Dickens was among its admirers.) But among his other works is a play, *Empsaël* (1797), which, while it rehearses the familiar arguments against the slave trade, is of interest here because its plot is animated by the idea of black revenge.

The plan of the play is set out in the prospectus that Bernardin de Saint-Pierre attached to it:

Having shown in my *Voyage à L'Ille de France* a negro enslaved

[1] Though it should be noted that in Southerne's popular stage version of Behn's novel, it is sexual jealousy (perhaps recalling *Othello*) that spurs Oroonoko to rebellion. And elsewhere we find occasional evocations of blacks' supposed physical spontaneity. The final couplet of *Les Nègres*, a one-act comedy published in 1783, has a modern ring:

> Pour danser, vivent nos amans,
> Les noirs dansent mieux que les blancs.

to Europeans, I thought it appropriate to show in turn Europeans enslaved to blacks, in order to demonstrate more forcefully our injustice towards them . . .[1]

The Empsaël of the title is the Negro chief minister to the Emperor of Morocco. Having been imprisoned himself as a boy by the Spanish and taken to San Domingo as a slave, he has now become a Muslim and devotes his life to satisfying his hatred of Europeans. 'His heart was magnanimous,' we are told, 'but his memories were bitter, and he had sworn to live only for vengeance.' He uses his position of power to capture by piracy and enslave as many Europeans as possible.[2] He is described as 'this fierce beast, who takes pleasure only in carnage', but Anthony Benezet – the abolitionist Quaker who appears as a character in the play – lays the blame for Empsaël's cruelty firmly at the feet of Europe. 'This black was born with all the good qualities of his race, but the Europeans changed him by lighting within him the fire of vengeance.' Bernardin de Saint-Pierre gets some satiric mileage out of the reversal of European and African situations, but eventually Empsaël is redeemed by the love of a good European woman, Zoaïde, and by the humanitarian arguments of Benezet. He frees the Europeans.

Maria Edgeworth's 'The Grateful Negro' (1802), included in her children's collection of *Popular Tales*, is set in Jamaica and built around a contrast between a grateful slave and a vengeful one, the contrast paralleling that between a kind master and a cruel one. The kind one is Mr Edwards. ('This gentleman treated his slaves with all possible humanity and kindness. He wished that there was no such thing as slavery in the world; but was convinced, by the arguments of those who have the best means of obtaining

[1] This simple scheme of reversing racial roles is the basis of a recent film starring John Travolta, *White Man's Burden*.
[2] The capture and enslavement of Christians by Muslims from the Barbary states of North Africa had exercised a fascination on the European mind for centuries. (For the historical basis of this fascination, see Stephen Clissold, *The Barbary Slaves* (London, 1977).) That this interest was still there at the end of the eighteenth century can be seen in the popular success of the comic operas *Die Entführung aus dem Serail* ('The Abduction from the Seraglio') (1782) by Mozart and *L'Italiana in Algeri* ('The Italian Girl in Algiers') (1813) by Rossini.

information, that the sudden emancipation of the negroes would rather increase than diminish their miseries.') He buys the slave couple Caesar and Clara from his neighbour, the cruel Mr Jeffries, because the latter is intending to sell Clara away separately. Mr Edwards's benevolence works its magic on Caesar:

> Kindness was new to him; it overpowered his manly heart; and at hearing the words 'my good friend', the tears gushed from his eyes: tears which no torture could have extorted! Gratitude swelled in his bosom...

When a slave revolt is planned by the fierce Coramantee slave Hector ('with them revenge was a virtue'), Caesar refuses to take part:

> The principle of gratitude conquered every other sensation. The mind of Caesar was not insensible to the charms of freedom... his heart beat light at the idea of recovering his liberty: but he was not to be seduced from his duty, not even by this delightful hope...

He dies defending his master's plantation, defending his own slavery. Edgeworth ends her tale with the pious hope that when they read of 'the treachery of the whole race of slaves, our readers ... will think that at least one exception may be made, in favour of THE GRATEFUL NEGRO.'

Edgeworth's docile Caesar and vengeful Hector are the summation of a long tradition. Both figures, both polarities, are present in anti-slavery literature of the eighteenth century, with only their relative prominence varying. And though they are conceived of as opposites, they are frequently presented in tandem, as opposed sides of a single coin. Where one is both product and expression of natural benevolence, the other is nature red in tooth and claw. Rebelliousness is a blind, instinctive lust for retribution, essentially irrational and even insane:

> Did then the Negro rear at last the sword
> Of vengeance? Did he plunge its thirsty blade
> In the hard heart of his inhuman lord?

Oh! who shall blame him? In the midnight shade
There came upon him the intolerable thought
Of every past delight; his native grove,
Friendship's best joys, and liberty and love,
For ever lost. Such recollections wrought
His brain to madness.

(Robert Southey, 'Poems concerning the Slave Trade')

It was common for eighteenth-century writers to depict disease and hurricanes – familiar dangers in the West Indies – as agents for natural or divine vengeance against slave traders and planters. Black rebellion was imagined by extension in a similar way, as a natural force that would engulf the whites in an ocean of blood. The black slave is seen as the bearer of some inner, natural authenticity – the 'hideous Moor' at the mouth of Diderot's cave. Naked of the trappings of civilisation, rendered authentic by the experience of suffering, his body speaks of a common humanity through the reduction of that humanity to a physical, 'natural' and instinctive essence.

The body is black – or, more commonly in the poetic diction of the time, 'sable' – and in the anti-slavery literature of the eighteenth century we find reproduced the association of blackness with the body and with physicality – and by extension, with sin and suffering. Whiteness, by contrast, is associated with an inner or hidden spirituality. Even in such an abolitionist piece as Day and Bicknell's *Dying Negro*, the African's nobility and spirituality are introduced as something in opposition to, and despite, his blackness:

What tho' the sun in his meridian blaze
Dart on their naked limbs his scorching rays;
What tho' no rosy tints adorn their face,
No silken tresses shine with flowing grace;
Yet of ethereal temper are their souls.

Elsewhere, the association of whiteness with spirituality is more explicit. In Moore's *Zeluco*, when a soldier tries to get a priest to give the last rites to Hammo, the Uncle Tom figure, the priest objects on the grounds that 'he is a black'. 'His soul,' counters the soldier, 'is whiter than a skinned potato.' In Mackenzie's *Slavery*, the spiritual equality of black and white is imagined as being despite the Negroes' blackness, pictured as a seeing through that black physicality to a light and fairness within. Adolphus says of Louisa Hamilton that 'her sensibility distinguished innate sincerity through the dark hue that shrouded Zimza's countenance. Yes, she looked to the heart for that equality the Christians deny us, nor shrank disgusted from the sable umbrage of an honest countenance.'

In Scottish poet James Montgomery's lengthy *The West Indies* there is a passage, an evocation of Africa and of the Negro in his primitive state, that perfectly expresses these intertwined dualities of darkness/light and physicality/spirituality. It is worth quoting in full:

> In these romantic regions man grows wild:
> Here dwells the Negro, nature's outcast child,
> Scorn'd by his brethren; but his mother's eye,
> That gazes on him from her warmest sky,
> Sees in his flexile limbs untutor'd grace,
> Power on his forehead, beauty in his face;
> Sees in his breast, where lawless passions rove,
> The heart of friendship and the home of love;
> Sees in his mind, where desolation reigns,
> Fierce as his clime, uncultur'd as his plains,
> A soil where virtue's fairest flowers might shoot,
> And trees of science bend with glorious fruit;
> Sees in his soul, involved with thickest night,
> An emanation of eternal light,
> Ordain'd, midst sinking worlds, his dust to fire,
> And shine for ever when the stars expire.

Hidden, 'involved' in the night of the African's body is the light, the whiteness of Christian spirituality. And Montgomery feminises the perception of the Negro's hidden qualities. It is the 'mother's eye' that sees, beneath his 'lawless passions', the possibilities within the African of benevolence ('the heart of friendship') and domest-icity ('the home of love'). Here again we encounter the pattern of a feminine sensibility observing and taking pity on the (male) slave. Montgomery was reflecting the fact that not only did women make up the bulk of the readership (and frequently the authorship) of sentimental anti-slavery literature, but they also played a crucial practical part in the grass-roots organisation of the anti-slavery movement.

From Oroonoko to 'The Grateful Negro' (1802), the European imaginative literature on slavery and the Negro is strikingly homogeneous. There are differences of emphasis and inflection, but *en masse* it presents a common idealisation of the African. He (for the most part the slave figure is male) is defined above all by his enslaved condition, his suffering. To the extent that he is thought to have any existence at all anterior to his being a slave, it is as the expression of a philosophically imagined Nature. He has, of course, no independent culture or history. Before slavery there is only the state of nature, a *tabula rasa*.

And in slavery, too, there is no culture, no economics, no shades of collaboration, no daily, covert acts of resistance. There is only the individual master confronting the individual slave. And hovering about them, moral absolutes. On the one side there are the opposites of benevolence and cruelty, and on the other of gratitude and vengeance. The African is always either kneeling or running amok. His gratitude is an expression of the natural benevolence he carries over from his Edenic, pre-slavery existence. But his vengeance, too, is a 'natural' response, the instinctual backlash of a cornered animal. Black rebellion is like a tropical storm breaking over the Caribbean, and just as much an act of God.

This image of the Negro is an aesthetic attitude, a collection of sometimes mutually contradictory perceptions, rather than a coherent theory. (Indeed, its ideological basis is a belief that morality and aesthetics can be conflated in 'sensibility'. Ethical conduct is not attained through rule-following or rationality; rather, it is the product of – perhaps even consists in – the exquisite aesthetic appreciation of others' pain.) 'Nature', to which the

Negro is closer than the European, is the source of both benevolence and savagery. In some later imperialist literature on Africa this tension is felt close to the surface of the narrative. But in the anti-slavery literature of the eighteenth century it is an ambiguity buried deep beneath the melodramatic rhetorical conventions of sentimentalism. Or in some formulations, both then and later, the Negro's benevolence and savagery are not contradictions at all, but rather opposed sides of the single coin of the African's 'authenticity'. Anna Maria Mackenzie speaks of 'the brilliant boldness which characterises the children of the sun'. They present all the (contradictory) passions that are buried within us all (Diderot's 'hideous Moor' again), but unrefined, in more vivid colours. The idea of black authenticity has had a highly visible presence in twentieth-century culture, but it is there in embryo among the tears and the whipped and kneeling slaves of the eighteenth-century sentimentalists.

The African's virtue could be said to derive from his body since both his current bodily suffering and his previous naked presence in the Eden of Africa speak of his authenticity. But his body is also black, polluted with sin. He is redeemed from his blackness by conversion, by the revelation and liberation of an inner spiritual whiteness and light. The Negro is liberated from his slavery, from the shackles of his physicality and hence his sin. He becomes free, Christian – and white.

If it is possible to discuss the eighteenth-century imaginative literature *en masse*, as different perspectives on a single anti-slavery aesthetic, this is in part a function of the fact that none of the works (with the possible exception of Aphra Behn's *Oroonoko*) have any originality or independent imaginative power. None of them have lasted, and none have deserved to. Their interest is historical and symptomatic rather than artistic. There are changes and shifts of emphasis, but these are collective, ideological shifts rather than instances of an individual artist forging something new out of the contradictions inherent in the old conventions. By the 1790s, as we have seen, there was a certain critical cynicism in the air concerning literary sentimentality. Harriet Martineau's *Demerara, A Tale* (1832) opens with a reprimand for those who set Negroes up as blameless heroes:

Our sympathy for slaves ought to increase in proportion to their vices and follies, if it can be proved that those vices and follies arise out of the position in which we place them, or allow them to remain. If the champion of the slave had but seen how his cause is aided by representing him as he is, – not only revengeful, but selfish and mean, – not only treacherous to his master, but knavish to his countrymen, indolent, conceited, hypocritical, and sensual, – we should have had fewer narratives of slaves more virtuous than a free peasantry, and exposed to the delicate miseries of a refined love of which they are incapable, or of social sensibilities which can never be generated in such social conditions as theirs.

Demerara is the fourth of Martineau's *Illustrations of Political Economy*, and her aim is to provide a critique of slavery as a social and economic system, rather than simply as a confrontation of moral absolutes. But her attack on sentimentalism amounts to little more than a prefatory platitude; the substance of the tale – its language, plot and characterisations – adheres to the wooden protocols of the existing European literature on slavery.

After 1791 we see less of the noble savage and more of the savage savage, less of the Negro kneeling and more of his running amok. The Saint-Domingue revolution of 1791–1804 had a profound impact on the European psyche. In the early nineteenth century it spawned a whole literary sub-genre of its own, including Victor Hugo's *Bug-Jurgal* and Harriet Martineau's *The Hour and the Man*, as well as poetic tributes, by Wordsworth and many others, to the revolution's leader, Toussaint L'Ouverture. After Saint-Domingue, gothic depictions of the dangers and consequences of black rebellion supplanted Rousseauesque dreams of black innocence. In 'Tamango' (1829), Prosper Mérimée – pioneer of the short story in French, whose penchant for southern exoticism found its most famous fulfilment in 'Carmen' – portrays an African slave dealer who is himself enslaved and leads a bloody rebellion aboard a slave ship. And in 'Benito Cereno' (1855), Herman Melville's consummate tale of duplicity, the slow seeping into the narrative of an atmosphere of gothic decay culminates in the revelation of a drastic dysfunction between appearance and reality aboard the doomed slave ship, and a terrifying inversion of the expected relationship between European master and African slave. 'Benito Cereno' stands well outside the sentimental tradition – Melville is more concerned with mood and narrative riddle than with the morality of slavery – but it is worth noting that the premise of the story is an anxiety concerning the precariousness of white overlordship and the possibility of the existing racial world being turned upside down. It is that that gives the story its eerie power.

According to a certain conventional wisdom, *Uncle Tom's Cabin* (1852) represents the nadir of the sentimental tradition. Although there has been some attempt in recent years by feminist critics to rehabilitate Harriet Beecher Stowe, placing her in the context of a tradition of female social reform, her most famous book still suffers from its association with those patronising and insulting racial attitudes summed up ever since in the two words 'Uncle Tom'. *Uncle Tom's Cabin* has been something of an embarrassment to literary historians, and the reaction of many has been simply to ignore it. But it sold 300,000 copies in its first year of publication alone, was translated into thirty-seven languages (three times into Welsh), and was credited by President Lincoln, in a famous but possibly apocryphal quip, with having started the American Civil War. Nor can its success be put down easily to the debased tastes of the book-buying public on both sides of the Atlantic. Respected critics compared it to Cervantes and Fielding, in Europe it was reviewed by Macaulay, George Sand and Heine (whom it led to study the Bible), and Tolstoy picked it out as representing the very highest type of novel.

In fact, for and because of all its faults, *Uncle Tom's Cabin* is a complex and powerful work. To the extent that it shares the anti-slavery aesthetic of its eighteenth-century predecessors, it raises certain elements of that aesthetic to such a fever pitch of intensity ('The Lord himself wrote it!' Harriet Beecher Stowe famously exclaimed) that it becomes something entirely individual. This intensity is felt above all in the book's relentless Manichean dualism of sin and redemption, slavery and freedom, darkness and light. Unlike the eighteenth-century works on slavery, there is no trace in Uncle Tom of the noble savage; instead, his black body is a scene of endless suffering. In the end, of course, Tom is a Christ figure; he dies to redeem us all. In a famous essay on the book, 'Everybody's Protest Novel', James Baldwin directs his coruscating prose right at the theological heart of the novel:

> [Uncle Tom] is phenomenally forbearing. He has to be; he is black: only through this forbearance can he survive or triumph ... His triumph is metaphysical, unearthly; since he is black, born without light, it is only through humility, the incessant mortification of the flesh, that he can enter into communion with God or man ... *Uncle Tom's Cabin* ... is activated by what might be called a theological terror, the terror of damnation; and the spirit that breathes in this book, hot, self-righteous, fearful, is not different from the spirit of mediaeval times which sought to exorcise evil by burning witches; and is not different from that terror which activates a lynch mob.

Baldwin's essay is in some respects an acute criticism of *Uncle Tom's Cabin*. But in others it is surely unfair. There is a contradiction in Baldwin's argument between his perception of a theological undertow to the book and his insistence that it is mere documentary, that '[Stowe] was not so much a novelist as an impassioned pamphleteer; her book was not intended to do anything more than prove that slavery was wrong; was, in fact, perfectly horrible. This makes material for a pamphlet but it is hardly enough for a novel ...'

Above all, his bald assertion that '*Uncle Tom's Cabin* is a very bad novel' fails to explain the book's extraordinary popularity or the different levels on which it can be read. Tolstoy may have been attracted by its didactic moralism, but one suspects that most of the book's millions of readers have been attracted by its 'incidental' features – its colourful social realism, its suspense, even its humour. These, the book's strictly novelistic virtues, are precisely what don't survive in the folk myth partly perpetuated by the dozens of stage and film versions. Anyone familiar only with these is bound to be surprised by, for example, the grim humour with which

Stowe brings to life the slave trader Haley and his associates, the slave catchers Tom Loker and Marks. Here the two slave catchers are contemplating the recapture of Eliza and her son Harry:

> – 'We'll do a business here on our own account; we does the catchin'; the boy, of course, goes to Mr. Haley – we takes the gal to Orleans to speculate on. Ain't it beautiful?'
>
> Tom, whose great, heavy mouth had stood ajar during this communication, now suddenly snapped it together, as a big dog closes on a piece of meat, and seemed to be digesting the idea at his leisure.

'As a big dog closes on a piece of meat' – this is surely the writing of a real novelist, not a pamphleteer. The escape and pursuit of Eliza and Harry – including the famous scene where Eliza leaps across the ice of the frozen Ohio River – recall the obsession with quest and chase in the historical romances of Scott and Fenimore Cooper, while the way in which she paints an involving top-to-bottom picture of Southern life is firmly in the tradition of Fielding and Dickens. This, from a scene set in the bar room of a Kentucky hotel, could comfortably grace one of the latter's novels:

> [E]verybody in the room bore on his head this characteristic emblem of man's sovereignty; whether it were felt hat, palm leaf, greasy beaver, or fine new chapeau, there it reposed with true republican independence. In truth, it appeared to be the characteristic mark of every individual. Some wore them tipped rakishly on one side – these were your men of humour, jolly, free-and-easy dogs; some had them jammed independently down over their noses – these were your hard characters, thorough men, who, when they wore hats, wanted to wear them, and to wear them just as they had a mind to; there were those who had them set far over back – wide-awake men, who wanted a clear prospect; while careless men, who did not know or care how their hats sat, had them shaking about in all directions. The various hats, in fact, were quite a Shaksperian study.

So *Uncle Tom's Cabin* deserves to be taken seriously as a novel.

But as soon as you do that, you come up against the book's gaping flaw – its portrayal of blacks. As Baldwin points out, apart from the procession of cut-out minstrel show characters (the field hands, house niggers, Aunt Chloe, Topsy, etc.), who are comic stereotypes rather than real people, there are really only three black characters in the book. Of them, as Baldwin again convincingly argues, the husband and wife George and Eliza are practically white. When we are first introduced to George, it is true, his role is to provide a defiant contrast to Uncle Tom's quietism. There is surely an echo, in this description of George's reaction to being humiliated by his master, of the late eighteenth-century image of the instinctual, vengeful African:

> He folded his arms, tightly pressed in his lips, but a whole volcano of bitter feelings burned in his bosom, and sent streams of fire through his veins. He breathed short, and his large dark eyes flashed like live coals . . . [T]he flashing eye, the gloomy and troubled brow, were part of a natural language that could not be repressed . . .

But as the novel progresses, the couple become more and more white. Eliza passes as white in order to escape, while George is able to pose as a Spanish gentleman. And by the end of the book, it has transpired that Eliza is connected to the French aristocracy. They are a model couple, the perfect romantic hero and heroine. If they made unlikely slaves to begin with, by the end of the book we have forgotten that they were ever in that condition.

That leaves Uncle Tom himself. And he is a theological idea (a 'moral miracle') rather than a human being. Throughout the book he remains curiously disembodied. Only on a couple of occasions do we get a sense of his physical presence and appearance:

> He was a large, broad-chested, powerfully-made man, of a full glossy black, and a face whose truly African features were characterised by an expression of grave and steady good sense, united with much kindliness and benevolence.

The physical description dissolves into moral abstractions. Much later, when Tom rescues little Eva from drowning, we get the same flat, uninvolving formula: 'a broad-chested, strong-armed fellow, it was nothing for him to keep afloat in the water'. These brief glimpses pull the reader up short because they contradict the impression that one otherwise gets that Tom is an old man. His relationship with Chloe is hardly that of a young or middle-aged man and wife (as Baldwin comments, 'Tom . . . has been robbed of his humanity and divested of his sex'), while the way he dandles his children on his knee is somehow more grandfatherly than paternal. His voice is described as 'tender as a woman's', and in his gentleness, his quiet stoicism and his instinct for the domestic, he bears out Stowe's contention that '[Negroes] are not naturally daring and enterprising, but home-loving and affectionate'.

To the thinness of characterisation, the inability to imagine the black characters as real human beings, one must add those asides in which Stowe casually assigns to the whole race characteristics that must have been highly congenial to the white abolitionist mind. Blacks are simple and childlike ('there is no more use in making believe be angry with a negro than with a child'), carrying with them as their African inheritance a susceptibility to immediate sensation:

> The negro, it must be remembered, is an exotic of the most gorgeous and superb countries of the world, and he has deep in his heart a passion for all that is splendid, rich, and fanciful; a passion which, rudely indulged by an untrained taste, draws on them the ridicule of the colder and more correct white race.

But for Stowe, their dominant characteristic is 'their childlike simplicity of affection, and facility of forgiveness'. In their gratitude, Stowe's Negroes are fully in line with that tradition of kneeling slaves described earlier. But their magnanimous generosity of spirit – which finds its highest expression in Tom's martyrdom – is but part of a wider universe that Stowe portrays as positively overflowing with magnanimity. Whites are magnanimous in their desire to liberate the slaves (epitomised, at the end, by the emancipation of his slaves by George Shelby, son of Uncle Tom's former owner); blacks are magnanimous in their forgiveness of the sins committed against them; but, above all, there is God, who, in a strikingly maternal image, is described as bearing 'the anguish of a world ... in his patient, generous bosom'.

If *Uncle Tom's Cabin* were simply the naturalistic documentary (the 'pamphlet') on slavery and its evils that Baldwin claims Stowe was aiming at, then these flaws in the realisation of its black characters would reduce it to the same level of artistic nullity as its forebears in the sentimental tradition. But there is more to the book than that. As Baldwin recognises elsewhere in his essay, *Uncle Tom's Cabin* is only secondarily a novel about slavery; it is first and foremost a religious novel. This may seem a perverse overall reading of the book in view of the fact that Stowe was famously spurred on to write it by the passing of the Fugitive Slave Law in 1850 and that she went on to write a follow-up book, *The Key to Uncle Tom's Cabin* (1853), which provided documentary support for the plausibility of key episodes in the novel. But although Stowe stresses thoughout that it is slavery as a system of law, rather than as a relationship between individuals, that she is attacking (and in this respect *Uncle Tom's Cabin* is more politically sophisticated than most of its anti-slavery predecessors), her evangelical world-view elevated the struggle over slavery to a divine battle for the hearts of men. When, in *The Key to Uncle Tom's Cabin*, she remarks that 'men are always seeking to begin their reforms with the outward and physical. Christ begins his reforms in the heart', we are reminded of that diary entry by Wilberforce linking the suppression of the slave trade with 'the transformation of manners'.[1]

The section of the book where this drama of redemption reaches its most feverish expression is the long episode in which Tom, having been sold down the river away from his family, fetches up in the eccentric household of Augustine St Clair. If this episode plumbs, in the death of Eva, the depths of maudlin sentimentality, it also contains some of the novel's most winning realism. St Clair, the aristocratic aesthete, the epitome of Southern languor, is counterpoised highly effectively by his charmless and puritanical

[1] Harriet Beecher Stowe was herself notoriously keen on 'the reformation of manners'. Not only did she abstain from drink herself, but she refused to appear at any function where alcohol was being served.

Northern cousin, Ophelia. The portrait of Ophelia St Clair is particularly surprising because it seems to satirise exactly the type of woman we might otherwise suppose Harriet Beecher Stowe to have been:

> Her theological tenets were all made up, labelled in the most positive and distinct forms, and put by, like the bundles in her patch trunk ... [She] was the absolute bond-slave of the 'ought.' Once make her certain that the 'path of duty', as she commonly phrased it, lay in any given direction, and fire and water could not keep her from it ... Her standard of right was so high, so all-embracing, so minute, and making so few concessions to human fraility, that though she strove with heroic ardour to reach it, she never actually did so, and of course was burdened with a constant and often harassing sense of deficiency. This gave a severe and somewhat gloomy cast to her religious character.

Ophelia inflicts her rigid abolitionism on the quixotic and hopelessly unpolitical Augustine, but in the end is forced by him to admit that her high-minded benevolence masks a secret, profound distaste:

> I know the feeling among some of you northerners well enough ... I have often noticed, in my travels north, how much stronger [colour prejudice] was with you than with us. You loathe them as you would a snake or a toad, yet you are indignant at their wrongs. You would not have them abused, but you don't want to have anything to do with them yourselves. You would send them to Africa, out of your sight and smell, and then send a missionary or two to do up all the self-denial of elevating them compendiously.

Augustine's strictures are reminiscent of the famous passage in *Bleak House* (1852–3) – itself an attack on the whole abolitionist ethos – in which Dickens satirises Mrs Jellyby's 'telescopic philanthropy'. But like most of the other characters in *Uncle Tom's Cabin*, Ophelia finds redemption. In her case this takes the form of conquering her prejudice in order to form a maternal relationship with the little slave girl Topsy. She is redeemed by becoming a surrogate mother.

In *The Key to Uncle Tom's Cabin*, Harriet Beecher Stowe is quite explicit that Eva, Augustine St Clair's daughter, is intended as 'an impersonation in childish form of the love of Christ'. It is Eva's death – an episode whose tear-jerking sentiment recalls, and was possibly modelled on, the demise of Little Nell in *The Old Curiosity Shop* – that forms the religious heart of the book. Eva – the white, golden-haired, blue-eyed virgin-child – redeems all around her by her love. Ophelia's utilitarian rigidities are softened, and her hidden prejudices wiped away. St Clair, Eva's father, turns from idle scepticism to active faith. And Topsy, the abused, delinquent slave girl, is transformed by the radiance of Eva's grace. Stowe makes much of the visual, racial contrast between the two girls:

> There stood the two children, representatives of the two extremes of society. The fair, high-bred child, with her golden hair, her deep eyes, her spiritual, noble brow, and her prince-like movements; and her black, keen, subtle, cringing, yet acute neighbour. They stood as representatives of their races. The Saxon, born of ages of cultivation, command, education, physical and moral eminence; the Afric, born of ages of oppression, ignorance, toil, and vice!

When Eva is close to death, she saves Topsy by her love. Stowe describes it in an extraordinary fevered paragraph:

> 'O Topsy, poor child, I love you!' said Eva, with a sudden burst of feeling, and laying her little, thin, white hand on Topsy's shoulder ... The round, keen eyes of the black child were overcast with tears; large, bright drops rolled heavily down, one by one, and fell on the little white hand. Yes, in that moment a ray of real belief, a ray of heavenly love, had penetrated the darkness of her heathen soul! She laid her head down between her knees, and wept and sobbed; while the beautiful child, bending over her, looked like the picture of some bright angel stooping to reclaim a sinner.

The cathartic tears of gratitude; the black, associated with sinfulness, contrasted with the white, associated with grace and heavenly love; the 'darkness' of a heathen soul illumined and made white by Christian redemption; the slave girl paying obeisance to, stooped over by, the 'bright angel' – beyond its obvious affinities with Blake's poem, the scene seems to encapsulate almost every image and idea of the sentimental abolitionist imagination.

Eva has a special love for Uncle Tom. Not that Tom needs redeeming, of course, since he is already half-way to heaven. The relationship between Eva and Tom is one of association and affinity. In some respects the two Christ-figures – the prepubescent, virginal white girl, and the sexless, feminised black man – are practically indistinguishable. After Eva's death, the grief-stricken St Clair, who has taken to reading his daughter's Bible, finds himself drawn more and more to Tom's company, for 'there was nothing that seemed to remind him so much of Eva'. St Clair begins the legal procedures necessary to give Tom his freedom, but is then murdered while intervening to stop a bar-room brawl. Tom is sold off by the heartless, pampered Marie, Eva's mother, and fetches up on the plantation of the evil Simon Legree.

If *Uncle Tom's Cabin* is a novel about redemption and damnation, it is heavily weighted in favour of the former. The only character who at the end of the book is truly damned – the slave trader Haley and his low-life associates Loker and Marks belong to the comic-adventure side of the novel, rather than to its metaphysical drama – is Legree, the brutal, alcoholic planter who feels so threatened by Tom's all-embracing goodness that in the end he has him beaten to death. The chapters set on Legree's grim, run-down plantation can be read on a number of different levels. The conflict between Legree and Tom is a conflict of master and slave and of Evil and Good – but there is another conflict going on in these chapters, a conflict between the sentimental and the gothic. There is no doubt which wins out. The gothic aspects – Legree's passionate relationship with Cassy, the half-crazed slave; his frustrated attempts to violate a fifteen-year-old quadroon, Emmeline; his apprehension of the hell that awaits him – are sketched rather than fully realised. And in the end the gothic aspect descends into theatrical farce, with Cassy and Emmeline mounting a charade of white sheets and spooky noises in order to frighten Legree and secure their escape. It is strange that Baldwin should lay so much stress in his criticism of *Uncle Tom's Cabin* on Stowe's playing on fears of hellfire and damnation. In fact it is the sentimental, radiant hope of salvation, epitomised by Eva and Tom, that has the greater force in the book, while the fear of hell is reduced to the flimsy, creaking scenery of Legree's mansion and the alcoholic vapours of his crazed, superstitious mind.

In some respects *Uncle Tom's Cabin* is a considerable advance on its eighteenth- and early nineteenth-century predecessors in the sentimental genre. Stowe does not reduce the institution of slavery to a set of individual relationships; she has grasped and constantly reiterates the point that the central issue is not whether the slave is treated cruelly or kindly, but the political one of legal property as against freedom. In novelist terms, her debt to Dickens and the historical romancers gives the book a range of tone that is far in advance of anything by the eighteenth-century novelists of slavery. And despite her failure to realise her black characters, she brought considerably more knowledge and curiosity about the details of slavery as a social reality. In this respect the great slave narratives, which were being published at about the same time as *Uncle Tom's Cabin*, must have been crucial. Frederick Douglass (who admired *Uncle Tom's Cabin*, a fact which should give us pause for a few thoughts on historical relativity before we blandly dismiss it as 'racist') published his *Narrative* in 1845, while in the decades following there appeared famous works by Henry Bibb, William Wells Brown, Josiah Henson and others. These well-known narratives were just the tip of an enormous iceberg. In some instances there was input from white abolitionists, who acted either as amanuenses or, at the extreme end of the spectrum, composed fictitious autobiographies; the slave narrative as a literary form both owed a debt to and – through the greater authenticity and realism that in many cases it brought – subverted the sentimental novel.

If *Uncle Tom's Cabin* transcended the sentimental anti-slavery genre in its realism and accomplishment, in other respects it merely epitomised that genre in a memorable way. In particular, Harriet Beecher Stowe brought into the foreground the evangelical theology that so often underscored both reform movements and the anti-slavery aesthetic. Being both a reformer's novel and a religious novel, *Uncle Tom*'s version of this evangelical world-view is especially, and optimistically, focused on the promise of redemption and liberation. The slave will be freed, the sinner will be saved. It took religious scepticism, such as that represented by Darwinism, and above all a crisis of confidence in European imperialism, to bring out the darker, more gothic and pessimistic aspect of this racial Manicheism.

Sources

Primary sources

Behn, Aphra, *Oroonoko, or the Royal Slave: A True History* in *The Works of Aphra Behn*, edited by Janet Todd (William Pickery, London, 1995).

Chatterton, Thomas, 'African Eclogues', in *Poetical Works* (Routledge, London, 1906), vol. I.

Colman, George (the Younger), *Inkle and Yarico: An Opera in Three Acts*, in Elizabeth Inchbald (ed.), *The British Theatre*, vol. XX (London, 1808).

The Poetical Works of William Cowper (Routledge, London, 1906).

Cumberland, Richard, *Henry* (London, 1795).

Day, Thomas, and John Bicknell, *The Dying Negro. A Poem* (London, 1793). First published 1773.

Diderot, Denis, 'Eloge de Richardson' and 'Supplément au voyage de Bougainville', in *Oeuvres complètes* (Le Club Français du Livre, Paris, 1970–1), vols V and X.

Dubois-Fontanelle, J., *Anecdotes africaines* (Paris, 1775).

Edgeworth, Maria, 'The Grateful Negro' (1802) in *Popular Tales* (London, 1852).

Grainger, James, 'The Sugar Cane' (1764), in Alexander Chalmers (ed.), *The Works of the English Poets* (London, 1810), vol. XIV.

La Vallée, Joseph, *The Negro as there are Few White Men* (London, 1790).

Mackenzie, Anna Maria, *Slavery; or the Times* (London, 1792).

Mackenzie, Henry, *Julia de Roubigné* and 'On Novel-Writing', in *The Works of Henry Mackenzie* (Edinburgh, 1808), vols III and V.

Mailhol, Gabriel, *Le Philosophe nègre et les Secrets des Grecs: Ouvrage trop nécessaire en Deux Parties* (Paris, 1764).

Martineau, Harriet, *Illustrations of Political Economy, Number IV: Demerara, A Tale* (London, 1832).

Melville, Herman, 'Benito Cereno', in *Great Short Works of Herman Melville* (Harper & Row, 1969).

Mérimée, Prosper, 'Tamango', in *Carmen and Other Stories* (Oxford, Oxford University Press, 1989).

Montgomery, James, *Poetical Works* (London, 1841), vols I and IV.

Moore, John, *Zeluco*, in *The Works of John Moore, M.D.*, vol. V (Edinburgh, 1820).

More, Hannah, 'Sensibility', in *Works*, vol. I (London, 1830).

Newton, John, *Letters and Sermons* (Edinburgh, 1787).

— *Posthumous Works* (London, 1808).

Saint-Pierre, J. H. Bernardin de, 'Empsaël' in *Oeuvres complètes* (Paris, 1834), vol. 12.

Smith, Adam, *The Theory of Moral Sentiments* (Bohn, London, 1853). First published 1759.

Southerne, Thomas, *Oroonoko, A Tragedy in Five Acts*, in Elizabeth Inchbald (ed.), *The British Theatre*, vol. VII (London, 1808).

Southey, Robert, *Poetical Works* (London, 1880).

Stanfield, James, *The Guinea Voyage, A Poem in Three Books* (Edinburgh, 1807).

Stowe, Harriet Beecher, *Uncle Tom's Cabin* (London, 1852).

Wilkinson, T., *An Appeal to England, on Behalf of the Abused Africans, A Poem* (London, 1789).

Secondary sources

Arendt, Hannah, *The Origins of Totalitarianism* (André Deutsch, London, 1986). First published 1951.

Baldwin, James, 'Everybody's Protest Novel', in *The Price of the Ticket. Collected Nonfiction 1948–1985* (Michael Joseph, London, 1985).

Blackburn, Robin, *The Overthrow of Colonial Slavery 1776–1848* (Verso, London, 1988).

Bolt, Christine, and S. Drescher (eds), *Anti-Slavery, Religion and Reform* (Archon, Folkestone, 1980).

Crozier, Alice C., *The Novels of Harriet Beecher Stowe* (Oxford University Press, London, 1969).

Curtin, Philip D., *The Image of Africa: British Ideas and Action 1780–1850* (Macmillan, London, 1965).

Davis, David Biron, *The Problem of Slavery in Western Culture* (Penguin, Harmondsworth, 1970).

— *The Problem of Slavery in the Age of Revolution 1770–1823* (Cornell University Press, Ithaca, 1975).

Dykes, E. V., *The Negro in English Romantic Thought* (Associated Publishers, Washington, DC, 1942).

Fairchild, Hoxie Neale, *The Noble Savage* (Columbia University Press, New York, 1928).

Fiedler, Leslie, *Love and Death in the American Novel* (Penguin, Harmondsworth, 1984).

Grégoire, Henri-Baptiste, *De la littérature des nègres* (Paris, 1808).

Hoffman, Léon-François, *Le Nègre romantique: Personnage littéraire et obsession collective* (Payot, Paris, 1973).

Honour, Hugh, *The Image of the Black in Western Art, Vol. IV Part 1: Slaves and Liberators* (Harvard University Press, Cambridge, Mass., 1989).

McKeon, Michael, 'Genetic Transformation and Social Change: Rethinking the Rise of the Novel', in Leopold Damrosch (ed.), *Modern Essays on Eighteenth-Century Literature* (Oxford University Press, New York, 1988).

Rice, C. Duncan, *The Rise and Fall of Black Slavery* (Macmillan, London, 1975).

Seeber, E. D., *Anti-Slavery Opinion in France during the Second Half of the Eighteenth Century* (Greenwood Press, New York, 1969).

Sypher, Wylie, *Guinea's Captive Kings: British Anti-Slavery Literature of the Eighteenth Century* (University of North Carolina Press, Chapel Press, Chapel Hill, 1942).

Todd, Janet, *Sensibility: An Introduction* (Methuen, London, 1986).

Watt, Ian, *The Rise of the Novel: Studies in Defoe, Richardson, and Fielding* (Penguin, Harmondsworth, 1963).

Whitney, Lois, *Primitivism and the Idea of Progress in English Popular Literature of the Eighteenth Century* (Johns Hopkins University Press, Baltimore, 1934).

3

The Invention of the Primitive: Race and Evolution

As far as my testimony goes, every individual who has the glory
of having exerted himself on the subject of slavery, may rely on it
his labours are exerted against miseries perhaps even greater than
he imagines.

> Charles Darwin, entry in the diary of the voyage
> of HMS *Beagle* for 12 March 1832

One of the most paradoxical features of early twentieth-century art
was the way the new was equated with the ancient, the avant-garde
with the atavistic. From Stravinsky's *Rite of Spring* to the works of
Picasso inspired by African sculpture, 'primitive' was one of the
strongest threads connecting the seminal works of high modernism. The motor rhythms of Stravinsky's 1913 ballet score evoke
both the machine age and the bleak world of pagan ritual on the
Russian steppes. Jazz became a cultural shorthand for that which
was both supremely modern and, through its African roots,
connected with the exotic origins of things. It was the music of the
urban jungle.

Race played an important part in the formation of this modern
atavism. The equation of blackness with the primitive, in the
temporal sense of the aboriginal, can be dated back to the impact of
Darwinism in the mid-nineteenth century, just as Darwinism was
the progenitor of the idea of nature not as a peaceful solace, but as a
battlefield of inexorable, machine-like forces. A line can be traced
from the modernist primitivism of the 1920s, back through what
one might call the *fin de siècle* imagination of imperialism, with its

violent or violently sexual atavism, to the idea put forward by Darwin's followers that the Negro represented a rudiment of human evolution, a throwback to prehistoric times.

Not that Darwin himself was a modernist or a radical by inclination. His scientific genius struggled against, and finally prevailed over, the innately conservative instincts of a Victorian gentleman. 'Cultural evolution', by reckoning societies along a single scale, was a way of reconciling fundamental unity with European superiority. Savages were living relics. They were what we had once been.

We have already seen how the questioning of the biblical time-scale for the history of the earth was a recurring theme of radical religious scepticism in the seventeenth and eighteenth centuries. For Darwin, chronology was vital to his theory of evolution. He freely accepted that if the discoveries of geologists such as his friend Sir Charles Lyell could be disproved, if it could be shown that the earth and biological life were much younger than he had supposed, then the entire edifice of his theory of evolution by natural selection would collapse. The vastly slow process would simply not have had time to happen. And when it came to race, the monogenism of the Darwinists was qualified by pushing the separation of the human races further and further back into the darkness of the prehistoric past. To understand how this new form of monogenism came about, how the racial gulf became a gulf of time, it helps to go back to the historical context of mid-nineteenth-century Britain and the hardening of racial attitudes that occurred as the abolitionist ethos began to be attacked and discredited.

Charles Darwin was steeped in the free thought and radical Christianity that were such important driving forces of the abolitionist movement. One of his grandfathers – also grandfather to his wife Emma – was Josiah Wedgwood, the Unitarian manufacturer responsible for abolitionism's most enduring icon, the 'Am I not a man and a brother?' medallion. His other grandfather was Erasmus Darwin, a flamboyant, atheistic physician who developed an early theory of evolution. The two grandfathers differed on practically everything – Erasmus Darwin described

Wedgwood's Unitarian beliefs as 'a featherbed to catch a falling Christian' – but on the question of slavery they were united.

The religious revival of the late eighteenth and early nineteenth centuries had a formative influence on British anthropology. There were particularly close links between the early Victorian anthropologists and that evangelical wing of Christianity that was so important in the abolition movement. James Cowles Prichard, who dominated British ethnology (as the subject was then called) in the early nineteenth century, and who devoted his career to defending the principle of monogenism, came from a Quaker family, as did Sir Edward Tylor, whose *Primitive Culture* (1871) and *Anthropology* (1881) were highly influential syntheses which formed cornerstones of the British anthropological tradition.

The connection between evangelical religion and Victorian ethnology can be seen, too, at an institutional level. In 1838 the Aborigines' Protection Society was formed by, among others, Thomas Fowell Buxton, a Quaker who had inherited the mantle of Wilberforce as leader of the anti-slavery movement in Parliament. Alongside its 'first object', which was to collect 'authentic information concerning the character, habits and wants of the uncivilised tribes', went a commitment to evangelism as the only 'effectual method to civilise' dark-skinned savage peoples. The Ethnological Society of London was formed in 1843 by the Quaker doctor Thomas Hodgkin (discoverer of Hodgkin's Disease) as an offshoot of the Aborigines' Protection Society. The formation of the Ethnological Society was symptomatic of a split within the Aborigines' Protection Society between those concerned with missionary work and those interested in 'scientific' observation.

Victorian 'cultural evolutionism' may have had its origins in Christian monogenism, but it came to be affected by the progressive hardening of racial attitudes that occurred during the course of the nineteenth century. By mid-century, the humanitarian impulses of abolitionism were becoming the object of increasingly jaundiced criticism. Sentimentalism was being replaced by cynicism. In 1834 Parliament passed the bill abolishing slavery throughout the British colonies, but abolitionism lived on in

Britain in the form of support for fellow campaigners in America and for missionary work to inculcate Christianity and stamp out the internal slave trade in Africa. In 1840 Buxton launched the African Civilization Society at Exeter Hall in London before an audience that included Prince Albert, leaders of the country's major religious organisations and dozens of Members of Parliament including William Gladstone and Sir Robert Peel. The list of seventy vice-presidents of the new society included three archbishops, five dukes, six marquises, fourteen earls and sixteen bishops. And in 1843 the Government sponsored an expensive and disastrous expedition up the river Niger, devised by Buxton, to stamp out the slave trade there and introduce to the interior of West Africa the benefits of Christian civilisation and 'legitimate trade'.

The ignominious failure of the 1843 Niger expedition was used thereafter as a cautionary tale, illustrative of the wishy-washy naïvety of the sentimental philanthropists who gathered at Exeter Hall. Charles Dickens, reviewing an account of the expedition published in 1848, suggested that 'it might be laid down as a very good general rule of social and political guidance, that whatever Exeter Hall champions, is the thing by no means to be done'. He was to exploit this material in the well-known 'Telescopic Philanthropy' chapter of *Bleak House* (1853), with its devastating portrait of Mrs Jellyby, who ignores the suffering around her while dreaming of a mission to 'Borrioboola-Gha, on the left bank of the Niger'. Her eyes, Dickens remarks, had 'a curious habit of seeming to look a long way off. As if . . . they could see nothing nearer than Africa.' The same criticism, and using a similar trope, had been used in a *Times* leader (quoting some verses that had appeared in *John Bull*) even before the Niger expedition set sail:

> The fact, my dear Philanthropy, is this –
> You're now like one upon a precipice,
> Or on the giddy top of some high steeple:
> Your dazzled thoughts are carried so far out
> 'Tis clear you know not what you are about:
> Come down, come down, look after your own people.

The attack on 'Exeter Hall philanthropy' extended from the issue of African missions to that of the apprenticeship system that had replaced slavery in Britain's West Indian colonies. The West Indian 'labour question' was addressed by Thomas Carlyle in his 'Occasional Discourse on the Nigger Qestion' (1849), which is cast as a mock lecture to 'My Philanthropic Friends'. Carlyle takes heavy-handed pleasure in goading the well-meaning Negrophile ('Do I, then, hate the Negro? No; except when the soul is killed out of him, I decidedly like poor Quashee ... With a pennyworth of oil, you can make a handsome, glossy thing of Quashee ... A swift, supple fellow; a merry-hearted, grinning, dancing, singing, affectionate kind of creature, with a great deal of melody and amenability in his composition') and in suggesting that the real slavery to which they should be addressing themselves is 'the slavery of the strong to the weak; of the great and noble-minded to the small and mean! The slavery of Wisdom to Folly.'

Carlyle poses as a courageous devil's advocate in 'The Nigger Question', but in fact he was swimming with the tide rather than against it. An illustration of how respectable anti-abolitionism had become by mid-century in Anthony Trollope's travel book *The West Indies and the Spanish Main* (1859), which is pervaded by casual prejudice and contempt for the philanthropists. The West Indian Negro, Trollope reports, 'has made no approach to the civilization of his white fellow creature, whom he imitates as a monkey does a man ... Their crimes are those of momentary impulse, as are also their virtues ... On the whole they laugh and sing and sleep through life ...' Philanthropy is a waste of time because 'God, for his own purposes ... has created men of inferior and superior race'. The abolition of slavery, he concludes, had led to the economic ruin of Jamaica.

Trollope's explanation of the decline in West Indian sugar production was by then a familiar one: blacks are inherently lazy, so without the discipline of slavery they simply refuse to work. Worries about the economic future of the West Indian colonies spawned a debate in the Victorian press and intellectual circles about the inherent character of the Negro race, a debate that was to come to a dramatic head in the mid-1860s. In October 1865 a local rising by black peasantry in the Morant Bay district of Jamaica was brutally crushed by Governor Eyre. Under rule of martial law, 439 blacks were shot or executed, 600 others flogged and a thousand homes of suspected rebels burned. News of this pogrom caused a furore in London. The governor was suspended and a Royal Commission of Inquiry established. When, in the summer of 1866, the Commission's report failed to satisfy those critical of the governor's actions, a group of anti-slavery philanthropists and political radicals formed the Jamaica Committee to pursue its own legal proceedings against Eyre. In response, a Governor Eyre Defence and Aid Committee was assembled.

According to Thomas Huxley, the naturalist and friend of Darwin, the Eyre controversy 'became the touchstone of ultimate political convictions'. Huxley himself supported the Jamaica Committee along with, among others, John Stuart Mill, Herbert Spencer, John Bright, Leslie Stephen, the geologist Sir Charles Lyell and Darwin himself. Luminaries lined up on the other side, in defence of Eyre, included Carlyle, John Ruskin, Alfred Lord Tennyson, Charles Kingsley and Charles Dickens. The Jamaica Committee argued that Eyre's arbitrary use of force threatened, by extension, the liberties of Englishmen (an argument with great resonance in the context of the agitation that was to lead to the passing of the Second Reform Bill the following year) while Eyre's supporters derided 'Nigger-philanthropy' and argued that the governor's actions had been an appropriate response to the Negro's innate indolence and viciousness. In an editorial, the *Morning Herald* remarked on this new trend in English opinion: '[T]he world-renowned question, once thought so convincing, of "Am I not a man and brother?" would nowadays be answered with some hesitation by many – with a flat negative to its latter half by those who regard the blacks as an inferior race.'

This general debate on the Negro's character, encouraged both by the West Indian 'labour question' and by the American Civil War (Dickens thought Harriet Beecher Stowe had weakened her case in *Uncle Tom's Cabin* by 'making out the African to be a great race') formed the context for a fierce scientific debate in Britain on the biological status of the Negro. The 1850s and 1860s saw a revival of the polygenist argument that Negroes were a separate species. In 1863 a breakaway group from the Ethnological Society was founded, the Anthropological Society of London, whose principal aim was to detail the supposed mental and physical differences between races. Its main preoccupation was summed up in the title of the inaugural address by the President of the Society, James Hunt: 'The Negro's Place in Nature'. In addition to a scholarly journal, the Society produced in 1866 a short-lived *Popular Magazine of Anthropology* dominated by articles on Jamaica ('the noble governor of the island ... [has] a most thorough insight into the Negro character') and on the supposed mental and physical differences between Negroes and Europeans. Among the vice-presidents of the Society was Sir Richard Burton, explorer and translator of the *Arabian Nights*, whose *Mission to Gelele, King of Dahome* (1864) contains his own essay on 'The Negro's place in Nature', addressed directly to James Hunt:

> Like other students of anthropology, I am truly grateful to you for having so graphically shown the great gulf, moral and physical, separating the black from the white races of Men and for having placed in so strong a light the physiological cause of the difference – namely the arrested development of the Negro. There is hardly a traveller, however unobservant, who has not remarked the peculiar and precocious intelligence of the African's childhood, his 'turning stupid' as the general phrase is, about the age of puberty, and the rapid declination of his mental powers in old age, a process reminding us of the simiad.

Burton goes on to comment on the backlash against abolitionism, linking it to the renewed debate on whether the human races constitute separate species:

> [The Negro] will lose *prestige* every year ... [T]hough there is little danger of our lapsing into the cruelties of which we read with shame, yet there is an ill time coming. For sons may avenge the credulity of their sires, by running into the clear contrary extremes, and the unnatural 'man and brother' of the day may

relapse into the 'nigger', the 'savage' and the 'semi-gorilla' of the morrow. Already there is a dawn of belief in a specific difference between the races, which carried out, leads to strange conclusions. Perhaps ... our society could do nothing more useful than to determine what signification the debased word 'species' should convey to the English anthropologist.

In Hunt's lecture on 'The Negro's Place in Nature', doubts are cast on whether Negro–white 'hybrids' are permanently fertile ('there is the best evidence to believe that the off-spring of the Negro and European are not indefinitely prolific'), and there is a crafty attempt to elide the terms 'race' and 'species':

> We have recently heard discussions respecting Man's place in nature: but it seems to me that we err in grouping all the different races of Man under one generic name, and then compare [sic] them with the anthropoid Apes. If we wish to make any advance in discussing such a subject, we must not speak of man generally, but must select one race or species, and draw our comparison in this manner.

Beyond such coy hints, Hunt wouldn't commit himself on the question of human origins. But the thrust of his approach to anthropology, and that of other speakers before the Society, was to present racial differences as being fixed and immutable, with extensive use made of the craniology that had been pioneered at the end of the eighteenth century and was being obsessively refined by, among others, the American Samuel Morton and the Frenchman Paul Broca. Broca's Société d'Anthropologie de Paris (1859 onwards) was the model for Hunt's Anthropological Society of London.

Hunt's motives for breaking away from the Ethnological Society were partly political – he had come into conflict with some of its older, abolitionist members – and partly arose out of a desire to replace the loose, descriptive practice of ethnology, ranging over linguistics and culture, with a rigid, classificatory discipline ('anthropology') that would concentrate on measurable physical differences between races. Although there was some overlap in membership between the two organisations, there was also considerable competition between them. A bitter institutional battle was fought over which of them should be represented at meetings of the British Association, and it was not until 1871 that a reconciliation of sorts was achieved when the two societies merged into the Anthropological Institute. In this battle between the 'Anthropologicals', with their overtly 'racist' agenda, and the 'Ethnologicals', with their broadly monogenist outlook, Darwin and his followers were firmly on the side of the 'Ethnologicals'. It was a conflict that was as much social as scientific. There was something vulgar in the way the Anthropologicals were willing to popularise scientific questions by linking them to political issues of the day such as the Eyre controversy. The Ethnologicals, by contrast, were the party of the respectable scientific establishment.

For all the air of monomaniacal crankiness surrounding it, the Anthropological Society of London represented more than just an obscure footnote to the history of science in Britain. The obsession with 'the Negro's place in nature', with drawing lines of racial demarcation, was symptomatic of the changing mood of the times. And it was into this context of increased Negrophobia that Darwin launched, in 1859, his *Origin of Species*, with its famous aside that the theory of evolution by natural selection would throw 'much light . . . on the origin of man and his history'. On the face of it, Darwin's theory of evolution provided powerful support for the monogenist position. It solved the old dilemma, the 'riddle' posed by Sir Thomas Browne, of how – short of invoking unsatisfactory environmentalist explanations – the variety of humans could have arisen from a single pair. Indeed, the earliest pre-Darwinian statement of a theory of evolution by natural selection – the exhaustively titled *An Account of a Female of the White Race of Mankind, Part of Whose Skin Resembles that of a Negro; with some Observations on the Causes of Differences in Colour and Form between the White and Negro Races of Man* (1813) by the Scottish physician William Charles Wells – proposes the theory precisely in the context of attempting to explain racial difference.[1]

[1] The *Account* is included in the volume *Two Essays* (London, 1818), though Darwin only became aware of its existence long after *On the Origin of Species* had

But if Darwin's theory of evolution seemed suited to supporting the monogenist position, it is a mark of how much the climate had changed by the 1860s that the Darwinians conceded so much to the polygenists and to those who would set up rigid taxonomic barriers within the human race.

The most striking and basic of these concessions is the notion that, though the European and the Negro may share common ancestors, racial differentiation was established at a very early stage of human evolution. In *The Descent of Man* (1871), Darwin identifies sexual selection as the mechanism by which racial differences arose. Rather than having anything to do with environmental adaptation, these differences have the same basic cause as the male peacock's flamboyant tail. Darwin goes on to speculate that sexual selection was a more powerful evolutionary force in early, 'primitive' man than in his modern descendants:

> [Man] would then ... have been guided more by his instinctive passions, and less by his foresight or reason. He would have jealously guarded his wife or wives ... Hence we may infer that the races of men were differentiated, as far as sexual selection is concerned, in chief part at a very remote epoch; and this conclusion throws light on the remarkable fact that at the most

been published, when an American bibliophile drew his attention to it. As Stephen Jay Gould points out in his essay 'Hannah West's Left Shoulder and the Origin of Natural Selection' (in *The Flamingo's Smile*), Wells proposes a particularly refined version of proto-Darwinism. The obvious marks of racial difference (skin colour, texture of hair, etc.) he describes as being not in themselves adaptive, but merely accidental by-products of more important but invisible changes, particularly related to immunity to certain diseases. They are, to use a modern language, 'correlations of growth' or 'non-adaptive consequences'. Darwin, similarly, did not regard the physical differences between races as the result of adaptations to the environment. They were, rather, like the peacock's feathers, the product of sexual selection. (The section specifically on human evolution in *The Descent of Man* is dwarfed by Darwin's accompanying account of the general principle of sexual selection.) For a modern statement of this theory, see Jared Diamond, *The Rise and Fall of the Third Chimpanzee* (Vintage, London, 1993), ch. 6, 'Sexual Selection, and the Origin of Human Races'. Using modern studies of correlations among married couples, Diamond argues that sexual selection (broadly, that one will marry someone who looks like oneself or one's parents) is not confined to 'primitive' man.

ancient period, of which we have as yet any record, the races of man had already come to differ nearly or quite as much as they do at the present day.

This evidence of the antiquity of racial differentiation to which Darwin alludes is that of the ancient Egyptian cave paintings at Abu Simbel, which demonstrated 'that negroes, apparently identical with existing negroes, had lived at least 4000 years ago'. The evidence of ancient Egyptian paintings, often adduced by polygenists in the nineteenth century, is referred to earlier in *The Descent of Man* when Darwin presents the prima facie case for polygeny – though there he is more careful to point out the dangers of drawing conclusions from highly subjective judgements about the similarity between ancient figures and modern racial types.[1]

So, for Darwin, the races are extremely ancient. Their differentiation belongs to an era before mental and cultural evolution rendered 'primitive' sexual selection inoperative as a shaping force on man's physical development. And it is difficult not to see the appeal of this association of racial differentiation with sexuality as a reflection of the old European equation of sexuality with blackness. Cultural progress towards 'civilisation' is seen as a process of liberation from – or, to put a different slant on it, repression of – the base physical instincts that had produced race.

Alfred Russel Wallace, co-originator with Darwin of the theory of evolution by natural selection, differed from Darwin over the issue of sexual selection. For Wallace, as for modern 'neo-Darwinists', natural selection (the 'struggle for survival') was everything.

---

[1] Modern scientists, of course, would regard 4,000 years as an insignificant blip in terms of the time-scale of human evolution. As Stephen Jay Gould has summarised the issue: '[Human races] are recent, poorly differentiated subpopulations of our modern species, *Homo Sapiens*, separated at most by tens or hundreds of thousands of years, and marked by remarkably small genetic differences.' But the nineteenth-century notion that racial differentiation occurred at a very early stage of human evolution is one that has had a long afterlife. Most famously, Carleton Coon argued in his *Origin of Races* (Jonathan Cape, London, 1962) that humanity divided into five distinct 'sub-species' during the time of our ancestor *Homo erectus*, and that subsequently (and by a somewhat implausible coincidence) these five sub-species underwent a parallel evolutionary development.

Mechanisms such as sexual selection which were not strictly adaptive had no place in his account of evolution. But in 'The Development of Human Races under the Law of Natural Selection' (first published in 1864 in the Anthropological Society's journal *Anthropological Review*), Wallace too puts the case for the antiquity of racial differentiation:

> Man may have been – indeed I believe must have been – once a homogeneous race; but it was at a period of which we have as yet discovered no remains – at a period so remote in his history that he had not yet acquired that wonderfully developed brain, the organ of the mind, which now, even in its lowest examples, raises him far above the highest brutes – at a period when he had the form but hardly the nature of man, when he neither possessed human speech, nor those sympathetic and moral feelings which in greater or lesser degree everywhere now distinguish the race.

For Wallace, the divergence of the human races, marked by differences in physical structure, must have occurred prior to the development of the modern human brain. The reason for thinking this is that, according to Wallace, the power that modern man's mental capacity has given him had rendered him immune to those external, adaptive forces that mould the animal world. Humans' physical form (including its existing racial variations) is in effect fixed:

> [M]an, by the mere act of clothing himself, and making weapons and tools, has taken away from nature that power of slowly but permanently changing the external form and structure in accordance with changes in the external world, which she exercises over all other animals.

Intelligence has enabled humans to escape the clutches of evolution. Indeed, in a later essay, 'The Limits of Natural Selection as Applied to Man', Wallace goes further and argues that modern humans were never really enmeshed in mundane evolution, that 'a superior intelligence has guided the development of man in a definite direction, and for a special purpose', and that 'if we are not the highest intelligences in the universe, some higher intelligence may have directed the process by which the human race was developed, by means of more subtle agencies than we are acquainted with'. This invocation of supernatural agency was extremely painful to Wallace's friend and colleague Darwin.

Wallace puts forward an ingenious argument for his theory, an argument which combines a racial egalitarianism that was unusual for its time with a cultural chauvinism that was, unfortunately, not:

> The brain of the lowest savage and, as far as we yet know, of the prehistoric races, is little inferior in size to that of the highest types of man, and immensely superior to that of the highest mammals ... Yet the mental requirements of savages, and the faculties actually exercised by them, are very little above those of animals. The higher feelings of pure morality and refined emotion, and the power of abstract reasoning and ideal conception, are useless to them, are rarely if ever manifested, and have no important relations to their habits, wants, desires or well-being. They possess a mental organ beyond their needs. Natural selection could only have endowed savage man with a brain a few degrees superior to that of an ape, whereas he actually possesses one very little inferior to that of a philosopher.

Darwin could not accept Wallace's removal of mankind from the scope of evolution. But he did represent man's cultural and intellectual development as opening up an ever-widening gap between (European) man and his natural roots. The terms in which he describes this process are chilling:

> At some future period, not very distant as measured by centuries, the civilised races of man will almost certainly exterminate, and replace, the savage races throughout the world. At the same time the anthropomorphous apes [chimpanzee, gorilla, orang-outang] will no doubt be exterminated. The break between man and his nearest allies will then be wider, for it will intervene between man in a more civilised state, as we may hope, even than the Caucasian, and some ape as low as a baboon,

instead of as now between the negro or Australian and the gorilla.

It is indicative of the engrainedness of racialist thinking in the late nineteenth century that Darwin – no rabid reactionary, indeed one of the most humane, enlightened and thoughtful men of his day – should regard the attainment of 'a more civilised state' as necessitating a holocaust of 'the savage races throughout the world'.

In his *Anthropology* (1881), Sir Edward Tylor was more forthright than Darwin in defence of the principle of monogenism: '[A]ll tribes of men, from the blackest to the whitest, the most savage to the most cultured, have yet such general likeness in the structure of their bodies and the working of their minds, as is easiest and best accounted for by their being descended from a common ancestry, however distant.' But the last two words are important, for 'the evidence of ancient monuments, geography and history, goes to prove that the great race divisions of mankind are of no recent growth, but were already settled before the beginning of the historical period'. Englishmen and Africans may have descended from a common stock, but they are now so different that they seem to have arisen separately: '[W]hole races are spread over vast regions as though they grew there, and the peculiar type of the race seems more or less connected with the climate it lives in.' And Tylor ends with the admission that though they are not separate species, their differences are such that they are almost separate species: '[I]t must not be supposed that such differences as between an Englishman and a Gold Coast Negro are due to slight variations of breed. On the contrary, they are of such zoological importance as to have been compared with the differences between animals which naturalists reckon distinct species.'

Tylor's rhetorical strategy, like that of Darwin, is to establish the principle that mankind is a single species, but then to obscure and qualify that statement, to make it more palatable, by denying that it implies any racial egalitarianism. The language of 'lower' and 'higher' races is adhered to.[1] And this spatial metaphor of

[1] There is a long tradition of this language within British liberalism. In the

ascendancy, this vision of the various races organised like the rungs of a ladder, represents more than simply a sloppy use of the popular language of the day. One of the most striking features of the writings of Darwin and his followers on the subject of anthropology and man's relationship to the rest of the natural world is the way they revert to the eighteenth-century notion of the 'Great Chain of Being'. The idea that everything in the natural world has its assigned place in a great metaphysical chain or ladder running from the lowest vegetable life up to man himself was a widespread literary trope, elaborated most famously in Alexander Pope's *Essay on Man* ('Mark how it mounts to man's imperial race, / From the green myriads in the peopled grass'). The last major English defence of it as a scientific explanation of the natural world was physician and biologist Charles White's 1799 treatise 'An account of the regular gradation in man, and in different animals and vegetables', in which, having assigned the rest of creation their places, he does the same for the human races, with African blacks at the bottom, Orientals in the middle and white Europeans on top. His crowning argument for the ascendancy of the European has often been quoted for its unintended humour:

> Ascending the line of gradation, we come at last to the white European; who being most removed from the brute creation, may, on that account, be considered as the most beautiful of the human race ... Where shall we find, unless in the European, that nobly arched head, containing such a quantity of brain, and supported by a hollow conical pillar, entering its centre? ... In what other quarter of the globe shall we find the blush that overspreads the soft features of the beautiful women of Europe, that emblem of modesty, of delicate feelings, and of sense? Where that nice expression of the amiable and softer passions in the countenance; and that general elegance of features and complexion? Where, except on the bosom of the European

twentieth century, British liberals who denounced Britain's colonial policies (Sydney and Beatrice Webb, J. A. Hobson, Leonard Woolf and others) did so on the grounds that they oppressed the 'lower races'. See Christopher Fyfe, 'Using race as an instrument of policy: a historical view', *Race and Class*, vol. 36, Oct.–Dec. 1994, p. 74, and the references there.

woman, two such plump and snowy white hemispheres, tipt with vermilion?

Pleasant though it was to detail the superiority of the white Europeans, there were problems with the Great Chain theory. Where, in particular, were the 'missing links' between the animal and vegetable kingdoms, between vertebrates and invertebrates? The chain seemed to have a lot of holes and gaps in it.

If the Great Chain were not already clearly inadequate as a scientific theory and description of the natural world, then surely Darwinism should have killed it off. What place could there be in the theory of evolution, with its picture of ever-branching natural diversity, for an arbitrary yoking together of distinct genealogical shoots in a fixed scale? Evolution is about bushes, not ladders. But the Great Chain or 'ladder' was precisely what the nineteenth-century Darwinians invoked when they discussed race. For the attraction of the Great Chain idea, the thing that outweighed its evident scientific shortcomings, was its reassuringly conservative message. Everything is bound up in a fixed and unbreakable hierarchy. That Darwin and his followers felt the need to resort to this deeply ideological language on this specific issue reflects the special place that the question of race had in the minds of mid-Victorian gentlemen.

The book which more than any other sparked the debate in the 1860s over 'man's place in nature' was Thomas Henry Huxley's *Evidence as to Man's Place in Nature* (1863), which followed up Darwin's hint at the end of *The Origin of Species* that the theory of evolution could be applied to man himself. In arguing for the affinities between man and the great apes, Huxley constantly refers to 'the scale'. Thus, in his conclusion, he explains how 'I have endeavoured to show that no absolute structural line of demarcation, wider than that between the animals which immediately succeed us in the scale, can be drawn between the animal world and ourselves'. On embryology, Huxley remarks that 'without question, the mode of origin and the early stages of the development of man are identical with those of the animals immediately below him in the scale'. And on the crucial question of brain size:

As if to demonstrate, by a striking example, the impossibility of erecting any cerebral barrier between man and the apes, Nature has provided us, in the latter animals, with an almost complete series of gradations from brains little higher than that of a rodent, to brains little lower than that of Man.

Like Darwin, with his predictions of a holocaust for the savage races, Huxley sees the 'lower races' as being closer to what he calls 'the under-world of life' – their ape relatives. Thus his argument that 'the difference in the volume of the cranial capacity of different races of mankind is far greater, absolutely, than that between the lowest Man and the highest Ape'.

Tylor, too, hovers uneasily between an eighteenth-century language of 'the scale' and a newer language of evolution:

By ... comparing their [the great apes'] skeletons, it will be seen that in any scale of nature or scheme of creation these animals must be placed in somewhat close relation to man. No competent anatomist who has examined the bodily structure of these apes considers it possible that man can be descended from any of them, but according to the doctrine of descent they appear as the nearest existing offshoots from the same primitive stock whence man also came.

The great apes may be our cousins, but they are also the next rung down in a ladder that ascends from the murkiest depths of brute creation, through the 'lower races', to the white European himself.

Tylor ends his discussion of race in *Anthropology* with the striking image of 'every Chinese and Negro bearing in his face evidence of the antiquity of man'. Even if one were to accept the argument for the antiquity of racial differentiation, there is, of course, no logical reason for seeing evidence of man's antiquity in the face of a Chinese or a Negro rather than in that of a white European. The reason for picking out the Chinese and the Negro as examples of antiquity has less to do with logic than with a prejudice that places them lower in a value-laden chain of living beings. The mid-Victorian evolutionists' contribution to the Great Chain idea was to temporalise the scale, so that evolution becomes a progress, the ascension of a ladder. Like their eighteenth-century predecessors, the Darwinians saw the Negro as being closer on the scale to the apes – thus adopting what had been perhaps the most popular racial slur since the seventeenth century – but they also saw him as a rudiment, a survival from man's primitive past. And this was linked to the idea that the races were formed early in man's evolutionary history.

Again it helps to place the argument in its historical context, for the 1860s saw a surge of interest in the early history of mankind, with books such as Lyell's *Geological Evidences of the Antiquity of Man* (1863), Tylor's *Researches into the Early History of Mankind* (1865) and Sir John Lubbock's *Pre-historic Times* (1865). This interest was sparked in part by the sensational discovery in 1857 of a fossil human skeleton at the Neanderthal Cave near Düsseldorf in Germany. Evolutionists were quick to point out the implications of 'Neanderthal man'. For Huxley, 'under whatever aspect we view this cranium . . . we meet with apelike characters, stamping it as the most pithecoid of human crania'. Furthermore, it 'manifests but an extreme degree of a state of degradation exhibited, as a natural condition, by the crania of certain races of mankind'. Huxley fits the Neanderthal cranium into a scale leading, via other ancient skulls and the 'lower races', to the 'highest' (European) crania:

> [T]hough truly the most pithecoid of known human skulls, the Neanderthal cranium is by no means so isolated as it appears to be at first but forms, in reality, the extreme term of a series leading gradually from it to the highest and best developed of human crania. On the one hand, it is closely approached by flattened Australian [Aboriginal] skulls . . . And, on the other hand, it is even more closely affined to the skulls of certain ancient people who inhabited Denmark during the 'stone period'.

Like Darwin, Huxley assimilates physical and cultural evolutionary 'scales', placing the 'lower races' broadly on a level with ancient peoples who are themselves just above the 'ape-like'. Sir John Lubbock's book – whose full title is *Pre-historic Times, as Illustrated by Ancient Remains, and the Manners and Customs of*

Modern Savages – makes explicit what was to become a standard anthropological comparison: 'If we wish clearly to understand the antiquities of Europe, we must compare them with the rude implements and weapons still, or until lately, used by savage races in other parts of the world.' A chapter of Tylor's *Researches* deals with 'The Stone Age Past and Present' – in which, though, it is conceded that Africa 'is now entirely in the Iron Age'.

An archaeological trench presents the passage of time spatially as the layers of a cross-section. Similarly, for the Darwinists, the human world carries within it traces of its journey, its ascent up the ladder of time. Darwin's account of human evolution opens with a description of 'rudiments' in human anatomy – those features (most famously the coccyx, our vestigial tail) whose existence can only be explained as the surviving traces of our earlier forms.[1] By analogy, the cultural evolutionists saw contemporary 'savages' as living rudiments of Europeans' prehistoric past. And rudiments could be found not just among savages, but even at the heart of civilisation. Tylor's *Researches into the Early History of Mankind* opens with the observation that 'the women of modern Europe mutilate their ears to hang jewels in them'. But 'the reason of their doing so is not to be found in the circumstances among which we are living now'. Tylor then asks the reader to think of bones and feathers thrust through noses, of 'wooden plugs as big as table-spoons stuck in the lower lip', of the teeth of animals stuck point outwards through holes in the cheeks – 'all familiar things among the lower races up and down in the world'. The conclusion to be drawn from these observations, according to Tylor, is that 'the

[1] Many nineteenth-century evolutionists adhered to the theory that rudiments were particularly pronounced in embryo and childhood, and indeed that embryonic development passed through stages representing, in sequence, the adult forms of ancestral lower creatures. The baby emerging from the womb, or the child emerging from infancy, represents, in effect, man emerging from his evolutionary past. This is the principle that 'ontogeny recapitulates phylogeny'. The nineteenth-century anthropologist Louis Agassiz explicitly proposed a 'threefold parallelism' of paleontology, comparative anatomy (the comparisons being primarily racial) and embryology. Adult members of 'lower races' are thus placed on a level with white children and fossil ancestors. Some recapitulations advocated a fourth parallel or 'throwback' – the mentally subnormal. See Stephen Jay Gould, 'Dr Down's Syndrome', in *The Panda's Thumb*.

modern earring of the higher nations stands not as a product of our own times, but as a relic of a ruder mental condition, one of the many cases in which the result of progress has not been positive in adding, but negative in taking away, something belonging to an earlier state of things'. Savages were not just what Europeans had once been, but at some level what they still were. It was the seed of an idea that would be developed by the writers of imperial romances at the end of the century.

The Victorian evolutionists' conflation of the old Great Chain idea with the new consciousness of 'deep time' reflected a faith in progress that was very much of its time and place. For the middle- or upper-class Englishman of the 1850s and 1860s – before economic depression and uncertainties about Empire set in – Britain seemed to have the world at its feet. God was in His heaven, hell was underground, and man had climbed out of the darkness and depth of his remote past, up into the light and ascendancy of his present position. It was an idea with the appeal of all metaphors of depth and ascent. The prisoners in Plato's cave climb out of the flickering darkness of ignorance into the light of knowledge and truth. One is reminded too of the dark cave – symbolically guarded by a 'hideous Moor' – into which according to Diderot, Samuel Richardson leads us when he leads us back to the wellsprings, the depths, of his characters' emotional life. And one looks forward to Freud, to the metaphor of depth embedded in the idea of the unconscious. The unconscious (or *sub*conscious) lies *beneath* the level of the everyday. As the historian Peter Gay has argued, it is surely no coincidence that Freud was fascinated by archaeology.

Perhaps the most striking characteristic of cultural evolutionism, and one which marks it out as being peculiarly of its historical moment, is its optimism. To the disillusioned eye of the late twentieth-century reader, the complacent tone of some evolutionist writings has an inadvertently comic ring. Huxley, surveying man's evolutionary 'progress', sounds like a headmaster commenting on a bright and promising pupil:

[T]houghtful men, once escaped from the blinding influence of traditional prejudice, will find in the lowly stock whence man has sprung, the best evidence of the splendour of his capacities; and will discern in his long progress through the Past, a reasonable ground of faith in his attainment of a nobler Future.

More philosophically, Sir Charles Lyell, in his peroration to *The Antiquity of Man*, portrays evolution as a progress from the material to the mental and spiritual:

It may be said that, so far from having a materialistic tendency, the supposed introduction into the earth, at successive geological periods, of life – sensation, – instinct, – the intelligence of the higher mammalia bordering on reason, – and lastly the improvable reason of Man himself, presents us with a picture of the ever increasing dominion of mind over matter.

As with the eighteenth-century sentimentalists, the 'lower races', on the lower rungs of the evolutionary ladder, are associated with the material, the body.

But for all their concessions to polygeny and to the hardening racial attitudes of their time, the Victorian anthropologists did believe – like their evangelical forebears – in mankind's basic unity. Given 'legitimate trade', European civilisation and Christianity, even the lowliest savage had at least the potential to follow the path marked out by Tylor as the 'three great stages . . . of human life': 'Savage, Barbaric, Civilized'. Indeed, there was no other place for them to go, no other possible path for them to follow. All paths led to the door of the Victorian anthropologist's study. Through its commerce, its missions, its stamping out of ancient barbarism such as the African slave trade, the British Empire was spreading light to all corners of the globe.

But this very confidence, this faith in the value of the Christian civilisation represented by the Empire, meant that there was a very dark side to the Victorians' view of those who lay beyond that civilisation, beyond the pale. One looks in vain in the writings of the Darwinists for hints of that eighteenth-century cultural relativism that could envision a 'noble savage', someone who through his authenticity could teach civilisation a lesson. The

Victorian anthropologist is much more struck by the enormous gulf – technological, cultural, moral – between the white European and the savage. The only conceivable instruction comes from Europe outwards, from Christian efforts to civilise the uncivilised. Darwin, for example, was haunted for decades afterwards by his encounter during the course of the *Beagle* voyage with the natives of Tierra del Fuego. He saw nothing 'noble' in them, as he records in his diary:

> I shall never forget how savage and wild one group was. Four or five men suddenly appeared on a cliff near to us: they were absolutely naked and with long streaming hair. Springing from the ground and waving their arms around their heads, they sent forth most hideous yells. Their appearance was so strange, that it was scarcely like that of earthly inhabitants.

The Fuegians were to crop up again in a crucial passage at the end of *The Descent of Man*:

> The astonishment which I felt on first seeing a party of Fuegians on a wild and broken shore will never be forgotten by me, for the reflection at once rushed into my mind – such were our ancestors. He who has seen a savage in his native land will not feel much shame, if forced to acknowledge that the blood of some more humble creature flows in his veins. For my own part I would as soon be descended from that heroic little monkey, who braved his dreaded enemy in order to save the life of his keeper, or from that old baboon, who descending from the mountains, carried away in triumph his young comrade from a crowd of astonished dogs – as from a savage who delights to torture his enemies, offers up blood sacrifices, practises infanticide without remorse, treats his women like slaves, knows no decency, and is haunted by the grossest superstitions.

In *The Descent of Man*, having even-handedly presented the evidence on both sides of the argument as to whether the human races had different origins, Darwin predicts that 'when the principle of evolution is generally accepted, as it surely will be before long, the dispute between the monogenists and polygenists will die a silent and unobserved death'. 'It is', he writes, 'almost a matter of indifference whether the so-called races of man are thus designated, or are ranked as species or sub-species; but the latter term appears the more appropriate.'[1] It may seem strange that Darwin should treat the issue so casually. It was, after all, one that had vexed generations of European intellectuals. But, for Darwin, taxonomy takes second place to genealogy; how we classify or name something is less important than our description of how it has evolved. In *The Descent of Man*, Darwin explains his indifference to the question of what title we give to the races by way of the analogy with which we are already familiar:

> Whether primeval man, when he possessed but few arts, and those of the rudest kind, and when his power of language was extremely imperfect, would have deserved to be called man, must depend on the definition which we employ. In a series of forms graduating insensibly from some ape-like creature to man as he now exists, it would be impossible to fix on any definite point when the term 'man' ought to be used. But this is a matter of very little importance.

'A matter of very little importance' – one can only marvel at the insouciance with which Darwin sweeps aside centuries of anthropocentric religion, art and philosophy.[2]

The extreme radicalism of Darwin's discovery – a radicalism which continues to disturb the way in which we think of ourselves – brought it into conflict with the certainties of Victorian society.

[1] Many modern biologists would wish to do away with the whole notion of 'races' or 'sub-species', whether applied to man or any other part of the animal kindom. As Stephen Jay Gould writes: 'The practice of naming sub-species has largely fallen into disfavour and few taxonomists use the term any more. Human variation exists; the formal designation of races is passé' ('Human Equality is a Contingent Fact of History' in *The Flamingo's Smile* (Penguin, 1986), p. 193). See also Gould's essay 'Why We Should Not Name Human Races – A Biological View', in *Ever Since Darwin* (Penguin, 1980), in which he argues forcefully that multivariate analysis has superseded the crude and arbitrary aggregation of characteristics in the form of 'races' or 'sub-species'.

[2] Compare the following, from Darwin's Notebooks: 'Plato says in *Phaedo* that our "imaginary ideas" arise from the preexistence of the soul, are not derivable from experience – read monkeys for preexistence.'

It was a conflict played out within the writings of Darwinists themselves. And one of the greatest stress-points was the issue of race, in dealing with which the evolutionists attempted to yoke together three quite separate series or progressions: the chronological progression from early, culturally 'primitive' to modern, culturally 'evolved' man; the physical evolution from ape-like creature to man; and the perceived hierarchy of the existing races, from 'lower' to 'higher'.

In this way, the Victorians focused the anxiety generated by the discovery of evolution onto specific fears. The 'lower races' epitomised the inhuman, primeval chaos from which we, the Europeans, had sprung. (And which, perhaps, we had never completely left behind.) In the writings of Darwin himself, and of his followers, the ameliorative, evangelical ethos – the ethos that had generated the abolitionist movement – was still strong enough to keep these fears suppressed. But a generation later the situation was different. Beneath the imperial pomp of late Victorian and Edwardian Britain were doubts and uncertainties. In the imaginative literature of *fin de siècle* Britain and France one finds the optimism of the evangelical outlook overturned. The seed sown by the Darwinists – in the form of the equation of the Negro with the primeval – began to bear darker fruit.

Sources

Primary sources

Burton, Richard F., *A Mission to Gelele, King of Dahome, With Notices of the so-called 'Amazons', the Grand Customs, the Yearly Customs, the Human Sacrifices, the Present State of the Slave Trade, and the Negro's Place in Nature* (London, 1864).

Carlyle, Thomas, 'Occasional Discourse on the Nigger Question' (1849), in *Critical and Miscellaneous Essays*, vol. VI (London, 1869).

Darwin, Charles, *The Descent of Man, and Selection in Relation to Sex* (London, 1882). First published 1871.

— *On the Origin of Species* (Mentor, New York, 1958). First published 1859.

Dickens, Charles, *Bleak House* (Oxford University Press, London, 1948). First published 1853.

Gobineau, Arthur de, *The Inequality of Human Races* (William Heinemann, London, 1915). First published 1854.

Haddon, Alfred C., *History of Anthropology* (Watts & Co., London, 1910).

Huxley, Thomas Henry, *Evidence as to Man's Place in Nature* (London, 1863).

Knox, Robert, *The Races of Man: A Philosophical Enquiry into the Influence of Race over the Destinies of Nations* (London, 1862). First published 1850.

Latham, Robert Gordon, *The Natural History of the Varieties of Man* (London, 1850).

Lubbock, Sir John, *Pre-historic Times, as Illustrated by Ancient Remains, and the Manners and Customs of Modern Savages* (London, 1865).

Lyell, Sir Charles, *The Geological Evidences of the Antiquity of Man* (John Murray, London, 1863).

Pope, Alexander, *An Essay on Man*, in *Poetical Works* (Oxford University Press, 1966).

Prichard, James Cowles, *Researches into the Physical History of Mankind* (London, 1837–41). First published 1813.

Trollope, Anthony, *The West Indies and the Spanish Main* (London, 1860). First published 1859.

Tylor, Edward B., *Researches into the Early History of Mankind* (London, 1865).
— *Primitive Culture* (London, 1871).
— *Anthropology: An Introduction to the Study of Man and Civilization* (London, 1881).

Wallace, Alfred Russel, *Natural Selection and Tropical Nature* (London, 1891).

Wells, William Charles, *Two Essays* (London, 1818).

Secondary sources

Barzun, Jacques, *Race: A Study in Modern Superstition* (Methuen, London, 1938).

Bolt, Christine, *Victorian Attitudes to Race* (Routledge & Kegan Paul, London, 1981).

Burrow, J. V., *Evolution and Society: A Study in Victorian Social Theory* (Cambridge University Press, 1966).

Coon, Carleton, *The Origins of Races* (Jonathan Cape, London, 1962).

Desmond, Adrian, and James Moore, *Darwin* (Michael Joseph, London, 1991).

Diamond, Jared, *The Rise and Fall of the Third Chimpanzee* (Vintage, London, 1993).

Gay, Peter, 'Sigmund Freud: A Partiality for the Prehistoric', in *Freud, Jews and Other Germans. Masters and Victims in Modernist Culture* (Oxford Univeristy Press, 1978).

Gould, Stephen Jay, *Ever Since Darwin* (Penguin, Harmondsworth, 1980).
— *The Panda's Thumb* (Penguin, Harmondsworth, 1980).
— *The Flamingo's Smile* (Penguin, Harmondsworth, 1986).

Lorimer, Douglas A., *Colour, Class and the Victorians: English Attitudes to the Negro in the Mid-Nineteenth Century* (Leicester University Press, 1978).

Lovejoy, Arthur O., *The Great Chain of Being: A Study in the History of an Idea* (Harvard University Press, Cambridge, Mass., 1942).

Montague, Ashley (ed.), *The Concept of the Primitive* (The Free Press, New York, 1968).

Rainger, Ronald, 'Race, Politics and Science: The Anthropological Society of London in the 1860s', *Victorian Studies*, vol. 22 (1978), pp. 51–70.

Stanton, William, *The Leopard's Spots: Scientific Attitudes Toward Race in America 1815–59* (University of Chicago Press, 1960).

Stocking, George W., *Victorian Anthropology* (The Free Press, New York, 1987).

Temperley, Howard, *White Dreams, Black Africa: The Anti-Slavery Expedition to the Niger, 1841–2* (Yale University Press, New Haven, 1991).

4

The Pessimism of Empire

In 1902 the economist J. A. Hobson published a classic study of European imperialism. He noted that since 1870 Britain had added 4,750,000 square miles of territory and 88 million people to its existing empire. And Britain was not alone. An unprecedented number of great powers had been involved in a scramble for territory in the tropics. Africa and Asia had become scenes of aggressive competition between the European states. This rapacious expansion into the tropics represented, for Hobson, the 'New Imperialism', something quite different in quantity and quality from the piecemeal colonisation that had taken place in the eighteenth and early nineteenth centuries. And on quantity, Hobson was right. Modern estimates are that in the years 1878 to 1914, the European colonial powers, the United States and Japan acquired about 17.4 per cent of the world's land surface at an average rate of 240,000 square miles per year.

Recent historians have questioned whether there was, in fact, anything new about the New Imperialism, or whether it was not a continuation, albeit on an increased level, of the kind of *ad hoc* acquisition that had been going on throughout the nineteenth century. There have also been debates about the root causes of the expansion. For Hobson, as later for Lenin, the roots of imperialism lay in economics, in the dysfunctions in the depressed capitalist economies that prompted the search for new markets and new investment opportunities for surplus capital. Again, revisionists have questioned whether the expansion had such deep, calculated causes, or whether it was not just a confused outcome of traditional diplomatic rivalries and insecurities between the European states.

But one thing that was indisputably new about the New Imperialism was the involvement of public opinion. Whether 'jingoism' (the word was coined in 1878) was cause or effect of the growth of Empire, it was clearly an important part of the domestic scene. Imperialism became as much a cultural phenomenon as it was a fact of international geopolitics. Rapid urbanisation and the expansion of education created a market for new newspapers aimed at the masses, and this 'yellow press' was quick to jump on the bandwagon of Empire. On its foundation in 1896, the *Daily Mail* stated that it stood 'for the power, the supremacy and the greatness of the British Empire ... The *Daily Mail* is the embodiment and mouthpiece of the imperial idea. Those who launched this journal had one definite aim in view ... to be the articulate voice of British progress and domination. We believe in England. We know that the advance of the Union Jack means protection for weaker races, justice for the oppressed, liberty for the down-trodden. Our Empire has not exhausted itself.'

This new 'imperialism', this self-consciousness about Britain's imperial destiny, was reflected in propagandist books such as Charles Dilke's *Greater Britain* (1868), John Seeley's *The Expansion of England* (1883) and James Froude's *Oceana, or England and Her Colonies* (1886). According to Seeley, in a famous phrase, Britain had 'conquered and peopled half the world in a fit of absence of mind'. It was time now to take pride in this achievement, to see its significance as reflecting the 'diffusion of the English race' across the earth. Social Darwinists, too, saw a greater significance in Empire, with the conflict between coloniser and colonised, and between competing European powers, reflecting a never-ending struggle for racial supremacy, a biological battle for the 'survival of the fittest'. For the Social Darwinist Karl Pearson, echoing Darwin himself, superior, efficiently organised societies would use the 'hecatombs of inferior races' as stepping stones to a 'higher intellectual and emotional life'.

Imaginative literature of the period, too, carried forward the imperial message. Popular writers like G. A. Henty built their careers on novels whose very titles – *Under Drake's Flag* (1883), *With Roberts to Pretoria* (1902) – proclaimed them as chronicles of Britain's glorious expansion. Stories in *Union Jack* and *Boy's Own Paper* gave a ringing call to Empire. At a more high-brow level, *Blackwood's Magazine* and other smoking-room journals provided a readership of army and navy officers and imperial administrators with adventure stories about men of action doing tough jobs in exotic locations. As Joseph Conrad commented: 'There isn't a single club and messroom and man-of-war in the British Seas and Dominions which hasn't a copy of Maga [*Blackwood's*].' At home, the romance of adventure transported the late Victorian and Edwardian reader from the drawing-room to the far-flung frontier, where European civilisation was imposing its will and order on primitive barbarism.

But the irony is that when one starts to look at this literature of Empire as it was created in Britain and France, one finds, not far below the surface, a profound pessimism and a fear that, transported into the realm of the primitive, European civilisation will 'go native', partaking of the chaos that surrounds it. The Empire, one senses, is already beginning to strike back. It was a pessimism that was very much of its time, as the mid-Victorian literature of meliorative balance, of faith in progress – the literature of Dickens, Mill and George Eliot – gave way to a literature of extremes, of the gothic, the decadent, the gloomily fatalistic, the *fin de siècle*.

In terms of literary history, the irony deepens when one considers the hopes that many held out that this turn to romance and exotic adventure would provide a healthy escape from fetid introspection. Take the case of Andrew Lang, a respected arbiter of taste in late Victorian literary London. As his biographer, Roger Lancelyn Green, has written: 'Lang's exaggeratedly sensitive nature prevented him from appreciating the more sordid or gloomy type of contemporary novel.' In his many columns and reviews he inveighed against the fashions for 'realism' – Zola, Tolstoy, Dostoevsky, Hardy – and for psychological analysis, lauding instead the virtues of escape into a boyhood world of imagination and adventure. He detested Henry James's later novels (James returned the compliment, writing of Lang's cultivation of 'the puerile imagination and the fourth-rate opinion'), while his heroes were Robert Louis Stevenson (a fellow Scotsman) and H. Rider Haggard (with whom Lang wrote a novel, *The World's Desire* (1891)). Stevenson carried forward in *Treasure Island* (1883) and *Kidnapped* (1886) the popularity of historical fiction that had been established in R. D. Blackmore's *Lorna Doone* (1869), while the extraordinary popularity of Rider Haggard's African adventure stories was a marked feature of the English publishing scene in the 1880s and 1890s.

Lang was much exercised by the question of The Future of the Novel, and in November 1887 he published 'Realism and Romance', his most considered treatment of the issue. It was a subject that was preoccupying the literary magazines at that time. A couple of months earlier, the well-known critic George Saintsbury had published a survey of 'The Present State of the Novel' in which he highlighted the 'return to the pure romance as distinguished from the analytic novel', citing in particular the recent successes of Stevenson and Rider Haggard. He predicted that this reappearance of the romance of adventure would not be a passing phenomenon, and contrasted English 'healthy beefiness and beeriness' with 'the sterile pessimism of Russian fiction'. The novel of society, of manners and characters, had 'bred in and in', producing feebleness of strain. By returning to 'the pure romance of adventure', narrative was returning to healthy primitive stock, to 'the earliest form of writing'.

Saintsbury's evolutionary analogy was taken up by Lang – either in direct imitation, or because Lang himself was something of an anthropologist. Influenced by Tylor, he has been credited with being one of the first to apply the evolutionary 'anthropological method' to the study of mythology. Romances, for Lang, were 'savage survivals' – or, to put it in evolutionary terms, rudiments. 'The Coming Man', he feared, 'may be bald, toothless, highly "cultured", and addicted to tales of introspective analysis. I don't envy him when he has got rid of that relic of the ape, his hair; those relics of the age of combat, his teeth and nails; that survival of barbarism, his delight in the last battles of Odysseus, Laertes' son. I don't envy him the novels he will admire ... Not for nothing did Nature leave us all savages under our white skins; she was wrought thus that we might have many delights, among others "the joy of adventurous living", and of reading about adventurous living.' He goes on to describe a society novel by Frances Hodgson Burnett which 'the civilised person within me, the Man of the Future within me, heartily delights to peruse', but the point of the example is to conclude that 'the natural man within me, the survival of some blue-painted Briton or of some gipsy, was equally pleased with a *true* Zulu love story, sketched in two pages, a story so terrible, so moving, in the long, gallant fight against odds, and the awful unheard-of death-agony of the two Zulu lovers, that I presume no civilized fancy could have invented the incidents that actually occurred'. The 'return to the primitive' was a description not only of the subject matter of imperial romance, but of its place in literary evolution.

Like Saintsbury, Lang contrasted this healthy extroversion and physicality with the gloomy self-absorption of the Russians. 'I, for one, admire M. Dostoieffsky so much, and so sincerely, that I pay him the supreme tribute of never reading him at all. I read [*Crime and Punishment*] till I was crushed and miserable; so bitterly true it is, so dreadfully exact, such a quintessence of all the imaginable misery of man. Then, after reaching the lowest deep of sympathetic abandonment (which I plumbed in about 4 chapters), I emerged feeling that I had enough of M. Dostoieffsky for one lifetime.'

The physicality that Lang preferred is definitely of the male variety. One of his most pointed criticisms of 'the modern Realists' is that they have become emasculated:

[S]ome of them have an almost unholy knowledge of the nature of women. One would as lief explore a girl's room, and tumble about her little household treasures, as examine so curiously the poor secrets of her heart and tremors of her frame ... Such analysis makes one feel intrusive and unmanly. It is like overhearing a confession by accident.

'The poor secrets of her heart and tremors of her frame ...
overhearing a confession' – it would be difficult to find a better
encapsulation of the sentimental aesthetic, the aesthetic of identification and empathy that, as we saw in Chapter 1, underlay the
culture of abolitionism. The essence of abolitionist sentimentalism,
surviving to some extent in evolutionary anthropology, was an
identification – and through that identification, an appropriation
and assimilation. Beneath and despite the blackness of his skin – in
itself a mark of ugliness and immorality – the Negro had a (white)
human soul or potentiality that might enable him, at least in
theory, to attain Christianity and civilisation. The imperialist
writers of the end of the nineteenth century, in rebelling against
that sentimentalism and what was seen as its feminine weakness,
broke that tenuous bond of identification. The Negro became
irredeemably Other. He became, in fact, inhuman. The notion of a
white soul masked by blackness was lost, and the Negro was
reduced to black physicality.

This reaction to the abolitionist aesthetic – a continuation of that
mid-century hardening of racial attitudes that had encouraged
Darwin and his followers to make concessions to polygenism – can
be seen clearly in Joseph Conrad's novels, especially *The Nigger of
the 'Narcissus'* (1898) and *Heart of Darkness* (1899). Conrad was a
writer who was highly conscious of his vocation as an artist, and
this made him touchily aware that his own early novels and stories,
far-flung adventure stories, shared the subject matter of the
popular fiction of the time. His first novels, *Almayer's Folly* (1895)
and *An Outcast of the Islands* (1896), with their Malayan settings,
owed much to the French tradition of 'exotic', escapist fiction.
Youth (1902) he described ironically as being fashioned from 'the
material of a boy's story', while with *The Nigger of the 'Narcissus'*
Conrad began a series of novels and stories about men at sea.

But Conrad had other objects in mind apart from telling a good
yarn. An early reviewer of *The Nigger of the 'Narcissus'*, perhaps
expecting from the novel the conventional melodramatic plot of
maritime tales, complained that

The tale is no tale, but merely an account of the uneventful voyage of the *Narcissus* from Bombay to the Thames. One of the ship's crew is an intelligent negro named James Wait. He lies in his bunk most of the voyage, and at last he dies and is buried at sea. This is positively all the story in the book. There is no plot, no villainy, no heroism, and, apart from a storm and the death and burial, no incident.

There is in fact more incident than the *Daily Mail* reviewer gave Conrad credit for – most notably a near-mutiny – but it is true that what gives the story its focus is not intrigue or heroic action but the figure of Wait himself.

James Wait is a malingerer. As we subsequently learn, he is in fact in the early stages of tuberculosis when he comes on the ship, but he exaggerates the seriousness of his illness and plays on the sympathy of his shipmates in order to avoid doing his duties. Wait's fellow sailors, encouraged by the malicious Donkin, take sides against those in authority. When his condition does genuinely worsen, he insists on returning to his duties, and the captain's attempt to confine him to his quarters results in the near-mutiny. Wait's presence is thus a divisive and subversive influence on the ship; he is literally a dead 'weight' on its progress. This symbolism is made explicit when he eventually dies. To the last, at its committal to the sea, his body clings to the ship:

> The men lifted the inboard end of the planks, the boatswain snatched off the Union Jack, and James Wait did not move . . . In death and swathed up for all eternity, he yet seemed to hang on to the ship with the grip of an undying fear . . . [T]he grey package started reluctantly to, all at once, whizz off the lifted planks with the suddenness of a flash of lightning. The crowd stepped forward like one man; a deep Ah-h-h! came out vibrating from the broad chests. The ship rolled as if relieved of an unfair burden . . .

In a preface 'To My Readers in America' added in 1914, Conrad makes a curious statement about Wait. '[I]n the book,' he writes, 'he is nothing; he is merely the centre of the ship's collective psychology and the pivot of the action.' When Wait first appears, at the muster of the ship's crew in Bombay, he is literally shrouded in darkness:

> The lamplight lit up the man's body. He was tall. His head was way up in the shadows of lifeboats that stood on skids above the deck. The whites of his eyes and his teeth gleamed distinctly, but the face was indistinguishable. His hands were big and seemed gloved ... The boy, amazed like the rest, raised the light to the man's face. It was black. A surprised hum – a faint hum that sounded like the suppressed mutter of the word 'Nigger' – ran along the deck and escaped out into the night.

Throughout the book there is an ambiguity and mystery about Wait. Physically, he first appears as commanding and imperious ('The nigger was calm, cool, towering, superb ... He was naturally scornful, unaffectedly condescending, as if from his height of six foot three he had surveyed all the vastness of human folly and had made up his mind not to be too hard on it'), but at other times becomes insubstantial. When he is rescued from his cabin by the other sailors, in the famous chapter describing the ship's near-loss in a storm, he is no more than a bag of wind:

> [H]e swung from one enemy to another, showing about as much life as an old bolster would do. His eyes made two narrow slits in the black face. He breathed slowly, and the air escaped through his lips like the sound of bellows.

Wait himself is blurred because what matters is not his being in its own right, but what he represents to the rest of the crew – his role as 'the centre of the ship's collective psychology'. He is a symbol. And the story of his corrupting influence on the *Narcissus* is a parable that warns of the dangers posed to loyalty and fidelity by an emasculating sentimentalism. If *Heart of Darkness* represents in an extreme form the inversion of the abolitionist aesthetic, Conrad's earlier novel marks a first step in that process of inversion. *The Nigger of the 'Narcissus'* may be 'A Tale of the Sea', the chronicle of a ship's journey from Bombay to London through storm, calm and potential mutiny, but, as we shall see, it is also a novel with a strong ideological project, a novel whose dense and varied symbolism is orchestrated to attack the sentimentalist world-view and furnish a warning as to its dangers. James Wait stands at the heart of that project.

Throughout the book, dreamy, self-serving philanthropy is set against that stern, practical application to the task in hand that Conrad sees as essential for keeping the crew together and getting the ship to its destination. Thus at the beginning, the evil Donkin, soon to become Wait's accomplice, is introduced as 'the man that cannot steer, that can't splice, that dodges the work on dark nights ... The pet of philanthropists and self-seeking landlubbers. The sympathetic and deserving creature that knows all about his rights, but knows nothing of courage, of endurance, and of the unexpressed faith, of the unspoken loyalty that knits together a ship's company.' The antithesis of Donkin is the old sailor Singleton, who stands for the silent and instinctive steadfastness of the seafaring life, a life that Conrad saw as being threatened by humanitarian campaigns on behalf of seamen:

> [A]lone in the dim emptiness of the sleeping forecastle he appeared bigger, colossal, very old ... Yet he was only a child of time, a lonely relic of a devoured and forgotten generation ... The men who could understand his silence were gone – those men who knew how to exist beyond the pale of life and within sight of eternity ... Well-meaning people had tried to represent those men who knew toil, privation, violence, debauchery – but knew not fear, and had no desire of spite in their hearts. Men hard to manage, but easy to inspire; voiceless men – but men enough to scorn in their hearts the sentimental voices that bewailed the hardness of their fate.

Singleton is the one member of the ship's crew who signally resists the 'subtle and dismal influence' of James Wait ('Jimmy') and forgoes sentimental pity:

> The old man, addressing Jimmy, asked: 'Are you dying?' Thus interrogated, James Wait appeared startled and confused. We were all startled ... 'Why? Can't you see I am?' he answered shakily. Singleton lifted a piece of soaked biscuit ... to his lips. –

133

'Well, get on with your dying,' he said with venerable mildness; 'don't raise a blamed fuss with us over that job. We can't help you.'

Conrad's attack on sentimentalism and philanthropy finds its main focus in the relationship of the crew to Jimmy. And the crucial point about Jimmy is that he is black, a 'nigger'.[1] Critics tackling the racial aspect of *The Nigger of the 'Narcissus'* have tended to do so by isolating certain 'racist' remarks in the book. Most conspicuous among these is a passage near the beginning, when Wait is first introduced, which begins with some of the light/dark imagery that pervades the novel, and ends – queasily for admirers of Conrad – with a thump:

> He held his head up in the glare of the lamp – a head vigorously modelled into deep shadows and shining lights – a head powerful and misshapen with a tormented and flattened face – a face pathetic and brutal: the tragic, the mysterious, the repulsive mask of a nigger's soul.

Both Ian Watt, in his *Conrad in the Nineteenth Century*, and Cedric Watts, in his introduction to the Penguin edition of the novel, put a gloss on this passage that shows how persistent is the white Christian and liberal attitude that it is less 'racist' to imagine that black people have a (good, fair) white soul than to imagine that black people have a (bad, ugly) black one. Cedric Watts's formulation, beneath its uneasy equivocation, appears to endorse the eighteenth-century evangelical picture of an inner whiteness: 'The racism of this passage can be mitigated by noting that it is the mask, rather than the soul, which is declared "repulsive"; but the

---

[1] The term 'nigger' was widely used in Britain in the 1890s, and its derogatory sense was explicit. In April 1897, four months before serialisation of *The Nigger of the 'Narcissus'*, Conrad's friend R. B. Cunninghame Graham published an article, 'Bloody Niggers', in which he denounced the use of the term: ' "Niggers" who have no cannons, and cannot construct a reasonable torpedo ... Cretans, Armenians, Cubans, Macedonians, we commiserate, subscribe, and feel for ... But "niggers", "bloody niggers", have no friends.' Conrad read the article and remarked that it was 'very good, very telling'.

declaration remains irredeemably racist.' After discussing such isolated remarks, Cedric Watts argues that though the novel 'is indeed tainted with racism ... this taint ... is greatly outweighed by various positive factors whose tenor is anti-racist'. Chief among these 'anti-racist factors' appears to be the fact that Donkin, a white character, is portrayed in an even more negative light than James Wait.

But surely a novel, particularly one as finely and densely wrought as *The Nigger of the 'Narcissus'*, should be considered as a whole rather than as a conglomeration of 'factors' that can be weighed against each other as though on an accountant's balance-sheet. Ian Watt argues that 'The main psycho-political thesis of the novel – the thesis that apparent solidarity based on "sympathy" may frequently be a false solidarity based on vicarious egoism – may be controversial, but it is not a racist thesis.' Both these critics are painfully aware of the spectre of political correctness peering over their shoulder as they write. It is their duty to weigh the book up on a balance-sheet of 'racism' and 'anti-racism'. But it is unhelpfully reductive, indeed practically meaningless, to argue about whether the book's central attack on sentimentalism is 'racist' or not. The fact is that it is charged with racial politics. James Wait is not incidentally black. His blackness would have struck a powerful chord with the late Victorian reader because blacks were, through missionary work and the memory of the abolition movement, particularly associated with the kind of philanthropy that Conrad is attacking as a philosophical world-view and a prescription for moral conduct. The language with which Conrad returns again and again to the theme reinforces the sense of its racial dimension, the sense that the power that Wait exerts over the crew is itself, for the whites, a kind of bondage, a 'weird servitude' that inverts the usual power relationship between black and white.

> [A] black mist emanated from him; a subtle and dismal influence ... With heavy eyes [he] swept over us a glance domineering and pained, like a sick tyrant overawing a crowd of abject but untrustworthy slaves.

[Belfast, the cook] tended him, talked to him; was as gentle as a woman, as tenderly gay as an old philanthropist, as sentimentally careful of his nigger as a model slave-owner.

Plunging into the consciousness of Belfast, the cook, Conrad highlights the association of sentimentalism and evangelical religion and its imagery of white and black, heaven and hell. In style, he even reproduces the effusions of a sentimental novel, before closing the jaws of his stream-of-consciousness paragraph with a snap of realism:

There was a great stir in his brain . . . an exciting row of rousing songs and groans of pain . . . His heart overflowed with tenderness, with comprehension, with the desire to meddle, with anxiety for the soul of that black man, with the pride of possessed eternity, with the feeling of might. Snatch him up in his arms and pitch him right into the middle of salvation . . . the black soul – blacker – body – rot – Devil. No! Talk – strength – Samson . . . There was a great din as of cymbals in his ears; he flashed through an ecstatic jumble of shining faces, lilies, prayer-books, unearthly joy, white shirts, gold harps, black coats, wings. He saw flowing garments, clean shaved faces, a sea of light – a lake of pitch. There were sweet scents, a smell of sulphur – red tongues of flame licking a white mist. An awesome voice thundered! . . . It lasted three seconds.

With its gothic religiosity, this could almost be a satire of *Uncle Tom's Cabin*.

Conrad's characterisation of sentimentalism focuses both on its self-regarding quality (the *Narcissus* was a real ship, but given Conrad's care with names and symbolism, the associations cannot be fortuitous) and on its femininity. Above all, he brings to the surface the sadism (or, given sentimentalism's egotistical bent, sado-masochism) latent within it, the violence contained within its tender touch:

[W]e hated James Wait. We could not get rid of the monstrous suspicion that this astounding black-man was shamming sick, had been malingering heartlessly in the face of our toil, of our scorn, of our patience ... The secret and ardent desire of our hearts was the desire to beat him viciously with our fists about the head: and we handled him as tenderly as though he had been made of glass ...

In his biography of Conrad, John Batchelor characterises the conflict at the heart of *The Nigger of the 'Narcissus'* as one between private and public values, between personal relationships and sympathy, on the one hand, and, on the other, the essential, eternal and authoritarian demands of life at sea. But it is surely more accurate to read the conflict not as one between private and public moralities, but as one between two ideologies, two moralities that encompass both private and public. On the one hand there is the sentimentalism characteristic of 'nigger philanthropy' and trade unionism; on the other is a conservative, fatalistic ethos that sees the world in terms of duties rather than rights. The reaction against abolitionism and its successor the missionary movement can be dated, as we saw in the last chapter, at least back to the writings of Dickens and others in the 1840s. Philanthropy, especially in its 'nigger' variety, is depicted as so much self-indulgent, impractical hogwash. *The Nigger of the 'Narcissus'* stands in that tradition, and it is a project that Conrad pursued in his two fictions about the Congo, 'An Outpost of Progress' and *Heart of Darkness*.

Both these stories are anti-imperialistic. But it is important to understand that in attacking 'imperialism', Conrad was attacking the belief in Europe's civilising mission among 'savage' peoples and the sentimentalism that he believed underlay it. He was not attacking it for the reason liberals would attack it now, and certainly not because he thought it 'racist'. 'An Outpost of Progress', written in July 1896, is a bleak comedy that draws, like *Heart of Darkness*, on the six months Conrad spent in the Belgian Congo in 1890. Kayerts and Carlier are two Belgian company officials left in charge of a trading station deep in the interior. ('The nearest trading-post was about three hundred miles away.') In their isolation, the two men form a needy, sentimental friendship. Both of them are weak characters who have been pampered by metropolitan life. Unprepared for the isolation and for the sense of menace that surrounds them, their minds begin to disintegrate. A petty argument leads to Kayerts accidentally shooting Carlier dead. Kayerts then hangs himself from the cross that marks the grave of the agent whom he and Carlier had been sent to replace. The end, with the discovery of Kayerts's body by his superior, is typical of the acid humour of the piece as a whole:

> His toes were only a couple of inches above the ground; his arms hung stiffly down; he seemed to be standing rigidly at attention, but with one purple cheek playfully posed on the shoulder. And, irreverently, he was putting out a swollen tongue at his Managing Director.

In the early stages of their ordeal, the two men take comfort from the illusion that they are furthering the great mission of civilising Africa. Conrad links their flight into this illusion with the sentimental escapism of their novel-reading:

> In the centre of Africa they made the acquaintance of Richelieu and of d'Artagnan, of Hawk's Eye and of Father Goriot, and of many other people ... The accounts of crimes filled them with indignation, while tender or pathetic passages moved them deeply. Carlier cleared his throat and said in a soldierly voice, 'What nonsense!' Kayerts, his round eyes suffused with tears, his fat cheeks quivering, rubbed his bald head, and declared, 'This is a splendid book ...' They also found some copies of a home paper. That print discussed what it was pleased to call 'Our Colonial Expansion' in high-flown language. It spoke much of the rights and duties of civilization, of the sacredness of the civilizing work, and extolling the merits of those who went about bringing light, and faith, and commerce to the dark places of the earth. Carlier and Kayerts read, wondered, and began to think better of themselves.

For Conrad, the faith in the 'civilizing work' of colonialism is based on a fundamental philosophical error, an error at once moral and aesthetic. This is made explicit when the two Belgians turn their addled attention to the greatest sentimental issue of all:

'Slavery is an awful thing,' stammered out Kayerts in an unsteady voice.

'Frightful – the sufferings,' grunted Carlier, with conviction. They believed their words. Everybody shows a respectful deference to certain sounds that he and his fellows can make. But about feelings people know nothing. We talk with indignation or enthusiasm; we talk about oppression, cruelty, crime, devotion, self-sacrifice, virtue, and we know nothing real beyond the words. Nobody knows what suffering or sacrifice mean – except, perhaps, the victims of the mysterious purpose of these illusions.

Thus Conrad cuts the thread of identification, of assimilation, that was the basis of sentimentalism. But what is to take sentimentalism's place? Already in the final sentence of the passage quoted above one can feel Conrad sliding into that windy fatalism ('the mysterious purpose') characteristic of his writing at its worst. Near the beginning of the story, Conrad announces the conflict that is to bring about the men's mental breakdown, and hence the brutal comedy:

They were two perfectly insignificant and incapable individuals, whose existence is only rendered possible through the high organisation of civilised crowds. Few men realise that their life, the very essence of their character, their capabilities and their audacities, are only an expression of their belief in the safety of their surroundings ... But the contact with pure unmitigated savagery, with primitive nature and primitive man, brings sudden and profound trouble into the heart. To the sentiment of being alone of one's kind, to the clear perception of the loneliness of one's thoughts, of one's sensations – to the negation of the habitual, which is safe, there is added the affirmation of the unusual, which is dangerous; a suggestion of things vague, uncontrollable, and repulsive, whose discomposing intrusion excites the imagination and tries the civilised nerves of the foolish and the wise alike.

Frontiers of civilisation are permeable. The primitive seeps back in, the Empire strikes back. Set in contrast to the womanish domesticity that Kayerts and Carlier try to construct around themselves (part of the comedy of 'An Outpost of Progress' is the way the two men become like a bickering married couple) is the reality of the vast, ever-present forest that surrounds them. This is the cue for some ripe Conradese:

> And stretching away in all directions, surrounding the insignificant cleared spot of the trading post, immense forests, hiding fateful complications of fantastic life, lay in the eloquent silence of mute greatness.

With its 'eloquent silence of mute greatness', the African forest plays the same role in 'An Outpost of Progress' that the sea does in *The Nigger of the 'Narcissus'*. Both testify to man's solitude and to the hollowness of civilisation and sentiment.

In 1897, the year that *The Nigger of the 'Narcissus'* appeared, Conrad began a fruitful association with the publisher William Blackwood. It was *Blackwood's Magazine* that in 1899 serialised in three parts perhaps the most famous of stories about Empire – *Heart of Darkness*. In December 1898 Conrad wrote to William Blackwood, telling him about the new story that he was finishing:

> The title I am thinking of is *The Heart of Darkness* but the narrative is not gloomy. The criminality of inefficiency and pure selfishness when tackling the civilising work in Africa is a justifiable idea. The subject is of our time distinc[t]ly – though not topically treated. It is a story as much as my *Outpost of Progress* was but, so to speak 'takes in' more – is a little wider – is less concentrated upon individuals.

Where 'An Outpost of Progress' focuses on the grotesque pantomime of Kayerts and Carlier, with the forest relegated to mute witness of the Belgians' impotence, the picture is indeed 'wider' in *Heart of Darkness*, with 'Africa' taking on a more active role in the metaphysical drama. 'Primitive nature and primitive man' have become an active agency for evil, infecting the white men who come into contact with it.

Kurtz, the maverick company official whom the narrator

Marlow has gone upriver to find, is the ultimate European 'gone native'. And the evil that seeps in from the forest, the blackness that infects the white coloniser, takes a regressive form. Marlow's journey upriver is a journey back to the distant past, a descent into the unconscious mind, a return to our animal ancestry, a falling-back on brute violence. 'Going up that river', says Marlow, 'was like travelling back to the earliest beginnings of the world ... The air was warm, thick, heavy, sluggish.' This idea of a journey back in time ('The smell of mud, of primeval mud, by Jove! was in my nostrils, the high stillness of primeval forest was before my eyes') is one to which Marlow constantly returns, and indeed one with which he introduces his story. True to the tradition of the Victorian smoking-room tale, *Heart of Darkness* has a framing device for the narrative, only here the audience are seated not around a fireplace but on board a yawl in the Thames estuary. As the sun sinks over London, Conrad/Marlow invokes the river's imperial history ('What greatness had not floated on the ebb of that river into the mystery of an unknown earth!'), taking his listeners right back to the time when the Romans landed, bringing with them civilisation:

> 'And this also,' said Marlow suddenly, 'has been one of the dark places of the earth.'

The pronouncement is echoed at the very end of the book, when 'the tranquil waterway leading to the uttermost ends of the earth flowed sombre under an overcast sky – seemed to lead into the heart of an immense darkness'.

Central to *Heart of Darkness* is the idea of surrender to something larger and darker than oneself, of self-sacrifice and self-destruction. Kurtz, who has gone all the way up the river, has done this. 'The thing', Marlow says of him, 'was to know what he belonged to, how many powers of darkness claimed him for their own.' In *The Nigger of the 'Narcissus'*, Conrad extols the mute surrender to duty and fate embodied in the old sailor Singleton, a surrender associated with the implacability of the sea itself. In *Heart of Darkness* the thing to which surrender is being made is much more nebulous, its intrinsic value more questionable. The passage where this comes out – in which Marlow is again drawing a comparison between the Roman conquest of Britain and the British penetration of Africa – is often quoted in support of the idea that *Heart of Darkness* is an anti-imperialist novel:

> It was just robbery with violence, aggravated murder on a great scale, and men going at it blind – as is very proper for those who tackled a darkness. The conquest of the earth, which mostly means the taking it away from those who have a different complexion or slightly flatter noses than ourselves, is not a pretty thing when you look into it too much. What redeems it is the idea only. An idea at the back of it; not a sentimental pretence but an idea; and an unselfish belief in the idea – something you can set up, and bow down before, and offer a sacrifice to . . .

The 'sentimental pretence' is the whole philanthropic, missionary ideology against which both *The Nigger of the 'Narcissus'* and 'An Outpost of Progress' are, in their different ways, directed. What then is the 'idea', the idol before which it is good to bow down? (The analogy is with paganism, with fetishism; the worship of imperialism is a post- (and pre-) Christian activity.) The answer can only be the 'aggravated murder on a great scale' that is the reality of imperialism, the reality behind the platitudes about progress and philanthropy.

Heart of Darkness is a nihilistic book. Colonialism is portrayed as, at heart, nothing but the mindless exercise of murderous power, with Kurtz as its natural, extreme expression. Yet the worship of colonialism as an ideal is a good thing because it is good to erase the self in the name of something 'higher', 'larger' than oneself. Far from being an 'anti-imperialist' book in any simple sense, Conrad's novella is a case study of how a deeply pessimistic imperialist ideology, pushed to an extreme, became a proto-fascism. For as with fascism, Conrad's nihilism is a nihilism without the courage of its own lack of convictions. If Conrad had honestly pursued the idea of a world without meaning, a world in which there is only the commitment to the act, then he might have written a more truthful book. As it is, *Heart of Darkness* shares with later fascist writings a windy pretentiousness and cosmetic mysticism. There is the heavy, portentous use of abstract nouns. ('It was the stillness of an implacable force brooding over an inscrutable intention.') There are the empty references to Buddha. (These are taken up enthusiastically in the final sequences of Francis Ford Coppola's film version, *Apocalypse Now*.) And above all there is the figure of 'Mistah Kurtz' himself, who is portrayed both as a mad charlatan and as the guardian of some profound if incommunicable secret. 'Mr Kurtz is a remarkable man,' says Marlow at one stage, and through Kurtz's acolyte at the station we get to hear, at second hand, of the man's 'magnificent eloquence':

> 'We talked of everything . . . I forgot there was such a thing as sleep. The night did not seem to last an hour. Everything! Everything! . . . Of love, too . . . he made me see things – things.'

Marlow intimates that though Kurtz is mad, it is the madness not of stupidity but of lucidity and insight:

> [H]is intelligence was perfectly clear – concentrated, it is true, upon himself with horrible intensity, yet clear . . . But his soul was mad.

And what is it that he knows as a result of this penetrating inner vision? What is Kurtz's dangerous secret? The reader never learns. When Marlow finally confronts Kurtz, we hear nothing of what the latter actually has to say. We learn only, in the vaguest terms, of the profound impression that he leaves:

> Kurtz discoursed. A voice! a voice! It rang deep to the very last. It survived his strength to hide in the magnificent folds of his eloquence the barren darkness of his heart.

In his portrayal of Kurtz, Conrad tapped into a strong vein in late Victorian and Edwardian smoking-room fiction: a fascination with men who have inside information, who are in the know. Kipling was attracted by individuals or groups who possessed arcane knowledge (such as technical knowledge of radio) that drew them together. The historian Richard Shannon, summarising Kipling's world-view, has linked this aspect of his fiction with the late nineteenth-century conservative reaction against liberalism, the kind of reaction that is the dominant theme of *The Nigger of the 'Narcissus'*.

Society did not function through the laws of melioristic Liberal or Socialist social science; it functioned through custom, convention, religion, law, duties, in-groups, codes of behaviour of pack and clan and the sanctions of discipline and leadership derived from them.

Similarly, the protagonist of Rider Haggard's African adventure stories, Allan Quatermain, is the epitome of the 'old Africa hand', the man (such people are always men, of course) who has seen it all, experienced it all, and knows the country and the natives for what they really are rather than for what sentimentalists would like them to be. The central role of the man-in-the-know (the narrator being the ultimate man-in-the-know, the only one with the whole story) both assumes and reinforces a conservative ideology of deference and authority. Conrad merely imparts to Kurtz's secret knowledge the grandeur of metaphysics.

There is a superficial irony in the fact that *Heart of Darkness*, which has been widely read as a radical attack on the imperialistic ethos, first appeared in the ultra-conservative *Blackwood's*. But the gloomy atavism of *Heart of Darkness* was of a piece with other tales of imperial adventure, albeit shrouded in greater pseudo-profundity. Such is the aura of reverence that surrounds the novella (a 'deeply troubling modernist masterpiece' according to one recent biography) that it is often forgotten that *Heart of Darkness* was written quickly, and for money. The picture of Africa and Africans that it paints was commonplace at the end of the nineteenth century. As the Nigerian novelist Chinua Achebe has observed:

> Conrad chose his subject well – one which was guaranteed not to put him in conflict with the psychological predisposition of his readers or raise the need for him to contend with that resistance. He chose the role of purveyor of comforting myth.

Conrad was steeped in French literature, and one can see the extent to which *Heart of Darkness* was of a piece with the ethos of its time if one looks at the imperialist literature that was being produced in France. Vigne d'Octon, for example, was primarily a novelist, a follower of the 'scientific' Naturalism of Zola that was so deplored by Andrew Lang. In a domestic setting, he wrote novels that analysed the place of distinct classes in an 'ethnological ladder', while in a colonial setting his *Chair noir* (1889) attempted to establish objectively that racial divisions are fixed and immutable. At the same time as Conrad was composing *Heart of Darkness*, d'Octon was writing his book of reportage, *La Gloire du sabre* (1900). And given Vigne d'Octon's undoubtedly racialist views, it at first comes as a surprise that the book is a passionate indictment (the title is deeply ironic) of atrocities committed by French forces in Senegal.

La Gloire du sabre may be reportage, but it is also highly impressionistic. The book opens not with an historical account of French involvement in Senegal but with an evocation of 'Africa' itself.

> This is Africa, man-eater, soul-destroyer, wrecker of men's strength, mother of fever and death, mysterious ghost which for centuries has sucked the blood of Europeans, draining them to the very marrow, or making them mad. Over there the smoke of the blue sea, lying in its eternal sleep under the implacable sun. The waves break and beat mercilessly over its narrow coasts and tortured estuaries, a constant terror to the bravest sailor. The innumerable inlets breathing out pestilence, which hide in the sickly shade of the mangroves, are the ever-open eyes of Africa, like sirens ready to engulf those hardy spirits who affront her ... The headlands, scarcely visible amidst the vast desolation of the scrubland ... are like teats, hideous udders wrinkled, withered, swollen only with the poisonous venom of reptiles, the deadly sap of mandrake and strychnine.

The French colonial soldiers 'are not savages, like their native comrades-in-arms', but are corrupted by Africa. Slavery continues in Africa under French auspices, but seems to grow out of the corrupt landscape of the continent. The Africans themselves have corruption written into their very features:

> A whole world of lust comes to life in their crude brain; strange, chaotic desires fill their yellow eyes and make their thick lips slobber.

The way in which Vigne d'Octon saturates every racial characteristic with lust fits into an established French literary tradition of making an imaginary Africa the arena for sexual fantasy, a tradition that overlaps with the orientalist fascination with the Arab world. In Guy de Maupassant's 'Allouma' (1889), one of his Algerian stories, a Monsieur Auballe has emigrated to Africa having spent his fortune on women in France. He becomes infatuated with a native girl who is introduced into his house. Maupassant's description of Allouma strikes a delicate balance between exotic allure and the socially acceptable:

> Her features were extraordinary, regular, slender and a little bestial, but mystical like those of a Buddha. Her lips, thick and coloured with a red lustre that one found on her body too, indicated a slight mixture of black blood although her hands and arms were of an irreproachable whiteness.

Auballe's attraction to her is to something inhuman and beyond his experience:

> She was nervy, lithe and healthy like an animal, with the air, the movements, the grace and a sort of odour of a gazelle, so that I found in her kisses a rare and unknown flavour, as strange to my senses as a taste of tropical fruit.

She moves in with him ('I would make her into a sort of slave mistress, hidden away in my house like the women in harems'), but then begins to steal away for periods to be with her tribe. Eventually she goes off for good with an Arab man, and Auballe is left alone to breathe the desert air from his window and reflect how 'I became attached in a strange way to this creature from another race, who seemed to me almost another species, born on a neighbouring planet'.

The most influential piece of French imperialist erotica was Pierre Loti's *Le Roman d'un spahi* (1881), in which the sensuality of the African woman is given an edge of danger with intimations of violence and magic. Where 'Allouma' is elegaic, Pierre Loti's novel is tragic, the story of a French soldier in the African colonies (a 'spahi' officer) who falls fatally under the spell of a native seductress. She too is animal-like:

> [She had] a Negro grace, a sensual charm, a tangible power of seduction, an indefinable quality that seemed at the same time simian, virginal and tigrish, – and which filled the soldier's veins with a strange intoxication.

The night before Jean, the hero, sleeps with Fatou-gaye for the first time, he feels as though he is 'passing over a deadly threshold, signing with this black race a fatal pact'. This atmosphere of melancholy fatalism – compounded of the soldier's isolation and homesickness, his immersion in a drug-like sensuality, and the baked, limitless horizons of the African landscape – pervades the book. In his heavy sleep, Jean dreams dark, atavistic dreams:

> Ideas awoke in him, sad, mixed-up and confused at first, shadowy thoughts, full of mystery, like the traces of an existence before the world ... the things of life viewed from below, from beyond the tomb; – the other side of what is, the reverse of the world ...

The melancholy of *Le Roman d'un spahi* is different in kind from that experienced by Auballe at the end of 'Allouma', which is the simple regret at time passing and passion ending. Jean's melancholy partakes of the depression of *Heart of Darkness*. It is abysmal, and he gets lost in it:

> [H]e seemed to hear the pulse of time, the beatings of a great, mysterious clock of eternity, and he felt time disappear, spin away, spin away with the speed of something falling into the void, and his life flowed through him without his being able to hold it.

At the end Jean is stabbed in an ambush, and as he lies dying he dreams that he is watching the natives' circle dance that has formed a motif throughout the book. The dancers spiral up into the blue sky 'like smoke whisked by the wind', and Jean has the sensation of following them, 'borne up on terrible wings.' When Fatou-gaye hears the news, she strangles their baby son and poisons herself, thus mixing sensuality with the sublime in its eighteenth-century sense – darkness, infinity, death.

The eroticism of the French exotic novel, and of *Le Roman d'un spahi* in particular, was a strong influence on Conrad's early *An Outcast of the Islands* (1896). But, unless one counts the undercurrents of necrophilia in Rider Haggard's *She* (1887), the sexual strain that is so strong in French literary treatments of Africa is largely absent in their English counterparts. The English imperial writers tended to specialise in sexual repression and exclusively masculine tales of quest and adventure. Allan Quatermain, hero of many of Rider Haggard's African tales, is driven not by dreams of African womanhood but by desire for gold, glory and knowledge. The only one of the Quatermain novels to have a significant romantic interest, *Allan's Wife* (1889), is beset by an ambivalence towards the feminine that ties in with his ambivalence towards Africa itself. Women are closer to nature, to the animal, than men. Thus, writing about jealousy, Haggard comments:

> [T]he lower one gets in the scale of humanity, the more readily this passion thrives; indeed, it may be said to come to its intensest perfection in brutes. Women are more jealous than men, small-hearted men are more jealous than those of larger mind and wider sympathy, and animals are the most jealous of all.

Stella, the woman who is to become Quatermain's wife, has been taken to South Africa by her father as a girl. Deserted by his wife (she ran off, predictably, with a Frenchman) and disillusioned with civilisation, Stella's father seeks to escape – like many of Haggard's characters – to a place where 'there are no white faces, no smooth, educated tongues'. He finds in the South African wilderness a kind of Eden, but his feelings about the nature represented by Africa are mixed:

At first I thought that I would let my daughter grow up in a state of complete ignorance, that she should be Nature's child. But as time went on, I saw the folly and wickedness of my plan. I had no right to degrade her to the level of the savages around me, for if the fruit of the tree of knowledge is a bitter fruit, still it teaches good from evil.

Rider Haggard inherited the Victorian ethnologists' cast-iron distinction between 'civilisation' and 'barbarism', and held strong, if confused, views about their relative merits. The corresponding ambivalence towards the female is expressed very starkly in *Allan's Wife*. Stella has been brought up in African innocence, but she is not like the savages around her – she learns French and German. She is the ideal of European womanhood, embodying the softer, refined virtues of civilisation. But there is another aspect to the female, the side that is closer to the animal, and this Rider Haggard embodies in the feral woman Hendrika, who has been brought up by baboons and then adopted by Stella. The affinity between the two aspects is underlined by a hint of lesbianism; when Hendrika, overcome by jealousy of Quatermain, kidnaps Stella, she kisses and caresses her. In the predictably violent denouement, Quatermain rescues Stella from the baboon's lair, but Stella only lives long enough to give birth to their son.

The descent into unadorned sensuality that one finds in French 'exotic' stories and, in a repressed form, in some English imperialist fiction, was but one of several forms of regression that one finds in *fin de siècle* literature. As we have already seen in the case of *Heart of Darkness*, late Victorian and Edwardian writers of romances were fascinated by the vast expanses of time opened up by Charles Lyell in geology and Darwin in biology. Conrad's book is dominated in particular by the idea of moving back in time, of returning to a state of atavism. The theme is introduced in the opening scene, when Marlow pictures the Thames as a primeval waterway, and is sustained with Conrad's evocations of the African forest. (These directly echo passages in *Le Roman d'un spahi*, for example Loti's description of the African sky as being 'heavy and static, making one think of primeval sunsets, of epoques when the atmosphere, hotter and more charged with vital substance, covered the primitive earth with its germs of mammoths and dinosaurs . . .') And above all the atavism is encapsulated in Conrad's depiction of the Africans themselves as a people stuck at man's darkest origins, a people without history, a *tabula rasa*:

> I don't think a single one of them had any clear idea of time, as we at the end of countless ages have. They still belonged to the beginnings of time – had no inherited experience to teach them as it were . . .

This is reminiscent of Olive Schreiner's evocation of the timeless antiquity of the African landscape in *The Story of an African Farm* (1883). There are echoes, too, of Rider Haggard's African fiction. At the beginning of *She*, Haggard describes Ayesha, the white goddess/ruler in the heart of Africa, as being 'a woman, clothed in the majesty of her almost endless years, on whom the shadow of Eternity itself lay like the dark wing of night'. Such flights as this, prompted by the passage of time, recur in Haggard. In *King Solomon's Mines*, on the night before a battle when many Zulus will die, Quatermain reflects that 'the old moon would shine serenely on, the night wind would stir the grasses, and the wide earth would take its happy rest, even as it did aeons before these were, and will do aeons after they have been forgotten'.

The temporal regression that one finds in imperial romances is of a piece with that which one finds in the 'scientific romances' of the period, fantasies such as H. G. Wells's *The Time Machine* (1895) and Arthur Conan Doyle's *The Lost World* (1912) in which the hero is transported, either literally or metaphorically, through aeons of time. The connection with imperialism is made explicit at the beginning of Conan Doyle's Darwinian fantasy, where the journalist-hero Malone is challenged by his girlfriend to be another Burton or Stanley. But as Malone's editor points out, 'The big blank spaces in the map are all being filled in, and there's no room for romance anywhere.' Malone joins an expedition to the Amazonian jungle that turns into a Jurassic Park-like journey back to the age of the dinosaurs. In *The Time Machine* the journey is one into the distant future, but in the form of the 'ape-like' Morlocks there is also the idea of regression, of humanity – or at least a portion of it – plunging back into a state of primitivism: 'Ages ago, thousands of generations ago, man had thrust his brother man out of the ease and the sunshine. And now that brother was coming back – changed!' The associations in the reader's mind with contemporary 'primitivism' are reinforced when the narrator compares his bewilderment faced by the civilisation of the far future with that experienced by an African visiting modern Europe: 'Conceive the tale of London which a negro, fresh from Central Africa, would take back to his tribe! ... Then, think how narrow the gap between a negro and a white man of our own times, and how wide the interval between myself and these of the Golden Age!'

Other forms of regression follow in the wake of this temporal rewinding in late Victorian fiction. There is the going-back to an animistic, pre-Christian religion. Rider Haggard, reflecting on 'the vast and secret forces that animate the world', often invokes the spirit world:

> Truly the universe is full of ghosts; not sheeted, churchyard spectres, but the inextinguishable and immortal elements of life, which, having once been, can never *die*, though they blend and change and change again forever.

Like Lang and Rudyard Kipling, Rider Haggard was drawn to the spiritualism that was so much a part of the late Victorian and Edwardian literary and intellectual scene. As Patrick Brantlinger writes in his study of imperialistic novels: 'If imperialist ideology is atavistic, occultism is obviously so, a rejection of individual and social rationality and a movement backward to primitive or infantile modes of perception and belief.' With the 'blank spaces' on the map fast disappearing, belief in reincarnation and the spirit world – central to the story of *She*, for example – opened up new realms for romantic adventure. And belief in spirits was associated particularly with 'savages'. *King Solomon's Mines*, like Haggard's other African tales, is peppered with tribesmen's wise sayings, beliefs which, while belonging to a lower level of civilisation, transcend the limited rationality of the European.

In addition to primitive religion there is violence. In Vigne d'Octon's documentary account of colonial atrocities, violence is seen as growing naturally out of the African landscape. Rider Haggard's fiction is marked by the pornographic intensity and vividness of its physical maimings. The following is representative, but there are countless other examples:

> Another second and he was up on his feet, the red blood streaming from the wound in his face, and so was Twala. Drawing the heavy tolla from his belt, he staggered straight at Curtis and struck him upon the breast ... Again Twala struck out with a savage yell, and again the heavy knife rebounded and Sir Henry went staggering back. Once more Twala came on, and as he came our great Englishman gathered himself together, and, swinging the heavy axe round his head, hit at him with all his force. There was a shriek of excitement from a thousand throats, and, behold! Twala's head seemed to spring from his shoulders, and then fell and came rolling and bounding along the ground towards Ignosi, stopping just at his feet. For a second the corpse stood upright, the blood spouting in fountains from the severed arteries; then with a dull crash it fell to the earth.

It is ironic that Andrew Lang saw in Haggard's work his ideal of a youthful, healthily physical literature of escape, for as time went on Haggard came under increasing critical attack for the almost pornographic obsession with violence that his novels evinced. No reader who has immersed him or herself in the necrophiliac world of *She* could describe Haggard's powerful, fetid imagination as being 'healthy'.

The atavism of *fin de siècle* imperial fiction involves, finally, the idea of a return to the roots of the human mind, to the unconscious, to that wellspring of psychic life guarded by Diderot's 'hideous Moor'. One senses in this literature not an imaginative turning outwards to brave new worlds, but rather a turning inward to the contemplation of an increasingly bleak view of human nature. Not that this introspection takes the form of psychologist analysis; the dark inner world is projected out on to 'the primitive'.

Both Freud and Jung were admirers of Haggard's fictions, seeing in them powerful projections of basic psychological instincts and processes. In *The Interpretation of Dreams* (1900), Freud analyses a dream that has been prompted by lending a friend a copy of *She*:

> 'Lend me something to read,' she had said. I offered her Rider Haggard's *She*. 'A *strange* book, but full of hidden meaning', I began to explain to her; 'the eternal feminine, the immortality of our emotions . . .'

And in his essay 'Psychology and Literature', Jung uses Rider Haggard as an example to draw a distinction between 'psychological' and 'visionary' literature. Psychological literature takes consciousness as its subject matter, while visionary literature 'derives its existence from the hinterland of man's mind, as if it had emerged from the abyss of prehuman ages, or from a superhuman world of contrasting light and darkness'. Visionary literature such as Rider Haggard's *She* and *Ayesha* is often crudely sensationalist, but while it may be looked down on by the literary critic, it is, according to Jung, a rich source of material for the psychologist. 'Rider Haggard', he writes, 'is generally regarded as a romantic story teller, but in his case . . . the tale is only a means – admittedly a rather lush one – for capturing a meaningful content.'

Whether Haggard was aware of this 'meaningful content' is irrelevant, according to Jung. Indeed, the very unselfconsciousness of visionary literature – which perhaps produces 'bad literature' in the eyes of the literary critic – may be a prerequisite for just that projection of unconscious psychic material that makes it of such interest to the psychologist. As Jung remarks: 'It seems as if we have to defend the seriousness of the visionary experience against the personal resistance of the poet himself.' Conrad is much more self-conscious than Rider Haggard, which perhaps disqualifies him from being 'visionary' in Jung's terms. But there is a psychological content, a sense that, in *Heart of Darkness*, he is projecting out on to his African smoking-room tale some deep inner trauma. It is known that he was going through a depression at the time of *Heart of Darkness*, and this certainly accords with the book's bleak vision.[1]

In late Victorian novels about Africa, these atavisms of time, sex, violence, spirituality and psychic life are focused on the figure of the Negro. The old associations of racial darkness with instinctual violence and sexual excess are perpetuated, but are now given a fixed intensity both by the pessimistic terms in which they are expressed, and by an elaborated ideological context that draws on evolutionary anthropology. There are echoes, when Rider Haggard celebrates the 'primitive wisdom' of the Zulus, of the eighteenth-century image of the 'noble savage', but on the whole by the late nineteenth century – even in French literature, which in the earlier period had done most to sustain it – this old idea has been superseded by a much gloomier notion of how the African embodies our oldest and basest instincts.

The belief that the Negro represents the nadir of primitivism finds its fullest and most inflated expression in *Heart of Darkness*. When it comes down to it, if one were to ask exactly what is being referred to when, at the end of the book, Kurtz speaks of 'The horror! The horror!' one would have to answer that it is Africa itself, and all that it represents. Rider Haggard's African novels may be full of pornographic violence, but to some extent this is

[1] Critics have debated whether *Heart of Darkness* should be read as a book about Africa or about Conrad's own depression. The answer, of course, is that it is both. For the debate, see John Batchelor, *The Life of Joseph Conrad: A Critical Biography* (Blackwell, Oxford, 1994), p. 95. Batchelor himself adheres to 'the now unfashionable approach' that 'the novella ... is a clinical document': 'The experience Marlow has undergone is restricted neither to him nor to Africa: it could be undergone by any of us, anywhere and at any time ... Conrad uses the river journey to put Marlow through a process which is like the process undergone by patients who are in psychotherapy. Marlow in his encounter with Kurtz looks into the abyss. Conrad himself is looking at the core of his depression.' But in claiming that *Heart of Darkness* is 'universal' in this sense of being non-specific to Africa (or, more accurately, the 'Africa' of Conrad's imagination), John Batchelor is surely cutting off one pole of Conrad's metaphoric use of 'the dark continent'. Metaphors consist of two terms, and Conrad's vision of an African 'heart of darkness' – like all imaginatively powerful metaphors – has an equivalence and interactivity between its two poles. It tells us as much about Conrad's view of Africa and Africans as it does about his view of 'human nature'.

balanced by occasional acknowledgements that Africa has cultures of its own. In *Heart of Darkness*, Africa's inhabitants are dehumanised, in description literally chopped up into the meaningless, robotic motion of body parts:

> But suddenly, as we struggled round a bend, there would be a glimpse of rush walls, of peaked grass-roofs, a burst of yells, a whirl of black limbs, a mass of hands clapping, of feet stamping, of bodies swaying, of eyes rolling, under the droop of heavy and motionless foliage. The steamer toiled along slowly on the edge of a black and incomprehensible frenzy. The prehistoric man was cursing us, praying to us, welcoming us – who could tell?

The African is no more than a physical object, and with Conrad's usual predilection for turning physical objects into grand symbols, the African in *Heart of Darkness* becomes a token of the metaphysical evil, the inner abyss, to which Kurtz has succumbed when he 'goes native'. The abolitionists, and to some extent their Darwinian successors, had envisaged the Negro as having a white soul beneath the mask of his blackness. Conrad not only denies the Negro a soul, but also inverts the old sentimentalist idea. For him, there is a black man inside every European. Beneath every white skin is a heart of darkness. In so far as the Africans are accorded any humanity, it is in that they represent this dark, primitive core of the European psyche:

> No, they were not inhuman. Well, you know, that was the worst of it – this suspicion of their not being inhuman. It would come slowly to one. They howled and leaped, and spun, and made horrid faces; but what thrilled you was just the thought of their humanity – like yours – the thought of your remote kinship with this wild and passionate uproar.

There is a strange Janus face to the imperial literature of the late Victorian and Edwardian period. On the one hand writers like Rider Haggard and Kipling, with their jingoistic cultural arrogance, seem to embody a past age, an age that died on the battlefields of the First World War. But there is also something in them – a neurotic pessimism, a taste for the demotic, a fractured conscious-ness – that sets them apart from mid-Victorian certainties and that seems to look, despite itself, into the future. For all his ideological Edwardianism, Kipling came to be admired by such gurus of the modern as T. S. Eliot and Bertolt Brecht. Freud and Jung, as we have seen, found beneath the surface Victorianism of Haggard's African adventure tales some very modern types of psychic disturbance. And Conrad, of course, has long been hailed as a modernist. Imperial romance turned mid-Victorian optimism on its head, creating an identification with the primitive and an aesthetic of nihilism and atavism that was both proto-fascistic and, for all its smoking-room trappings, avant-garde. Imperial romance merged into imperial modernism.

The symbolism of blackness was at the heart of that process, just as it was to be at the heart of the modernist primitivism of the 1920s. The writers of imperial romance took from Darwin and his followers an identification of the 'lower races' with everything that was earliest and closest to nature in humanity, but took it as a sign not of how far man could progress, but of how far he could fall. The movement is not a projected one of the savage eventually pulling himself up to a state of civilisation, but rather one of the civilised man tumbling helplessly back into savagery. Even the most civilised products of European society are subject to – indeed, embody – the ancient, inhuman mechanisms of evolution. Nature, for the imperial modernists, is a machine, and the African is the missing link to that machine.

Sources

Primary sources

Buchan, John, *Prester John* (Thomas Nelson, London, 1910).

Conrad, Joseph, 'An Outpost of Progress', in *Tales of Unrest* (Eveleigh Nash & Grayson, London, 1922).

— *Heart of Darkness* (Penguin, Harmondsworth, 1973). First published 1902.

— *The Nigger of the 'Narcissus'* (Penguin, London, 1988). First published 1898.

— *An Outcast of the Islands* (Oxford University Press, 1992). First published 1896.

d'Octon, Paul Vigne, *La Gloire du sabre* (Flammarion, Paris, 1900).

Doyle, Arthur Conan, *The Lost World* (Hodder & Stoughton, London, 1912).

Haggard, H. Rider, *King Solomon's Mines* (London, 1886).

— *She: A History of Adventure* (London, 1887).

— *Allan's Wife* (London, 1889).

Hobson, J. A., *Imperialism: A Study* (James Nisbet & Co., London, 1902).

Lang, Andrew, 'Realism and Romance', *Contemporary Review*, vol. LII (November 1887).

Loti, Pierre, *Le Roman d'un spahi* (Gallimard, Paris, 1992). First published 1881.

Maupassant, Guy de, 'Allouma', in *Eighty-eight Short Stories* (Cassell, London, 1961).

Mille, Pierre, *Sur la vaste terre* (Calman-Lévy, Paris, 1905).

Psichari, Ernest, *Terres de soleil et de sommeil* (Paris, 1908).

— *L'Appel des armes* (G. Oudin, Paris, 1913).

Saintsbury, George, 'The Present State of the Novel', *Fortnightly Review*, vol. XLII (September 1887).

Schreiner, Olive, *The Story of an African Farm* (London, 1883).

Stevenson, Robert Louis, 'A Gossip on Romance', in *Memories and Portraits* (London, 1887).

Wells, H. G., *The Time Machine: An Invention* (William Heinemann, London, 1927). First published 1895.

Secondary sources

Achebe, Chinua, 'An Image of Africa: Racism in Conrad's *Heart of Darkness'* in *Hopes and Impediments: Selected Essays 1965–87* (Heinemann Educational Books, Oxford, 1988).

Baines, Jocelyn, *Joseph Conrad: A Critical Biography* (Penguin, Harmondsworth, 1971).

Batchelor, John, *The Life of Joseph Conrad: A Critical Biography* (Blackwell, Oxford, 1994).

Brantlinger, Patrick, 'Victorians and Africans: The Genealogy of the Myth of the Dark Continent', *Critical Inquiry*, vol. 12 (Autumn 1985).

— *Rule of Darkness: British Literature and Imperialism 1830–1914* (Cornell University Press, Ithaca, 1988).

Dabydeen, David (ed.), *The Black Presence in English Literature* (Manchester University Press, 1985).

Etherington, Norman A., 'Rider Haggard, Imperialism and the Layered Personality', *Victorian Studies*, vol. XX (1978).

Freud, Sigmund, *The Interpretation of Dreams* (Avon Books, New York, 1965). First published 1900.

Hargreaves, Alec G., *The Colonial Experience in French Fiction* (London, 1983).

Hervouet, Yves, *The French Face of Joseph Conrad* (Cambridge University Press, 1990).

Jung, C. G., *Collected Works*, Vol. XV, *The Spirit in Man, Art and Literature* (Routledge & Kegan Paul, London 1966).

Katz, Wendy R., *Rider Haggard and the Fiction of Empire: A Critical Study of British Imperial Fiction* (Cambridge University Press, 1987).

Miller, Christopher, *Blank Darkness: Africanist Discourse in French Literature* (Chicago University Press, 1985).

Rich, Paul B., *Race and Empire in British Politics* (Cambridge University Press, 1986).

Ridley, Hugh, *Images of Imperial Rule* (Croom Helm, London, 1983).

Sandison, Alan, *The Wheel of Empire: A Study of the Imperial Idea in Some Late Nineteenth- and Early Twentieth-Century Fiction* (Macmillan, London, 1967).

Shannon, Richard, *The Crisis of Imperialism, 1865–1915* (Paladin, London, 1976).

Watt, Ian, *Conrad in the Nineteenth Century* (Chatto & Windus, London, 1980).

Part Two

5

'Passing': A Question of Identity

To shift one's gaze from eighteenth- and nineteenth-century European conceptions of Africa to the racial culture of early twentieth-century America is to move from fantasy to reality. Not that slavery and Empire were not real, with devastating consequences for those that experienced them. But the commentaries that they generated – in fiction, poetry, reportage, propaganda and critique – were composed and consumed for the most part far from the action. Their projections of what was signified by the African were determined as much by the internals of the European psyche – the legacies of Christianity, the fears for the future – as they were by the realities of what was happening thousands of miles away across oceans. Above all, the objects of those projections were, as far as their authors were concerned, silent. If the African answered back, the European didn't hear. In America, by contrast, the racial divide was immediate and intimate, a matter of employment and housing, economics and marriage, of everyday life and everyday social interaction. And the American Negro could and did answer back to the white man. Even under slavery, African-Americans had evolved a distinctive folk culture that had a palpable effect on the wider society. The abolition movement had given literate black Americans an opportunity to answer back in the form of slave narratives. Like it or not, white America couldn't help but hear the voice of blacks.

Yet in important respects Europe and America are parts of the same story. As Paul Gilroy has argued at length in *The Black Atlantic*, racial attitudes were forged in the geopolitical crucible of the 'triangular trade', the slaving and commercial connections that tied together Africa, Europe and the Americas. Those racial attitudes may have had immediate consequences for white Americans that they did not for European contemporaries, but the attitudes themselves were born of the same cultural inheritance, and shared a similar history. As we have already seen in the case of *Uncle Tom's Cabin*, evangelical Protestantism played the same important part in moulding the world-view of American abolitionism as it did in forging liberal racial attitudes in Europe. Darwinism had a similar intellectual impact both sides of the Atlantic, and the hardening of racial attitudes that one finds in Europe in the last quarter of the nineteenth century can be broadly paralleled in the United States. The prejudices of white America may have had concrete and close-at-hand consequences that they didn't for white Europeans, but white Americans and white Europeans shared many roots. American reality was not without its admixture of European fantasy.

The most visible signs of the hardening of racial attitudes in America were the 'Jim Crow' segregation laws that spread across the South from the 1880s onwards. Jim Crow laws began on the railroads, with designated (and inferior) carriages for blacks, but multiplied to cover just about every aspect of public life. In 1898 we find the editor of the Charlestown *News and Courier* resisting the spread of the new Jim Crow railroad laws to South Carolina in the following sarcastic terms:

> If there must be Jim Crow cars on the railroads, there should be Jim Crow cars on the street railways. Also on all passenger boats ... If there are to be Jim Crow cars, moreover, there should be Jim Crow waiting saloons at all stations, and Jim Crow eating houses ... There should be Jim Crow sections of the jury box, and a separate Jim Crow dock and witness stand in every court – and a Jim Crow Bible for colored witnesses to kiss. It would be advisable also to have a Jim Crow section in county auditors' and treasurers' offices for the accommodation of colored

taxpayers. The two races are dreadfully mixed in these offices for weeks every year, especially about Christmas ... There should be a Jim Crow department for making returns and paying for the privileges and blessings of citizenship. Perhaps, the best plan would be, after all, to take the short cut to the general end ... by establishing two or three Jim Crow counties at once, and turning them over to our colored citizens for their special and exclusive accommodation.

As C. Vann Woodward, the distinguished Southern historian, goes on to remark after quoting this passage: '[W]hat he intended as a *reductio ad absurdum* and obviously regarded as an absurdity became in a very short time a reality ... Apart from the Jim Crow counties and the Jim Crow witness stand, all the improbable applications of the principle suggested by the editor in derision had been put into practice – down to and including the Jim Crow Bible.' In the momentous *Plessy* v. *Ferguson* decision of 1896, the Supreme Court ruled that 'legislation is powerless to eradicate racial instincts', and laid down the 'separate but equal' rule as a justification of segregation. The actions of the Southern states had federal sanction.

The new segregation laws were more than merely a continuation of or harking back to the social situation of slavery. With many slaves being employed as domestic servants, social intermingling of the races was commonplace in the antebellum period. Even into the 1870s, Northern observers were surprised and even shocked at the close coexistence of black and white in the South. As Edward Ayers writes in his recent history of the South: 'Railroad segregation was not a throwback to old-fashioned racism; indeed, segregation became, to whites, a badge of sophisticated, modern, managed race relations.' In their enthusiasm for the new legislation, the Southern states went into minute and very modern bureau-cratic detail, often prescribing the exact dimensions for 'Whites Only' and 'Colored' signs, and in one case the kind and colour of paint. In *The Origins of Totalitarianism*, her monumental study of the historical roots of twentieth-century fascism, Hannah Arendt argues for the close connection between racism and bureaucracy in the context of the European New Imperialism of the late nineteenth century. The same argument can be made for the American context. Driven by the expansion of the railroads, segregation was an emblem of the new South.

Segregated societies rely on legal definitions of who is to count as 'black', and such definitions, which were particularly important for laws against interracial marriage, varied wildly across the South. In applying for school admission in some states, for example, 'one drop of Negro blood' made one a black, while in applying for a marriage licence seven-eighths 'white blood' made one white. In practice, visual appearance and reputation were crucial, and these vaguer criteria enabled many mulattos to slip across the colour line, to 'pass'. (There was a large increase in the number of mulattos in the South after the Civil War. The number of blacks increased by 129 per cent between 1850 and 1920, while that of mulattos increased by 498 per cent.) 'I am a Negro,' proclaimed Walter White, novelist and a senior official of the NAACP. 'My skin is white, my eyes are blue, my hair is blond. The traits of my race are nowhere visible upon me.' White chose to affirm his 'blackness', but, writing in 1948, he estimated that 'every year approximately twelve thousand white-skinned Negroes disappear – whose absence cannot be explained by death or emigration. Nearly every one of the fourteen million discernible Negroes in the United States knows at least one member of his race who is "passing".'[1]

The strange, tangled life-histories produced by this looking-glass world of American racial identity can be illustrated with two literary examples, both leading figures of the Harlem Renaissance of the 1920s. Nella Larsen, author of the novels *Quicksand* (1928) and *Passing* (1929), was born as Nellie Walker in 1891 in the State Street neighbourhood of Chicago. It was a district where, at the turn of the century, the lines of racial demarcation were particularly blurred. 'Coloured' families mixed with recent European

[1] Walter White, *A Man Called White* (Gollancz, London, 1949), pp. 3–4. One 1921 estimate suggested that between 1900 and 1910 anywhere from 10,000 to 25,000 passed each year. See Eric J. Lundquist, *To Wake the Nations: Race in the Making of American Literature* (Harvard University Press, Cambridge, Mass., 1993), p. 393.

immigrants. Nella Larsen, as she became, did everything to obscure her origins, including changing her name several times, but the basic story she told in later life was that her mother was Danish and her natural father a 'coloured' from the Danish Virgin Islands, who had died when she was a young child and been replaced by a white stepfather. Thadious Davis's recent biography, however, has produced detailed evidence to show that this was not the true story, and that Larsen was in fact born into a 'coloured' family that subsequently became 'white'. Larsen herself was too dark-skinned to cross the colour line permanently, though not so dark as to prevent her from passing on at least one occasion when the situation demanded it. During the years of her literary celebrity she lived among an aristocracy of predominantly light-skinned Negroes, and tended to look down on the black proletariat of Harlem. The awful secret of her upbringing – its cruelty almost defies comprehension – seems to have been that while the rest of her family were light-skinned enough to pass into that 'other world' of which Du Bois wrote, Nella was too dark to make the grade. And so she was cast out. Her subsequent story that her natural father had died and been replaced by a white man may therefore have had a kind of metaphorical truth: in 'passing', Larsen's father had 'died' as a Negro and been born again as a white man.

With a background like that, it is perhaps no wonder that Nella Larsen seems to have developed a brittle toughness. Rejected by her family, she worked hard to put herself through some of the most prestigious black educational institutions of the time – Fisk University, New York's Lincoln Hospital Nursing School and Booker T. Washington's Tuskegee Institute in Alabama, where she spent an unhappy year teaching. During the 1920s she revelled in the bohemian, somewhat snobby world of the Harlem literati, but in the late Thirties, after the break-up of her marriage, she systematically cut off all ties with her old Harlem friends and returned to nursing. She died, alone and entirely forgotten by the literary world, in Brooklyn in 1964.

Another writer who lived at the margins of racial identity was Jean Toomer, who was born as Nathan Eugene Toomer in 1894.

His *Cane* (1923) is the most brilliant and lasting product of the Harlem Renaissance, an incandescent blend of fiction and poetry that achieves coherence through mood, imagery and an intense, dream-like evocation of rural Georgia. It has become a classic of African-American literature. But Toomer himself moved for most of his life in a white world, and was only ever identified as 'Negro' because he had written a 'Negro novel'. The dominant figure in Toomer's upbringing (his own father disappeared before his birth) was his maternal grandfather, Pinckney Benton Stuart Pinchback, who presents the unusual example of a 'white' man becoming 'coloured'. Pinchback had a flamboyant political career that began in 1862 with his declaration – to the surprise of those who knew him – that he was a Negro. He was thus qualified to command a Negro regiment, and his subsequent rise to power as a 'Negro' politician during Reconstruction was rapid, culminating in his election to the Senate and, briefly, to the governorship of Louisiana. In his *Black Reconstruction in America*, Du Bois wrote of Pinchback that he was 'to all intents and purposes ... an educated, well-to-do, congenial white man, with but a few drops of Negro blood, which he did not stoop to deny, as so many of his fellow whites did'. This was a generous construction to put on Pinchback's conversion to blackness, as was Toomer's that it was a result of his grandfather's boyish romanticism, his 'passion for the dramatic'. Political opportunism is equally plausible as a motive.

Toomer himself was 'white' for most of his youth, and his first prolonged exposure to an exclusively black community came in 1921, when he took a position as temporary head of a black school in rural Georgia. The job lasted only a few weeks, but the experience of the landscape, and of the disappearing folk culture of the Black Belt, had an enormous impact on him. The result was *Cane*. Partly on the advice of his friend the novelist Waldo Frank, Toomer identified himself as a Negro for the purposes of *Cane*'s publication, but subsequently came to regret the decision. He had no literary success after *Cane*, and blamed this on publishers' blinkered expectations of another 'Negro novel'. There is no evidence that Toomer went through a long night of the soul on the subject of his racial identity. As he recalls in one of his many unpublished autobiographical writings, he had fixed on his own, somewhat eccentric, views on race before *Cane*:

> I ... worked over my position, and formulated it with more fullness and exactitude. I wrote a poem called, 'The First American' the idea of which was, that here in America we are in process of forming a new race, that I was one of the first conscious members of this race...

Toomer's prediction that American apartheid would be overcome by the evolution of a 'new race' remained a personal fantasy, but – as the examples of Larsen and Toomer indicate – there were changes occurring in America in the early years of this century that did cut against the enforcement of white supremacy through segregation. The black population was becoming increasingly mobile and urbanised. Between 1900 and 1930, about two and a quarter million Negroes left the farms and villages of the South for the cities of the North. During the decade from 1910 to 1920 alone, the total Negro population of New York, Chicago, Philadelphia and Detroit grew by nearly three-quarters of a million. As a result, 1919 saw bloody race riots in these cities. With the urbanisation of the black community went the growth of the black bourgeoisie. The National Negro Business League was founded in 1900 by Booker T. Washington, apostle of black self-help, with the aim of encouraging African-Americans to turn segregation to their own advantage by patronising their own businesses. And with increased education and economic self-confidence went an expansion of the black press. Newspapers like the Chicago *Defender*, founded in 1905, played an important proselytising role in the northward migration by painting a favourable picture of life in the North compared with Southern oppression. *The Crisis* (1910–), *The Messenger* (1917–) and *Opportunity* (1923–) carried the expansion of black publishing into magazines, giving a voice to the educated middle class and, through campaigns on civil rights issues, opposing the conciliatory attitude of Booker T. Washington towards the white establishment.

The cultural fruit of these developments in the American black community was the 'Harlem Renaissance', a label that reflected the leading – though not exclusive – role of 'Black Manhattan', and also the sense that something was happening that had a deep significance in terms of the history of the African diaspora. Indeed, the Harlem Renaissance of the early years of this century can lay claim to be the first self-consciously 'black' literary and artistic movement – that is, the first movement arising in a racially divided society that addressed itself to the significance of racial identity, of 'blackness'.[1]

Not, of course, that there hadn't been black writers before then. The decades before the American Civil War saw the publication of hundreds of slave narratives, establishing the autobiographical as a central mode of African-American literary expression. A few of these narratives – such as those by Frederick Douglass, William Wells Brown and Sojourner Truth – had great power and individuality. Nobody who has read the account in Douglass's *Narrative* of his battle with an overseer can be in doubt as to the realities of slavery, its realities not just in terms of chains, blood and whippings but in terms of the psychological subjugation of the will that it demanded. These well-known narratives were only the tip of the iceberg, though at its lower levels this iceberg included much material that was heavily ghosted or even entirely composed by white abolitionists. The relationship between the slave narratives and the sentimentalist aesthetic is a complex one. The penetrating psychological realism of Douglass presented a direct challenge to it, as did the sly, undercutting reminders in William Wells Brown that duplicity rather than authenticity was a vital tool of survival for the slave. But in many other cases the sentimental novel provided the model, the literary template, on to which the

[1] Cultural movements do not conform to strict chronological limits. The Harlem Renaissance, the advent of the 'New Negro', is commonly identified with the years immediately after the First World War, when New York, like other Northern cities, was the destination of a wave of black immigration from the South. But the influx had in fact been going on since the 1890s, and recently historians have identified a black cultural community of musicians, performers and writers in New York in the 1900s centred around cabaret, musical theatre and ragtime. James Weldon Johnson – himself, along with his younger brother Rosamond, an important songwriter, and a connecting figure with the Renaissance of the Twenties – used this community as a setting for portions of his 1912 novel *The Autobiography of an Ex-Colored Man.*

slave experience was fitted. In the narratives, the issue of race or colour is largely subsumed in the larger one of slavery. After Emancipation, the problem of racial prejudice, and of the true meaning of racial identity, comes to the fore. What does it mean to be black? The first book to address the question directly was W. E. B. Du Bois's *The Souls of Black Folk* (1903), a bold and potent mixture of historical research, autobiography and fictional excursion. The opening chapter, 'Of Our Spiritual Strivings', has become probably the most anthologised piece in the African-American canon, particularly for the passage in which he describes the American Negro's 'double-consciousness', his 'two-ness':

> The Negro is ... gifted with second-sight in this American world, – a world which yields him no true self-consciousness, but only lets him see himself through the revelation of the other world. It is a peculiar sensation, this double-consciousness, this sense of always looking at one's self through the eyes of others, of measuring one's soul by the tape of a world that looks on in amused contempt and pity.

The passage continues:

> One ever feels this two-ness, – an American, a Negro; two souls, two thoughts, two unreconciled strivings; two warring ideals in one dark body, whose dogged strength alone keeps it from being torn asunder.

The passages are continuous in the original, but I have separated them here because there seems to me to be an important discontinuity in thought corresponding to two quite different definitions of 'doubleness'. In the second passage Du Bois talks the language of national and racial essences or 'souls', of 'American-ness' and 'Negroness' as Platonic Ideals wrestling within individuals. This romantic racialism was very much of its time – one finds it, too, in the rhetoric of Marcus Garvey's black nationalism in the 1920s – but it also reflects a spirit in Du Bois's own personality that we see throughout his long writing life (he died in 1963 aged ninety-three) between a florid if somewhat repressed romanticism and a cool social scientific attitude towards the world.

The 'doubleness' in the first passage, by contrast, is existential. It describes a split or 'doubling' between 'true self-consciousness' or authenticity and the false consciousness of seeing oneself through the eyes of others, of living by the definitions that others put on us. The 'American world' in which one's soul is measured by a 'tape' is a vivid, specific reference to the modern, bureaucratic racialism of Jim Crow segregation. But by formulating in this way the problem of identity for the American Negro, Du Bois was also anticipating a general question that has preoccupied artists and intellectuals in the twentieth century: is there a true 'self', or are we composed of the shifting roles that a complex society forces us to play out? Can we be 'true' to ourselves, or are we lost in a hall of mirrors? Are we – like the hero of Ralph Ellison's *Invisible Man*, who can only believe in his own existence by illuminating himself with hundreds of light bulbs – forever alienated from ourselves? It is a preoccupation reflected in modernism's taste for surfaces, for masks and pastiche, and it has strong roots in the black experience. For the African-American's 'double consciousness' could be seen as standing in general for the twentieth century's fractured, dissociated consciousness, their problem of identity as pointing to the fluidity and open-endedness of all forms of personal identity. It was for this reason, as we shall see in the next chapter, that Sartre and Genet came to regard the American Negro as the epitome of modernity.

The dilemma of personal identity raised by racial labelling arises in its most dramatic form at the margins, in those cases when by physical appearance a person can neither be said to be definitively 'white', nor definitively 'black'. (Racial purity being a myth, we could all, of course, strictly be said to be at the margins.) And herein lies the significance of a series of novels written around the turn of the century on the theme of 'passing', from Mark Twain's *Pudd'nhead Wilson* (1894) to Nella Larsen's *Passing* (1928). Nineteenth-century white writers of the Southern 'plantation school' often featured light-skinned Negroes in their melodramatic novels, but for Thomas Nelson Page and Thomas Dixon the 'tragic mulatto' was a freak of nature, the mixture of racial bloods – the conflict of racial 'souls' in Du Bois's romantic sense – causing a tendency towards criminality, deception and arrogance. By contrast, black writers such as Charles W. Chesnutt (*The House Behind the Cedars*), James Weldon Johnson (*The Autobiography of an Ex-Colored Man*), Jessie Fauset (*Plum Bun*) and Nella Larsen were interested in the way that the story of a 'black' who passed as 'white' could illustrate the arbitrariness and absurdity of all racial identity. The melodramatic quality of the 'tragic mulatto' theme was not entirely lost, but their use of the genre highlighted the way in which melodrama – with its secrets and lies, its role-playing, its sense of the individual being the puppet of a larger plot – could be a metaphor for existence in a racially divided society.

The starting-point for considering the literature of passing in this light is Mark Twain's *Pudd'nhead Wilson*. As is the case with Twain's other post-*Huckleberry Finn* novels, the book's patchiness and sheer eccentricity have flummoxed many critics, though it has also had its champions (including, somewhat surprisingly, F. R. Leavis). In mood and spirit it is related to those final chapters of *Huckleberry Finn* – chapters that have been seen (wrongly) by many critics as marring that great novel – in which the story abandons its rich realism and poignant irony, making a lurching descent into farcical burlesque as Tom and Huck stage-manage an absurd and unnecessary rescue of Jim from the woodshed. ('[T]o set a nigger free that was already free before', as Huck puts it.) Twain plays a dangerous game in those final chapters of *Huckleberry Finn*, teetering on the edge of minstrelsy, but the risk brings rich rewards. *Pudd'nhead Wilson* has, throughout, the same sense of schematic unreality, with its deliberate mixing of genres – detective story, melodrama, small-town humour – and its self-conscious play on certain formal motifs. Even the setting, though painted in detail, has a strange quality of abstraction. 'The scene of this chronicle', the book begins, in 'once upon a time' fashion, 'is the town of Dawson's Landing, on the Missouri side of the Mississippi . . .' And then we are given a description:

> In 1830 it was a snug little collection of modest one- and two-storey frame dwellings whose whitewashed exteriors were almost concealed from sight by climbing tangles of rose-vines,

honeysuckles, and morning-glories. Each of these pretty homes had a garden in front, fenced with white palings and opulently stocked with hollyhocks, marigolds, touch-me-nots, prince's-feathers and other old-fashioned flowers; while on the window-sills of the houses stood wooden boxes containing moss-rose plants and terracotta pots in which grew a breed of geranium whose spread of intensely red blossoms accented the prevailing pink tint of the rose-clad house-front like an explosion of flame. When there was room on the ledge outside of the pots and boxes for a cat, the cat was there – in sunny weather – stretched at full length, asleep and blissful, with her furry belly to the sun and a paw curved over her nose. Then that home was complete, and its contentment and peace were made manifest to the world by this symbol, whose testimony is infallible.

It is picturesque and carefully drawn, but strangely bland, undifferentiated (all the houses are the same) and dreamlike – a generic 'small town America' down to the white palings.

Despite Twain's precision about the year in which it is set, there is also a sense of freefloating timelessness about *Pudd'nhead Wilson*. Leaving aside for the moment the book's large and crucial anachronism, there are only two elements in Twain's story that give it any kind of historical or cultural anchor. One is the obsession of the citizens of Dawson's Landing with the language and ethos of medieval chivalry, an aspect of Southern life that Twain lampoons to great effect elsewhere in his fiction, most notably in *Huckleberry Finn*. The other, much more crucial to the narrative, is slipped into the opening panorama with a deliberately shocking insouciance:

Dawson's Landing was a slaveholding town, with a rich, slave-worked grain and pork country back of it. The town was sleepy and comfortable and contented.

The main story of *Pudd'nhead Wilson* concerns Roxana, a slave girl belonging to Percy Northumberland Driscoll, one of the leading citizens of the town. 'To all intents and purposes,' Twain explains with a typically mordant conceit, 'Roxy was as white as anybody, but the one sixteenth of her which was black outvoted the other fifteen parts and made her a negro.' Roxy gives birth to a son on the same day as her mistress does the same. This new slave baby is thirty-one parts white and has 'blue eyes and flaxen curls like his white comrade'. When, shortly afterward, the mistress dies, it is given to Roxy to bring up both babies.

Already the reader can sense the way in which the plot is to be set in motion. Some money is stolen from the house. Driscoll gathers the domestic slaves together, threatening to sell them 'down the river' unless they reveal the culprit, and this incident brings home to Roxy the awful precariousness of her precious son's future. She resolves to drown both herself and the baby. Seized by a sense of theatre, she dresses herself for death in a new Sunday gown, then dresses her son in one of the pretty baby-gowns belonging to her master's son.

She stepped over and glanced at the other infant; she flung a glance back at her own; then one more at the heir of the house. Now a strange light dawned in her eyes, and in a moment she was lost in thought. She seemed in a trance; when she came out of it she muttered, 'When I 'uz a-washin' 'em in de tub, yistiddy, his own pappy asked me which of 'em was his'n.'

And so the story proper begins: Roxy decides to switch the two babies. 'Marse Tom,' she exclaims, addressing her own son, '– oh, thank de good Lord in heaven, you's saved, you's saved! – dey ain't no man kin ever sell mammy's po' little honey down de river now!'

The switch is but part of a pattern of doubles in the book. The bizarre secondary plot concerns a pair of Italian twins whose European exoticism ruptures the paling-fenced insularity of the town. (In the short story that was the germ of the novel, 'Those Extraordinary Twins', they are actually Siamese twins. Twain subsequently separated them but his slapdash editing has left incongruous traces of these origins in the final text.) Even small touches reveal Twain's fascination for this idea of the double, of a twin-poled or mirrored figure bound as one by some formal connection. The 'Pudd'nhead' of the title is one David Wilson, a lawyer and outsider who arrives in Dawson's Landing only to find himself pityingly treated as a fool. His undoing is to remark one day of a dog that wouldn't stop yelping:

'I wish I owned half of that dog.'
'Why?' somebody asked.
'Because I would kill my half.'

Failing to cotton on to the fact that he was making a joke, the citizenry give him his nickname and seal his fate; thereafter he is to be the town's 'pudd'nhead'. But it is to be Pudd'nhead Wilson, of course, who is to astound his fellow townsfolk by unravelling, in a final courtroom scene, the mystery of Roxy's switch.

But the complications of plot lie ahead. The reader's initial response to Roxy's action, which is more important in the present context, is to reflect on the terrible contradiction and paradox at its heart. For in saving 'her son' she has changed his identity so that he is no longer 'her son'. It is surely no coincidence that Twain has Roxy see the possibility of the switch when she is on the point of murdering him. For in so changing his identity she is in effect killing him as the person that he was and causing him to be born again as someone else, someone whom he is not. One thinks of Nella Larsen's father, dying as a 'black man' and being born again as a 'white man'. Roxy's son grows up as her master, and Twain spells out the vertiginous loss of identity involved in these roles' hardening into reality:

[T]he little counterfeit rift of separation between imitation-slave and imitation-master widened and widened and became an abyss, and a very real one – and on one side of it stood Roxy, the dupe of her own deceptions, and on the other stood her child, no longer a usurper to her, but her accepted and recognised master. He was her darling, her master and her deity all in one, and in her worship of him she forgot who she was and what he had been.

Tom, the counterfeit young master, proves a bad apple. Not only does he take to gambling and general dissolution, but he treats his mother, his 'slave', with the vicious contempt he reserves for all 'niggers' – a contempt to which Roxy reacts with irrational rage at her son's ingratitude. (Tom has no inkling of his true history.) When Tom's supposed father dies, Roxy is given her freedom and leaves Dawson's Landing to work as a chambermaid aboard the river steamboats. But eight years later she is back, penniless. When Tom refuses to help her out she blackmails him, revealing to him his true identity as a 'nigger' and threatening to tell the world. His interior monologue reveals a mental world turned, briefly, upside down:

> 'Why were niggers *and* whites made? What crime did the uncreated first nigger commit that the curse of birth was decreed for him? And why this awful difference made between black and white? . . . How hard the nigger's fate seems, this morning! – yet until last night such a thought never entered my head.'

Tom's perturbation lasts about a week, until – with Twain's characteristically laconic realism – he lapses back into his old carefree ways and resolves to make the best of maintaining the deception by entering into an unholy conspiracy with his mother.

A complex plot ensues involving a disputed inheritance and the murder of Tom's guardian uncle, for which the Italian twins are wrongly accused. Puddn'head Wilson defends the twins in court, and in revealing the actual culprit he also reveals Tom's true parentage. The means by which he does so is the big anachronism in the book, but also an inspired focus for the novel's theme of identity. While Twain was working on *Pudd'nhead Wilson* he read Sir Francis Galton's *Finger Prints*, published in 1892, and incorporated this new technique of forensic science into his story.[1] Throughout the book Pudd'nhead Wilson obsessively takes and collates the finger marks of everyone whom he comes across, a foolishness which his fellow citizens indulge. He takes the fingerprints of the two babies before the switch, and after it. And he finds fingerprints at the scene of the murder. Hence he is able to solve the mystery.

Plot summaries inevitably have a bald, schematic quality, a

---

[1] An incidental irony, given the novel's turning on a question of racial identity, is that Galton was also to pioneer the racial 'science' of eugenics.

quality that usually misrepresents the book. But *Pudd'nhead Wilson*, despite the rich reality of Twain's humour, is in fact a novel of almost surreal abstraction, as announced at the outset in the never-never land of its setting. And its strange power lies in the fact that its irreality accords precisely with its theme of the absence of identity. For the point we are left with at the end of the book is not that Tom was 'really' black and a slave, or that his double was really white and free, but that all these fundamental social definitions of who we are as people are arbitrary and, with an awful comedy, absurd.[1] The only sure guide as to who we are is something as ultimately meaningless as ridges of skin on the ends of our fingers.

At the end of the novel the strange order of things is restored. Tom is indeed sold down the river, and his double – about whom we have heard little during the course of the story – is restored to his rightful property. But even this restitution has a hollow, absurd quality, leaving the reader with true laughter in the dark:

> The real heir suddenly found himself rich and free, but in a most embarrassing situation. He could neither read nor write, and his speech was the basest dialect of the negro quarter. His gait, his attitudes, his gestures, his bearing, his laugh – all were vulgar and uncouth; his manners were the manners of a slave. Money and fine clothes could not mend these defects or cover them up, they only made them the more glaring and the more pathetic. The poor fellow could not endure the terrors of the white man's parlour, and felt at home and at peace nowhere but in the kitchen. The family pew was a misery to him, yet he could nevermore enter into the solacing refuge of the 'nigger gallery' – that was closed to him for good and all. But we cannot follow his curious fate further – that would be a long story.

Humour, melodrama, murder-mystery – the curiously effective

---

[1] It can and has been argued that Tom's proving a bad apple is an expression of Twain's racialism, that he proves a ne'er-do-well because black blood will out. But this is a weighted and partial reading; one can more convincingly argue that Tom goes to the bad because that is what the plot requires.

abstraction of *Pudd'nhead Wilson*, its schematic quality, is in part a function of the way it is driven by genres. There is also the point that in so far as it is a novel about passing, there is no psychological issue of motivation. Tom does not decide to pass for white. He simply finds himself, without choice, to be one who has passed. But in other novels of the colour line, the issue of motivation, the decision of the individual to change identity and pass, is crucial. Charles W. Chesnutt, the best-known African-American novelist prior to the Harlem Renaissance, was himself light-skinned enough to have considered passing at one stage of his life. He was a lawyer by profession, and it no doubt would have helped his legal career to have done so, as it helps John Warwick, brother of the heroine of his novel about passing, *The House Behind the Cedars* (1900). But in exploring the motivation of John and Rena Warwick in deciding to become 'white', Chesnutt is not judgemental. Indeed, his propagandist mission in writing the novel was to urge that mulattos, and in particular mulattos who made the decision to pass, should be viewed with humanity rather than as doomed freaks of nature or underhand deceivers. The fault is not with them, but with society. Rena is unmasked by society as a 'black' because she puts love for her mother before prudence. Had she not done so, as Chesnutt points out, society, with all its hypocrisy, would have been happy to laud her as 'white'. Thus segregation turns the true world of human values upside down:

> If there be a dainty reader of this tale who scorns a lie and who writes the story of his life upon his sleeve for all the world to read, let him uncurl his scornful lip and come down from the pedestal of superior morality, to which assured position and wide opportunity have lifted him, and put himself in the place of Rena and her brother, upon whom God had lavished his best gifts and from whom society would have withheld all that made these gifts valuable. To undertake what they tried to do required great courage. Had they possessed the sneaking, cringing, treacherous character traditionally ascribed to people of mixed blood ... had they been selfish enough to sacrifice to their ambition the mother who gave them birth, society would have

been placated or humbugged and the voyage of their life might have been one of unbroken smoothness.

The interest of *The House Behind the Cedars* lies in this quality it has of spelling out the ways in which segregation – and the racialist world-view on which it is based – comes into conflict with and inverts the fundamentals of our humanity. Truth becomes lie, love becomes hate, John Warwick returns to his home town of Patesville, to the 'house behind the cedars', after some years away – years during which he has redefined himself as white and built a successful career as a lawyer. He and his sister Rena are the illegitimate offspring of their mother and a white man. After much persuading, Rena agrees to leave their mother and make a future for herself in the white world. In this new world she falls in love with and becomes engaged to her brother's best friend George Tryon, who is from a respectable Southern white family and comes equipped with the conventional views of his class and colour.

The ensuing revelations are predictable, but even before they come Rena identifies how their love is corrupted by the lie on which it is based:

> But would her lover still love her, if he knew all? ... She had read that love was a conqueror, that neither life nor death, nor creed nor caste, could stay its triumphant course. Her secret was no legal bar to their union. If Rena could forget the secret and Tryon should never know it, it would be no obstacle to their happiness. But Rena felt, with a sinking of the heart, that happiness was not a matter of law or fact, but lay entirely within the domain of sentiment. We are happy when we think ourselves happy and with a strange perversity we often differ from others with regard to what should constitute our happiness. Rena's secret was the worm in the bud, the skeleton in the closet.

Behind the somewhat archaic language this is psychologically acute, and also contains a sense that one finds in later African-American fiction that race is paradoxically both everything and nothing, both trivial and fundamental. It has nothing to do with who one is as an individual, and yet socially it can define almost everything one is as a person. The individual may rebel against that social definition – may seek to escape it and may even succeed – yet such a flight will be a denial of something that, willy-nilly, constitutes one's identity. In terms of its artistic representation, it is a paradox that can lead to absurdity, or tragedy, or both.

The inevitable happens. Tryon discovers Rena's secret and breaks off the engagement. His realisation that the woman he loves is really 'black' takes the novel to the brink of deep and fascinating psychological territory. At first he is outraged: 'A negro girl had been foisted on him for a white woman and he had almost committed the unpardonable sin against his race of marrying her.' But his thoughts change, and an inner conflict emerges:

> Tryon's race impulse and social prejudice had carried him too far and the swing of the pendulum brought his thoughts rapidly back in the opposite direction. Tossing uneasily on the bed where he had thrown himself down without undressing, the air of the room oppressed him and he threw open the window . . . He burst into tears, bitter tears that strained his heartstrings. He was only a youth. She was his first love and he had lost her forever . . . He had felt the power and charm of love and no ordinary shock could have loosened its hold, but this catastrophe, which had so rudely swept away the groundwork of this passion, had stirred into new life all the slumbering pride of race and ancestry which characterized his caste. How much of this sensitive superiority was essential and how much was accidental? . . . How much of it was ignorance and self-conceit? . . . He tried to be angry with her, but after the first hour he found it impossible . . . But for the sheerest accident, no, rather, but for providential interference, he would have married her and might have gone to the grave unconscious that she was other than she seemed.

So the same thought occurs to Tryon as had occurred to Rena: that they might have lived happily if Tryon had remained ignorant of the truth – this 'truth' being itself based on a lie, the lie of racial identity. Well might he be unsure whether it was 'providential interference' that he should have found out, or 'sheerest accident'.

The territory to the brink of which Chesnutt takes us is that of betrayal and its varieties. Rena and Tryon are both betrayed and burnt out by love. Rena is betrayed by a person, by Tryon's inability to overcome his upbringing and his prejudices, by the failure of his love. Tryon's first instinct is also to believe that he has been betrayed by a person, but there dawns in him the realisation that he may have been betrayed by the way that he looks at the world – that he may have been betrayed, in fact, by himself. He decides to go back to her, to overcome himself and mend things between them:

'She ought to have been born white,' he muttered, adding weakly, 'I would to God that I had never found her out!'

This is a potentially fascinating scenario, but one whose psychological depths it would need a Dostoevsky to explore fully. Chesnutt, unfortunately, was no Dostoevsky, and it is at this point, on the brink of this murky but potentially illuminating spiritual territory, that the novel fumbles and collapses fully into melo-drama. Rena, burnt out by love, has returned to 'her people' and become a teacher in a black school. She is lasciviously pursued by Wain, a mulatto who fits all the stereotypes Chesnutt had originally set out to combat. When Tryon returns to Rena, he sees her with Wain and misinterprets what he sees. She has become in his eyes just another nigger wench, though one for whom he still has a passion. In time-honoured fashion, he decides to try and take her for his mistress. Physically pursued by both Wain and Tryon, Rena loses herself in the swamp, catches a fever and dies. As an ending it is disappointingly perfunctory, and also absurd. By killing off his heroine, by grasping on to the most hackneyed closure of romantic fiction, Chesnutt slams the door on his own psychological drama. The final failure of *The House Behind the Cedars* is a failure of psychological action; psychological action is replaced by sensational, physical action, and it is in that sense that the book ends as melodrama, as absurdity.

Passing as a subject for fictional treatment lends itself to melodrama in two ways. At the basic level of plot there is the idea of a dark secret hidden in the past, of a final revelation that may bring about the hero or heroine's downfall. That – with its accompanying factor of betrayal, of both those from whom and to whom one has 'passed' – has always been a feature of melodramatic and sensational literature. At a profounder level, the confusion or loss of identity involved in passing – the sense that people have become, whether they pass or not, the puppets of social categories beyond their control – complements melodrama's tendency to treat character as subservient to plot. In *Pudd'nhead Wilson* Twain uses genre with some self-consciousness as a way of extrapolating the absurdity inherent in the idea of racial identity. The absurdity of *The House Behind the Cedars'* ending is unintended, a deflation of the novel's psychological possibilities. But this very artistic failure is itself testimony to the way that 'passing' as fictional subject matter subverts psychological realism and the notion of personal identity upon which it rests.

Two women writers of the 'Harlem Renaissance', Nella Larsen and Jessie Redmon Fauset, use genre with conscious irony to portray passing as essentially subversive, a disruption of conventional categories of both art and life. Fauset's *Plum Bun* (1929), like *Pudd'nhead Wilson*, signals its generic quality from the start, with a fairy-tale-like description of setting. In 'an unpretentious little street lined with unpretentious little houses, inhabited for the most part by unpretentious little people . . . dwelt a father, a mother and two daughters'. The two daughters absorb wish-fulfilment at an early age:

> When Angela and Virgina were little children and their mother used to read them fairy tales she would add to the ending, 'And so they lived happily ever after, just like your father and me.'

Angela, the lighter skinned of the sisters, grows up adhering to a creed of idealised freedom and happiness. And, with a canny intelligence, she early on identifies the key to that wonderful world:

> Colour or rather the lack of it seemed to the child the one absolute prerequisite to the life of which she was always dreaming . . . very often early she began thanking Fate for the

chance which in that household of four had bestowed on her the heritage of her mother's fair skin.

Angela learns the trick of passing from her mother, but with a vital difference in the attitude they bring to the practice. For her mother, devotedly in love with her darker skinned husband, it is an occasional frivolity, a way of cocking a snook at silly rules and regulations. When forced to choose between passing and loyalty to her husband, she chooses her husband without hesitation. For Angela, passing is a much more serious matter, a instinctive expression of her deep need to reach out towards visions of freedom and happiness. At first, in school, she passes by default, by not correcting those that take her for white. On each occasion when she is discovered her reply is straightforward but disingenuous:

> 'Coloured! Angela, you never told me that you were coloured!'
> And then her own voice in tragic but proud bewilderment.
> 'Tell you that I was coloured! Why of course I never told you that I was coloured. Why should I?'

On the occasions when the sisters' coloured friends engage in tortured debates on how far the individual should sacrifice him- or herself for loyalty to 'the race', Angela's contributions are similarly simple:

> 'What do you think, Angela?'
> 'Just the same as I've always thought. I don't see any sense in living unless you're going to be happy.'

With her directness and intelligence, Angela doesn't make the mistake of attaching any innate or metaphysical significance to whiteness. She sees through it, understands its arbitrariness. She sees simply that, with the world as it is, whiteness is the means towards an end that she desires:

> [I]t seemed to Angela that all the things which she most wanted were wrapped up with white people. All the good things were theirs. Not, some coldly reasoning instinct within her was saying, because they were white. But because for the present

they had power and the badge of that power was whiteness, very like the colours on the escutcheon of a powerful house. She possessed the badge, and unless there was someone to tell she could possess the power for which it stood.

'The escutcheon of a powerful house' – into Angela's realistic, cynical appraisal of her prospects, Fauset already introduces the language of chivalry, romance and fantasy. This disruptive conflict between innocently idealistic invention and harsh realism is felt at different levels throughout the novel, and announced even in its title and nursery-rhyme epigraph:

> To Market, to Market,
>   To Buy a Plum Bun;
> Home again, Home again,
>   Market is Done.

This seems innocent enough, but when used for the titles of the five parts into which the narrative is divided ('Home', 'Market', 'Plum Bun', 'Home Again', 'Market is Done') it acquires less innocent, sexual connotations. Angela is herself the 'Plum Bun'. With the death of her parents, Angela deserts her sister and leaves 'Home' in Philadelphia for New York. She has made the decision to join the white world, and specifically to get herself a white husband. The market to which she has gone is the marriage market. And 'Plum Bun', with its strong sexual overtones, refers to the commodity that is dealt and exchanged in this market. Tutored by a girlfriend, Angela (or 'Angele', as she now calls herself) learns how she must extract from her wealthy white suitor, Roger, the maximum price – marriage – for her sexual favours:

> 'It is a game, and the hardest game in the world for a woman, but the most fascinating; the hardest in which to strike a happy medium. You see, you have to be careful not to withhold too much and yet to give very little. If we don't give enough we lose them. If we give too much we lose ourselves.'

Angela plays the game badly. As happens in such emotional games, she only 'wins' when she has given up playing, when she no longer even wants marriage to Roger when he offers it. And the reason that she plays the game badly is that she allows herself to be seduced by romantic illusions, by the very visions of idealised personal happiness that drew her to take up the game in the first place. Roger becomes for her 'a blond glorious god ... [radiating] light and gladness ... the finest flower of chivalry and devotion ... rounding out [her life] like a fairy tale'. She takes her eye off the ball. When Roger initially offers her not marriage but a position as kept mistress, she is at first shocked but then gives way, mistakenly thinking that sexual acquiescence will keep him hooked. Angela's seduction is played out, with a wry nod towards the conventions of the romantic genre, against the backdrop of a stormy, turbulent night.

Thus far *Plum Bun* is a deconstruction of romantic myths, justifying its subtitle, 'A Novel Without a Moral'. But in the end, just as Chesnutt succumbs to melodrama in *The House Behind the Chedars*, Jessie Redmon Fauset ceases playing ironic riffs on the theme of romance and instead starts singing straight from the songsheet. The book ends with not one but two marriages. There have been two men in Angela's life apart from Roger – the dark-skinned Matthew and Anthony, a fellow art student who Angela thinks is white but who is actually passing too. After Angela has rejected Roger and discovered her vocation as a painter, she and Anthony confess their secret to each other. Anthony, who had thought for a time that perhaps he loved Angela's darker, race-conscious sister Virginia, decides that he does love Angela after all. Everything is sorted out. All have rejected the lures of the white world and come to terms with their true racial identity. But, as the black nationalist literary critic Addison Gayle points out, there is a hidden agenda to the way in which things are sorted out and racial identities are come to terms with at the end of *Plum Bun*:

> Lost on Miss Fauset, but obvious to the reader, is the fact that the mulattos, Anthony and Angela, and the Blacks, Virginia and Matthew, enter into union with each other and not with their differently complexioned partners of either sex ... Few middle-class-black families would not understand Miss Fauset's inten-

tions, subconsciously or otherwise, in uniting Anthony with Angela and Virginia with Matthew. Pride in race does not mean that one surrender the white aesthetic, that he opt for the formula that Black is beautiful. The successful marriage from which all else might spring demands a union between like people, mulattos with mulattos, Blacks with Blacks.

It was not incompatible for the Negro middle class to adhere to an idea of racial belonging, of collective 'racial uplift', and yet at the same time regard themselves as a distinct group, marked out from the rest of the black population perhaps unspokenly by skin tone, but also by attitudes to life and by the path they were destined to follow. Indeed, the two ideas – of being part of the race and distinct from it – could be fused in a philosophy of vanguardism. In the 1900s, W. E. B. Du Bois led a political and intellectual movement opposed to the social accommodationist ideology of Booker T. Washington. According to Washington, African-Americans should play down antagonistic political demands and concentrate on pulling themselves up by their own economic bootstraps. The Tuskegee Institute that he founded put its emphasis on technical and vocational education. Du Bois, himself educated at Harvard and the University of Berlin, campaigned on civil rights issues and argued for the vanguard role of a black intelligentsia, the 'Talented Tenth', in demonstrating to American society at large the capabilities of African-Americans. Fauset, who in the 1920s was literary editor of *Crisis*, the journal that Du Bois founded, adhered to the 'Talented Tenth' idea and the values of the class it sustained. At the end of *Plum Bun*, Angela's transgressive individuality evaporates as she stabilises her identity within a racial niche. It would take the more acerbic eye of Nella Larsen to expose, in a highly personal way, the blandishments and hypocrisies of the new black middle class.

Larsen's *Passing* (1929) ends, like *The House Behind the Cedars*, with the sudden death of the heroine, but is saved from bathos – if not from a certain terse sketchiness – by the ambiguities surrounding that death and the life that it ended. The story is told from the point of view of Irene Redfield, a light-skinned mother of two who is married to a doctor. On a visit to Chicago, while casually 'passing' to get a drink in a hotel, Irene runs into Clare Kendry, whom she had known as a girl. Clare, it becomes clear, has passed and is married to a white man who knows nothing of her background. Clare is anxious to renew the friendship with Irene, but Irene holds back, fearing an instability and wildness in Clare that she fears could introduce unwanted complications into the domestic certainties of her own life. Irene's disapproval of Clare blends sexual puritanism with a censorious belief that Clare has betrayed 'her people'. She had, in Irene's eyes, 'no allegiance beyond her own immediate desire. She was selfish, cold and hard.' Irene, by contrast, is the self-sacrificing mother and, with her constant round of charity dinners, a member of the vanguard of her race. She returns to New York, seeing the episode as finished. But Clare follows her there, hoping for an opportunity of re-entry into that black milieu that she had abandoned. Clare attaches herself to Irene's world, and an awful certainty takes hold of Irene that Clare has begun to have an affair with her husband, that she is in the process of destroying that safe world which Irene has painstakingly constructed and maintained. In the final and undeniably melodramatic scene of the book, they are at a party high in an apartment block. Clare is standing at an open window. Her white husband, who has discovered her secret, rushes in. In the confusion, Clare falls from the window to her death. Did she jump? Was it an accident? Or – and this is the clear though coded impression with which the reader is left – did Irene push her in a fit of insane jealousy and hatred?

Despite its title, *Passing* is only secondarily about crossing the colour-line – or rather, that transgression is a medium by which she approaches her main subject matter, which is a certain kind of marriage and a certain kind of woman. Irene Redfield is an unreliable narrator. Even as she depicts her happy marriage and family life, it becomes apparent to the reader that its seeming stability is in fact built on shifting sands, on Irene's compulsion to manipulate and control those around her under the cloak of self-sacrifice. Her husband Brian had cherished the dream of the family's escaping Harlem and emigrating to Brazil, but Irene had quashed that dream. ('Not for her, oh no, not for her – she had never really considered herself – but for him and the boys.') It is in fact Irene, not Clare, who emerges as selfish, cold and hard:

> [S]he understood him so well, because she had, actually, a special talent for understanding him. It was, as she saw it, the one thing that had been the basis of the success she had made of a marriage that had threatened to fail. She knew him as well as he knew himself, or better . . . She had only to direct and guide her man, to keep him going in the right direction.
>
> She put on her coat and adjusted her hat.

Furthermore, Irene's puritanical disapproval of Clare is a cloak for deeply repressed erotic feelings. The descriptions of the two women's encounters are soaked in the language of sensuality, of beauty and allure. Larsen hints at a sexual content to Irene's inability to shake off her wayward friend's attentions, and these hints – bold for a writer of the 1920s – are all the more striking for working against the grain of the 'society novel' language (she was influenced by Henry James and Edith Wharton) in which she couches them. Indeed, it is not at all clear to the reader that there has been any affair with Irene's husband, that these suspicions are not in fact projections – not just of her fundamental insecurities concerning her marriage, but of her own sexual fantasies.

Clare is a dangerous, transgressive force in the novel. As Irene remarks to her husband:

> 'It's funny about "passing". We disapprove of it and at the same time condone it. It excites our contempt and yet we rather admire it. We shy away from it with an odd kind of revulsion, but we protect it.'

The 'odd kind of revulsion' that Irene feels towards Clare contains a particular fascination which reflects the ambiguities and internal conflicts of her own sexuality. Clare is destructive, in that one senses that she will be a catalyst for the dissolution of a marriage, but one gets a clear sense that Larsen regards that marriage – and the hypocritical ideology of sacrifice for race and family on which it is based – as ripe for destruction. Already in her first novel,

Quicksand (1928), Larsen had attacked the straitjacketing, almost militaristic ethos of 'racial uplift' embodied in places like Tuskegee. *Passing* shows that she regarded the ethos of the 'Talented Tenth' in a similar light. The sad irony of Larsen's own life was that she was herself a part of that world (her own husband was a physicist, in the days when a black physicist was a rare thing indeed) and seems, from the evidence we have, to have shared some of its brittle snobberies. ('Furious at being connected with all these niggers,' she writes to a friend, of living in Harlem.) Unlike Claude McKay and other more 'primitivist' writers of the Harlem Renaissance, she was unable to celebrate the black proletariat or embrace the idea of an 'authentic' black culture. Her writing is fascinating for its lack of comfort, its marginality, its sense of being on an edge. But in the end that was not enough to sustain it, and after two sharp, acidic novels she fell into permanent silence.

Reading the literature of the Harlem Renaissance, one constantly comes up against the issue of social class – and, closely allied to it, that of skin tone. In his coolly ironic, picaresque novel *The Autobiography of an Ex-Colored Man* (1912), James Weldon Johnson offers an economic explanation for the tendency of the nascent African-American middle class to be lighter skinned than their working-class brothers and sisters.

> [B]lack men generally marry women fairer than themselves; while, on the other hand, the dark women of stronger mental endowment are very often married to light-complexioned men; the effect is a tendency toward lighter complexions, especially among the more active elements in the race. Some might claim that this is a tacit admission of colored people among themselves of their own inferiority judged by the color line. I do not think so ... [I]t is, in fact, a tendency in accordance with what might be called an economic necessity ... I have seen advertisements in newspapers for waiters, bell-boys, or elevator men, which read: 'Light-colored man wanted' ... There is involved not only the question of higher opportunity, but often the question of earning a livelihood ...

The couples in *Plum Bun* pair off at the end of the novel by skin tone. One of the appurtenances of the Redfields' comfortable domesticity in *Passing* is a dark-skinned maid – 'Zulena, a small mahogany-colored creature'. In the bitter and highly personalised political feud carried on in the 1920s between Du Bois and Marcus Garvey – whose United Negro Improvement Association spectacularly, if briefly, marshalled black masses behind an ideology of nationalist separatism – the rhetoric was frequently determined by the issue of skin colour. For Garvey – coming originally from Jamaica, where lighter-skinned blacks formed more of a distinct caste than in the United States – the skin tone of middle-class leaders like Du Bois was a visible sign of racial betrayal. Du Bois, for his part, hardly helped his cause in the argument by allowing himself to describe Garvey as 'a little, fat, black man; ugly, but with intelligent eyes and a big head'. Garvey leapt on the gaffe with glee.

So 'passing' shades into the wider issue of colour prejudice, a prejudice that can take in the black community itself. If one is unable to pass as white, one can at least distance oneself from those at the bottom of the racial heap and obtain membership of a distinct 'blue-vein' caste. And over generations, with the right discrimination as to mates, that caste might itself pass. The grandmother of Emma Lou, heroine of Wallace Thurman's satirical novel *The Blacker the Berry* (1929), is founder of the blue-veins in Boise, Idaho. Her motto is ' "Whiter and whiter every generation," until the grandchildren of the blue veins could easily go over into the white race and become assimilated so that problems of race would plague them no more.' One of the liveliest novels of the Harlem Renaissance, *The Blacker the Berry* tackles head-on this issue of intra-racial colour prejudice. (It was roundly condemned by some at the time for hanging out dirty washing in public.) The book's sharp, bleak humour lies in the character of Emma Lou herself. 'The tragedy of her life', the reader is told at the outset, 'was that she was too black.' Too black, that is, in her own eyes as well as in the eyes of her blue-vein family. For the awful comedy of Emma Lou's predicament, the root of her flailing, pathetic attempts to find a life for herself, is that from birth she has absorbed and internalised the prejudices of those around her. She has become 'possessed of a perverse bitterness [for] she idolized the one thing one would naturally expect her to hate.' Her worship of all things pale leads her to regard her own skin with disgust. She mutilates her face with bleaching agents and plasters it with rouge and lipstick. One is reminded of Edmund Burke writing 150 years earlier of man's instinctive horror of blackness in terms of a young child's fear at the sight of a Negro woman – with its implication that had that child been black, it would have regarded itself with the same horror.

Emma Lou's world-view is that of white society at large, learnt at second hand through the blue-veins. As a Harlem intellectual character puts it late in the novel:

'[Y]ou can't blame light Negroes for being prejudiced against dark ones. All of you know that white is the symbol of everything pure and good ... [V]irtue and virginity are always represented as being clothed in white garments ... [T]he God we ... worship is a patriarchal white man, seated on a white throne, in a spotless white Heaven, radiant with white streets and white-apparelled angels eating white honey and drinking white milk.'

By the time she hears this, Emma Lou has been rendered so paranoid by the continual snubs and setbacks that she has received on account of her black skin, that she takes the remarks to be in some obscure way an insult directed at herself. But the thing that has thus made her so vulnerable – and herein lies the novel's somewhat cruel humour – is her own snobbery. At college in Los Angeles she shuns those who are black like her on account of what she sees as their vulgarity of speech and manner, and desperately seeks the society of 'sophisticated' light-skinned Negroes. A dark-skinned man with other things to recommend him – wealth, looks, talent – might make it into that society, but the door is closed to a black-skinned woman.

Emma Lou throws up her college course and moves to New York, where her black skin is a formidable obstacle to respectable employment. She ends up – like the mother of Angela Murray in *Plum Bun* – working as maid to a white actress who blacks up to play sexy mulatto women. Her desperate attempts to obtain a lighter-skinned husband – as well as a transgressive impulse that echoes that of Angela in *Plum Bun* and Clare in *Passing* – makes her easy prey to a variety of rakes and seducers. She becomes the victim, in particular, of Alva, a thoroughly unpleasant character, a drunkard and wholesale exploiter of women. (One cannot help the feeling that Thurman's desire to combat the elitism of light-skinned Negroes led him to create in Alva – and here perhaps there is an analogy with Wain in Chesnutt's *The House Behind the Cedars* – a character who echoes, consciously or not, old stereotypes of the mulatto as an abomination of the natural and moral order. Not only is Alva almost wholly evil, but the baby he has by a light-skinned woman is born physically weak and deformed.) By the end of the book, Emma Lou has become exactly that which she had always sought to avoid becoming – the stereotypical black mammy, sexually exploited and looking after another woman's baby. At this point Emma Lou takes a long hard look at herself and sees that her problem lies in self-hatred, in her inability to love herself for who she is as a black woman. The realisation enables her to walk out on Alva. So far, so therapeutic and heart-warmingly redemptive, but although this is how the novel ends in terms of plot, with Emma Lou 'finding herself' much as Angela 'finds herself' at the end of *Plum Bun*, *The Blacker the Berry* remains in spirit, and working against its formal optimism, a bleak novel, a satirist's novel, a novel of laughter in the dark.[1] Its title is taken from an old saying, 'The blacker the berry the sweeter the juice', but the only time that the saying is quoted in the book is not in the context of Emma Lou's self-affirmation, but ironically, as Alva cynically licks his lips at the prospect of the sexual delights she has to offer. And the last sentence of the book leaves us not with Emma Lou's redemption, but with the crying of the baby abandoned by her to Alva's tender mercies.

[1] Born in 1902, Thurman died at the age of thirty-two, a victim of alcoholism and tuberculosis. In *The Negro Novel in America* (Yale University Press, New Haven, 1958), Robert Bone puts forward the theory, without any evidence to back it up, that the anti-black self-hatred of Emma Lou in *The Blacker the Berry* was by way of a self-portrait, and that this explains Thurman's self-destructive tendencies.

Thurman's dark satire strains against the formal pattern it shares with *Plum Bun* as a novel of personal redemption. This quality of being ill at ease with its chosen form is one it shares more generally with the other novels described so far. The subject matter of racial identity – or, more accurately, of that identity being transgressed, exposed as something fundamental and at the same time flimsy and arbitrary – lends itself to genres such as melodrama and romance in so far as the impulse of genre is to subordinate integral, interior personality to the operation of external forces. Characters become the creatures of plot, just as they become creatures of society's racial definitions. But if genre in this way offers an opportunity to open up the field of racial identity, it also, in the way that it works towards a final closure (whether as melodramatic tragedy or heart-warming redemption), flinches from the abyssal paradox of race, the aporia of a phenomenon that is both as literally superficial as a matter of skin colour and also capable of putting at stake one's deepest attachments of love and loyalty. Put more bluntly, the novels of Chesnutt, Larsen and Fauset are let down by their endings.

It took an artist more forward-looking, more self-assured in his recognition of the possibilities of modernist and expressionist techniques, to follow this particular path further, to perceive the connections between the question of racial identity in America's segregated society of the 1920s and the wider, peculiarly modern question of whether individuals have a coherent identity at all. Eugene O'Neill was establishing himself as America's leading playwright just as the Harlem Renaissance was getting into its swing, and he provides a good example of how white artists of the time were influenced by the new awareness of African-American culture. Not only did he actively promote Negro theatre – serving, for example, on judging panels for competitions – but he also made race a prominent theme of his early plays. Highly conscious of his own Irish-American identity, O'Neill was drawn to the Negro as a figure of the outsider, someone marked out by society for ostracism.

Nowhere can this be seen more clearly than in the play that first made his name, *The Emperor Jones* (1920), which presents in a starkly expressionistic form the racial atavism that was developed in the literature of the 1880s and 1890s. (Conrad was a favourite author of O'Neill's, and *Heart of Darkness* is an obvious influence on *The Emperor Jones*.) Brutus Jones is a former Pullman porter who has become 'emperor' of an island in the Caribbean. Faced with a rebellion, he attempts an escape through the forest to the coast, but his journey becomes a symbolic one, a flight from the trappings of civilisation with which he had cloaked himself into a primitive terror. The pursuit is marked by the beating of tom-toms, which get gradually faster over the course of the play until they cease with Jones's death.

The same retreat into the primitive (though without the overt racial dimension) marks the course of *The Hairy Ape* (1922), which depicts a 'Neanderthal'-looking ship's stoker's flight from civilisation to death – and a kind of communion – in an ape's cage at the city zoo. Yank, the stoker, has affinities both with the ape and with the machinery that surrounds him in the ship's engine room. As he says himself:

> I'm de ting in coal dat makes it boin; I'm steel and oil for de engines; I'm de ting in noise dat makes yuh hear it; I'm smoke and express trains and steamers and factory whistles; I'm de ting in gold dat makes it money! And I'm what makes iron into steel! Steel, dat stands for de whole ting!

It is this equation of man, machine and ape that makes *The Hairy Ape* a classic expression of modernist primitivism. Like Conrad, O'Neill finds the same heart of darkness, the same atavistic pulse, beating both in the jungle and in the innermost bowels of the city.

These two early plays seem dated now, and the racial characterisation offered in *The Emperor Jones* appears both hackneyed and offensive to a modern audience. But in *All God's Chillun Got Wings* (1924), O'Neill produced a very different take on race – one which, like the novels of 'passing', focuses on the issue of how far we are free to choose our 'identity', or how far this identity is thrust upon us. It does this by combining the issue of racial identity with two other themes that run through O'Neill's plays of the 1920s – the Strindbergian one of marriage as a self-destructive struggle, and the use of masks both as a feature of production and as a metaphor for the human condition.

In 'Memoranda on Masks', an essay published in 1932, O'Neill set out to formulate his views on the use of masks in the theatre:

> *Dogma for the new masked drama.* One's outer life passes in a solitude haunted by the masks of others; one's inner life passes in a solitude hounded by the masks of oneself.

Far from hiding a true identity, masks, according to O'Neill, provide 'a fresh insight into the inner forces motivating the actions and reactions of men and women'. Identity is to be found in the loss of identity, the mask. The truth about human beings lies in 'the masks that govern them and constitute their fates'. Thus, in going on to review how he would now use masks more extensively and to more profound effect than he had in the original productions of his plays of the 1920s, he writes:

> In *The Great God Brown* I would now make the masks symbolise more definitely the abstract theme of the play instead of, as in the old production, stressing the more superficial meaning that people wear masks before other people and are mistaken by them for their masks.

The Emperor Jones and *The Hairy Ape* could be said to use the idea of the mask according to this 'more superficial meaning', with the mask of civilisation torn off to reveal the primitive truth within.

All God's Chillun Got Wings, by contrast, treats the mask as a means not of concealment but of tragic revelation. The racial theme is combined with a portrayal of marriage as an abyss in which two personalities, two identities, are locked in an unending embrace and struggle of mutual definition and self-destruction. But this abyss of marriage is also a celebration, an acting out, of life's tragic commitment, and thus something about which one can be darkly exultant. Like the masks of race, the roles played out in marriage may be false and destructive, but in the commitment to them there is a transcending truth. In *Welded*, the Strindbergian play written the year before *All God's Chillun Got Wings*, O'Neill makes a passing connection between the two themes, writing in a stage direction that the couple 'act for the moment like two persons of different races, deeply in love, but separated by a barrier of language'. In *All God's Chillun Got Wings* that connection is made the heart of the drama, with the characters caught in the mutual self-definition of black and white, man and woman.

Jim Harris and Ella Downey are, respectively, black and white, growing up in a New York district where white and coloured communities sit side by side. The gulf between the juxtaposed groups is represented in a stark, stylised form:

> In *All God's Chillun Got Wings*, all save the seven leading characters should be masked; for all the secondary figures are part and parcel of the Expressionistic background of the play, a world at first indifferent, then cruelly hostile, against which the tragedy of Jim Harris is outlined.

Blacks and whites sing different songs, move with a different body language. 'The Negroes', O'Neill writes in the stage directions, are 'frankly participants in the spirit of Spring', while 'the whites [laugh] constrainedly, awkward in natural emotion ... it expresses the difference in race.' In successive scenes we are shown Jim and Ella as children, teenagers and young adults. As children they are sweethearts, the bond between them mediated innocently by the playground language of racial taunt. As teenagers, however, they grow apart. Ella falls in with 'my own kind' and spurns him. Jim struggles to remove himself from his background, but – as in this exchange with his black friend Joe – reality keeps pulling him back:

> *Joe*: ... What's all dis dressin' up and graduatin' an' sayin' you gwine study be a lawyer? ... What's all dis denyin' you's a nigger ... is you a nigger or isn't you? (*Shaking him.*) Is you a nigger, Nigger? Nigger, is you a nigger?
> *Jim*: (*Looking into his eyes – quietly.*) Yes. I'm a nigger. We're both niggers.

In the third scene Ella appears as an ex-prostitute. Her illegitimate child has died, and now Jim is her only friend in the world, her protector. Jim, for his part, continues to struggle at and fail in his law exams. Faced with a sea of white faces in the exam room, his nerve always gives way. They resolve to get married, Jim expressing his love in a frenzy of devotion:

> *Jim*: ... I don't ask you to love me ... I don't want nothing – only to wait ... – to give my life and my blood and all my strength that's in me to give you peace and joy – to become your slave! – yes, be your slave – your black slave that adores you as sacred!
> *He has sunk to his knees. In a frenzy of self-abnegation, as he says the last words, he beats his head on the flagstones.*

At least one commentator has highlighted this passage as being embarrassing and offensive, illustrative of the fact that the play as a whole is 'both dated and retrograde' rather than 'progressive'. But this is to treat *All God's Chillun Got Wings* merely as a 'problem' play on a social issue, rather than as an exploration of the way that the masks we wear (of which the masks of racial stereotype, such as that of the self-abnegating 'slave', are a kind of archetype) can act as the means by which we identify and become involved with the other. This expressive and symbolic aspect of race is underlined visually by the use of masks and, in the last scene of Act 1, by the way in which, at Jim and Ella's wedding, the communities 'form into two racial lines on each side of the gate, rigid and unyielding, staring across at each other with bitter hostile eyes'.

Act 1 of *All God's Chillun Got Wings* is a sociological prelude to the true drama of the play. Contemporary reviewers tended to see the play as straightforwardly a commentary on the 'race question', and had it been such a simple commentary the story of Jim and Ella might have followed a Romeo-and-Juliet scenario: love thwarted by the racial divide. For the first of its two acts that is the direction in which the play seems to be going. But in the second act, the racial stand-off – which is portrayed in the first act through externals, by the stand-off between the two communities – becomes internal and psychological. The masks worn for others are replaced by the masks one presents to oneself. O'Neill emphasises this movement of withdrawal to an interior, this sense of a journey into psychological claustrophobia, by directing that in the successive scenes of the act the walls and ceiling of the set should close in, so that the individual characters – and the African mask that plays an important symbolic role in the act – loom increasingly and grotesquely large.

Two years have passed since Jim and Ella's wedding, two years in which they have played out their dream of living in France, free from American racial tensions. But Ella has grown increasingly withdrawn and mentally disturbed. They have returned to New York and Jim plans to devote himself to passing his law exams and becoming a member of the bar. This issue of whether Jim will 'pass' is the central one around which the complex elements of their relationship whirl. And the double meaning of 'pass' is deliberate. The law exams have come to represent the threshold between black and white worlds. Ella tells Jim 'with tenderness and love':

> I want you to pass ... I want you to show 'em – all the dirty, sneaking, gossiping liars that talk behind our backs – what a man I married. I want the whole world to know you're the whitest of the white!

She says she wants Jim to pass, to become white. But she is lying, because really she wants Jim to fail, to remain the black man she both loves and despises, the black man who will remain her self-abnegating slave, looking after her and nurturing her most basic weaknesses. She does everything she can to disappoint her husband's most cherished ambition, to make him fail the exams, and when in the final scene he learns that he has indeed failed, she is exultant. And at this moment, Jim's language and humour appear at their 'blackest', an outpouring of biblical rhetoric that recalls some black storefront preacher:

> Jim: (*looking at her wildly*). Pass? Pass? (*He begins to chuckle and laugh between sentences and phrases, rich, Negro laughter, but heartbreaking in its mocking grief.*) Good Lord, child, how come you can ever imagine such a crazy idea? ... It'd be miraculous, there'd be earthquakes and catastrophes, the Seven

Plagues'd come again and locusts'd devour all the money in the banks, the second Flood'd come roaring and Noah'd fall overboard, the sun'd drop out of the sky like a ripe fig, and the Devil'd perform miracles, and God'd be tipped head first right out of the Judgment Seat! (*He laughs, maudlinly uproarious.*)

Ella takes down the African mask and stabs it in triumph. 'It's dead. The devil's dead ... If you'd passed it would have lived in you.' For Ella, the African mask represents the frightening possibility of a blackness liberated, a blackness released from its prison of subservience and stereotype. For a second, as Ella stabs the mask, Jim glimpses her destructiveness ('You devil! You white devil woman!') but then he slumps, literally, back into his old role. They are both automata, the wearers of masks hardly even of their own making:

> *Ella*: (*after a pause – like a child*). Will God forgive me, Jim?
> *Jim*: Maybe He can forgive what you've done to me; and maybe He can forgive what I've done to you; but I don't see how He's going to forgive – Himself.

And at the end, they revert to the world of children that was shown in the very first scene of the play, a world of childish atavism that dwells on racial difference. ('I'll put shoe blacking on my face and pretend I'm black, and you can put chalk on your face and pretend you're white, just as we used to.') Jim throws himself on his knees in a fit of religious exultation and, in the last line of the play, vows to play the game with her to the bitter end: 'Honey, Honey, I'll play right up to the gates of heaven with you!'

It is a horrifying picture of a mutually destructive marriage, of a love that feeds voraciously on the weakness of the Other. And yet it is still love and to be exalted as such – a point that goes to the heart of O'Neill's tragic view of life. The point is brought out earlier in the act, in the exchange between Jim and his sister Hattie. Hattie is a minor character in the drama, yet a remarkably forward-looking one. A strong, independent-minded young black woman ('with a high-strung, defiant face – an intelligent head showing both power and courage'), she is almost like a character out of a play from the late Fifties or Sixties. The lines with which she describes the African mask, her wedding present to her brother, could come from Lorraine Hansberry:

It's a mask which used to be worn in religious ceremonies by my people in Africa. But aside from that, it's beautifully made, a work of Art by a real artist – as real in his way as your Michael Angelo.

It is Hattie who sees Ella's true hatred for Jim as a black man and attempts to warn him against it, urging him to send her to an asylum. Jim's reply is that a tragic and destructive love is still love – indeed, perhaps a greater love for being tragic and destructive:

Let her call me nigger! Let her call me the whitest of the white! I'm all she's got in the world, ain't I? She's all I've got! You with your fool talk of the black race and the white race! Where does the human race get a chance to come in? I suppose that's simple for you. You lock it up in asylums and throw away the key.

It is in this sense that the love between Ella and Jim is both founded on race and at the same time transcends it. There is a tragic truth in the mask.

The literature of marginal racial identity, of 'passing', is a literature of imposed identities, of the masks that society forces one to wear. Composing the masks are those images, ideas and associations of blackness that reach back to premodern times and that were elaborated and systematised during the centuries of slavery. Slavery was abolished, but the masks remained. Indeed, the abolition of slavery gave the masks new importance, and in the twentieth century the 'battle of the color-line' that Du Bois predicted in the *The Souls of Black Folk* has been fought out not just on the streets of Montgomery and Detroit, but at the level of representation, of culture. All this began with the Harlem Renaissance, when a newly urbanised black American population became aware in a new way of its collective significance, its cultural gift. Artists of the Renaissance celebrated blackness, but they also asked what is left of the individual when his or her identity is defined (whether positively or negatively) in terms of such masks. Herein lies the significance of the literature of passing.

The literature of passing is a literature of existential choice: the hero or heroine has the choice of which mask to don, of whether to 'be' black or white. Either choice is unsatisfactory, though. Even in Jessie Fauset's *Plum Bun* and Nella Larsen's first novel, *Quicksand*, when the heroine does the 'right' thing and returns from the white world, there is an element of regret despite (and enhancing) the moral rewards reaped. The case of Jim in *All God's Chillun Got Wings* is quite different. There is no chance, of course, that Jim could literally pass and become white. But he could 'pass' his law exams and, above all, he could leave Ella, whose love for him is horribly bound up with thinking of him as a 'nigger'. He chooses not to leave Ella, to accept all that means in terms of remaining a 'nigger', and he does this, at the end, without regret or anticipation of reward. Faced with an existential choice, he hurls himself into the choice without reserve and not just accepting, but embracing, the suffering that it will bring.

There is one point, a crucial one, that O'Neill makes very carefully: the bond between Jim and Ella is not a sexual one. At the beginning of Act 2, Jim tells Hattie that he and Ella lived for the first year of their marriage 'like friends – like a brother and sister'. Jim sacrifices his own identity in his love for Ella – but not by dissolving in an ocean of sexual passion, which is the nineteenth-century romantic way. The union of Jim and Ella is one of shared suffering, and it is this tragic outlook, reflecting O'Neill's interest in Greek drama, that marks him out from the other writers on the 'colour question' in the first couple of decades of this century. Chesnutt, Larsen and Fauset recognise the subversion of self embodied in racial labelling and mirror this in their use of generic forms where characters are liable to be puppets, to wear masks. But none of these writers go far enough. At the end they conceive a closure, an end of suffering – either through death or through the heroine 'finding herself', discovering a true identity. In *All God's Chillun Got Wings* by contrast, the loss of identity has no end ('right up to the gates of heaven'), and is embraced, celebrated as an expression of tragic love achieved through suffering. Jim embraces his 'niggerhood', accepting with joy and laughter his darkest destiny. It was a theme, a tragic twist on old conceptions of racial identity, that has been taken up by other writers – both black and white – on the 'black' condition.

Sources

Sources

Ayers, Edward L., *Southern Crossing: A History of the American South 1877–1906* (Oxford University Press, 1995).
Berry, Mary Francis, and John W. Blassingame, *Long Memory: The Black Experience in America* (Oxford University Press, 1982).
Chesnutt, Charles W., *The House Behind the Cedars* (The X Press, London, 1995). First published 1900.
Davis, Thadious M., *Nella Larsen, Novelist of the Harlem Renaissance: A Woman's Life Unveiled* (Louisiana State University Press, Baton Rouge, 1994).
Douglass, Frederick, *Narrative of the Life of Frederick Douglass, An American Slave*, edited with an Introduction by Houston A. Baker, Jr (Penguin, New York, 1982).
Du Bois, W. E. B., *The Souls of Black Folk: Essays and Sketches* (Archibald Constable, London, 1905). First published 1903.
— *Black Reconstruction in America* (Harcourt Brace & Co., New York, 1935).
Fauset, Jessie Redmon, *Plum Bun: A Novel Without a Moral* (Pandora Press, London, 1985). First published 1929.
Gayle, Addison, *The Way of the New World: The Black Novel in America* (Doubleday, New York, 1976).
Gilroy, Paul, *The Black Atlantic: Modernity and Double Consciousness* (Verso, London, 1993).
Huggins, Nathan, *The Harlem Renaissance: The Growth of American Negro Culture in the 1920s* (Oxford University Press, New York, 1971).
Johnson, James Weldon, *The Autobiography of an Ex-Colored Man* (Penguin, New York, 1990). First published 1912.
Larsen, Nella, *Quicksand and Passing* (Serpent's Tail, London, 1989). First published 1928 and 1929.
Larson, Charles R., *Invisible Darkness: Jean Toomer and Nella Larsen* (University of Iowa Press, Iowa City, 1993).
O'Neill, Eugene, *The Emperor Jones*, in *Plays: First Series* (Jonathan Cape, London, 1922).
— *'Memoranda and Masks' in Eugene O'Neill and his plays. A survey of his life*

and works, edited by O. Cargill, N. B. Fagin and W. J. Fisher (Peter Owen, London, 1962). First published 1932.

— *The Hairy Ape* and *All God's Chillun Got Wings* (Nick Hern, London, 1993). First published 1923 and 1924.

Thurman, Wallace, *The Blacker the Berry* (The X Press, London, 1994). First published 1929.

Toomer, Jean, *Cane* (Liveright, New York, 1975). First published 1923.

Twain, Mark, *Tom Sawyer and Huckleberry Finn* (J. M. Dent, London, 1943). First published 1876 and 1884.

— *Pudd'nhead Wilson and other tales* (Oxford University Press, 1992). First published 1894.

Vincent, Theodore G. (ed.), *Voices of a Black Nation: Political Journalism in the Harlem Renaissance* (Ramparts Press, San Francisco, 1973).

White, Walter, *A Man Called White* (Gollancz, London, 1949).

Woodward, C. Vann, *The Strange Career of Jim Crow* (Oxford University Press, New York, 1955).

6

The Black Hero

The reputation of the Harlem Renaissance has waned and waxed within the African-American community. By the mid-1930s many of its leading members had either died or were no longer publishing significant works. And given the impact that the Harlem writers had at the time, one is struck by how little influence they had on the next generation of African-American writers. The concerns of Richard Wright, Ralph Ellison and James Baldwin were quite different, and for them the Harlem generation hardly seem to have figured as precursors. Black critics worried about what seemed like stereotypical images projected by some Harlem writers, and about the links between the Harlem Renaissance and white patronage. Blackness, these critics felt, should be more a matter of politics and protest than of romantic, sepia-tinted exoticism. The Harlem Renaissance is scarcely mentioned in Baldwin's incendiary essays, despite the fact that one of its most prominent poets, Countee Cullen, taught him in high school. One of the most influential books of the Sixties, black nationalist Harold Cruse's *The Crisis of the Negro Intellectual*, includes a damning indictment of the Harlem generation for their alleged pandering to white patronage and general Uncle Tomism.

But in the post-Civil Rights era, another reaction has taken place. With the ever-increasing role that the media plays in people's lives, racial politics has moved to the field of culture. The issue of how people of colour should be represented – and who should represent them – has become recognised as political. And cultural power means first of all reclaiming and celebrating one's own 'roots', to quote the title of one of the biggest best-sellers of the 1970s and perhaps the most popular book ever by a black American. Since the 1970s a number of powerful historical novels about the black community have been published, including works by Toni Morrison, Alice Walker and David Bradley. In this context, the Harlem Renaissance is both something to celebrate in itself, for its cultural wealth, and a precursor for the idea of a cultural rebirth of black people. When Alain Locke published his famous *New Negro* anthology in 1925, the spiritual and artistic renewal of the American Negro was portrayed in terms of a 'Renaissance' that invited a provocative comparison with the Renaissance of the fifteenth and sixteenth centuries in Europe. Just as Europe had rediscovered its Roman and Hellenic roots, had rescued them from the intervening Dark Ages, so the Afro-Americans would redeem their African heritage from the dark ages of slavery. In the 1970s, in the wake of the political upheavals of the 1960s, there was a renewed concern with capturing the essence of blackness as a historical continuity reaching back to an African origin. 'Afrocentricity' is the extreme contemporary form of this impulse, and its language often echoes that of Marcus Garvey and other black nationalists of the early part of this century.

At the same time, this historical interest in the Harlem Renaissance has also led to an awareness of its specificity, to the way that it was a part of the complex cultural politics and economics of America in the Twenties. Ann Douglas's *Terrible Honesty*, for example, shows how the Harlem Renaissance was an integral component of a broad American modernism that flowered in the years after the First World War. The centre of American publishing moved from Boston, capital of New England, to the melting-pot of New York. Many of the new publishing houses were founded by non-Anglo-Saxon immigrants. And it was these houses – Knopf in particular – that published the writers of the Harlem Renaissance. The thread running through this modernism that found itself so at home in New York was pluralism, an openness to the diversity that America had to offer. American artists were seeking an alternative to the materialist corruption of America's Gilded Age, but they sought it not in imitations of

Europe, but right at home in the diversity of American life itself. It was this native pluralism that led Zora Neale Hurston, Sherwood Anderson, Waldo Frank, Jean Toomer and DuBose Heyward to find inspiration in the folk culture of the Deep South.

So there was a distinctively American modernism, and the Harlem Renaissance was a vital component of it. But black Americans also entered European consciousness, primarily through music. The nascent recording industry and a proliferation of European imitators made jazz the first 'popular music' of the machine age, and simultaneously an international phenomenon. Debussy, Stravinsky, Ravel, Shostakovich, Weill, Britten – all were influenced by jazz. With the exception of old romantics like Richard Strauss and Sibelius, it is difficult to think of an important European composer of the inter-war years who was not. And the stereotypical images associated with jazz fixed the American Negro in the European mind as the very embodiment of modern city life – the hustler, the bootlegger, the king of the urban jungle.

America's participation in the First World War (including the participation of thousands of black troops) gave it a new importance in world politics, and its control over the new media projected images of America around the world. The cultural prominence of Harlem ('Black Manhattan') reinforced an image of the American Negro as being, like New York itself, at the cutting edge of modernity. Black music became synonymous with the times. Already by 1922, Scott Fitzgerald was writing *Tales of the Jazz Age*. It was the time when, in Langston Hughes's phrase, 'the Negro was in vogue'.

The phrase 'urban jungle', which began to be commonly used at about this time, hints at part of the attraction of jazz to artists and writers. For while jazz was the music of the modern city, it also carried traces of its African ancestry, and thereby provided a sudden, ecstatic access, straight from the sidewalks, to that primal authenticity that had for a hundred years and more been central to European myths about Africa. Black writers themselves encouraged the idea. This image of an Africa blossoming in the smoke-filled air of a New York nightclub, from Claude McKay's *Home to*

Harlem (1928), could be paralleled in several other novels of the Harlem Renaissance:

The piano-player had wandered off into some dim, far-away, ancestral source of music. Far, far away from the music-hall syncopation and jazz, he was lost in some sensual dream of his own ... Tum-tum ... tum-tum ... tum-tum ... The notes were naked, acute, alert. Like black youth burning naked in the bush. Love in the deep heart of the jungle ... The sharp spring of a leopard from a leafy limb, the snarl of a jackal, green lizards in amorous play, the flight of a plumed bird, and the sudden laughter of mischievous monkeys in their green homes. Tum-tum ... tum-tum ... tum-tum ... tum-tum ... Simple-clear and quivering. Like a primitive dance of war or of love ... the marshalling of spears or the sacred frenzy of a phallic celebration.

Jazz was quintessentially modern and urban, but – as in Darius Milhaud's 'ballet nègre' *La Création du monde* (1923), to a scenario by Blaise Cendrars, who had himself compiled an anthology of African folklore – it could also speak of the primitive, of the origin of things. The interest in black American culture, and especially music, could thus be assimilated to that European colonial tradition – the tradition that is so strongly represented in Darwinian and post-Darwinian literature – of associating blackness with that which is oldest, most animal-like, most physical, in humanity.

This primitivism was the target of *Paleface* (1929), a polemic by one of the most acerbic surveyors of the cultural scene in the inter-war years (and himself a signed-up modernist), the painter-novel-ist-philosopher Wyndham Lewis. Lewis argued that primitivism was a significant international phenomenon (he took his examples from both Europe and America, from D. H. Lawrence, for example, and from Sherwood Anderson) and also that it had a strong racial dimension. This racialism manifested itself as a neurotic, self-lacerating sentimentalism:

Everywhere to-day the White European (both as a European and also among the great White colonies and nations) is profoundly uneasy, and looks apprehensively behind him at all moments, conscious of a watchful presence at his back, or somewhere concealed in his neighbourhood, which he does not understand. *Dark Laughter* [the title of Sherwood Anderson's 'Southern' novel] of the hidden watching negro servants is a typical concrete expression of this uneasiness: evidently, when masters become obsessed with their servants, they are then only masters in name . . . [W]here the White Man is confronted by the Black, the Red or the Brown, he now feels inside himself a novel sensation of *inferiority*. He has, in short, an 'inferiority complex' where every non-White, or simply alien personality or consciousness, is concerned. Especially is it in his capacity of *civilized* (as opposed to *primitive*, 'savage', 'animal') that he has been taught to feel *inferior*.

With the feeling of inferiority that Lewis identified went fear. Violence, atavism, a spontaneity that could cut both ways – all were components of the European image of the African in its sentimental, Darwinian and imperialist guises. The Negro could be seen as closer to nature not in some comforting eighteenth-century sense, but in a threatening sense of being more in touch with inhuman, mechanical forces. In *Paleface* Lewis quotes a passage from *Dark Laughter* in which Anderson describes some Negro workers:

The bodies of all the men running up and down the landing-stage were one body. One could not be distinguished from another. They were lost in each other. Could the bodies of people be so lost in each other?

They are deprived of their individuality, while the repetition of 'body' has the effect of reducing them to the physical. Anderson's description is intended to be celebratory, but the effect is not that much different from *Heart of Darkness*:

But suddenly, as we struggled round a bend, there would be a glimpse of rush walls, of peaked grass-roofs, a burst of yells, a whirl of black limbs, a mass of hands clapping, of feet stamping, of bodies swaying, of eyes rolling, under the droop of heavy and motionless foliage. The steamer toiled along slowly on the edge of a black and incomprehensible frenzy.

The modernist primitivism of the 1920s often has mechanical associations. The rhythms hammered out by the orchestra in Stravinsky's *Rite of Spring* sound like a machine, as does the drumming that forms the aural backdrop of Eugene O'Neill's *Emperor Jones*. And in *The Hairy Ape*, the Neanderthal-looking ship's stoker – whose life is spent deep in the engine room, almost as a part of the engine – expresses his atavism, his kinship, by climbing into a cage with a gorilla at the end of the play.

The influence that black culture and a certain primitivist view of blackness had on writers between the wars was not confined to Europe and the United States. The Harlem Renaissance was paralleled by developments in the Caribbean and Latin America, such as the Indigenist movement in Haiti and the Afrociollo movement in Brazil. Afro-Cubanism, which flowered between the mid-1920s and 1940 – 'in 1928,' as the folklorist Fernando Ortiz wrote, 'the drums began to beat in Cuban poetry' – was an example both of how primitivism was inflected by particular political circumstances, and of how Africanism could become, for a time at least, an interracial lingua franca. African cultural forms, especially religion, survived in a purer form in Cuba than in many parts of the New World, and these African survivals had an importance in Cuban culture disproportionate to the size of Cuba's black population. They seemed to provide a way of defining a distinct Cuban national identity as against the claims of Europe and of the rest of the Americas. As Ortiz wrote:

Up to that time Cuban culture was Spanish in flavour, and not Cubano; it was Latin American in taste, and not Afro-Cuban; it was European in outlook, and not American: in short, it lacked a specifically Cuban soul.

Of the leading figures of Afro-Cubanism, only one, Nicolas Guillen, was black himself. And Guillen was to turn his back on *negrismo* in the 1930s, criticising it for failing to recognise that in the black world 'all is not drum, macumba, rumba and voudou'. His own poetry became more concerned with economic and social realities.

Sexuality was often at the heart of the process whereby blackness seemed to generate a modern, anti-Victorian culture. In the 1900s, black dances such as the foxtrot and the charleston began to take over from the waltz in respectable upper-middle-class American society. The seeming lack of restraint and the sexual expressiveness of these dances alarmed critics, just as they had alarmed critics of the waltz a hundred years earlier. The same issue of respectability was prominent in discussions of literature by blacks or on black themes. The case of Carl Van Vechten illustrates how the debate between respectability and sexuality was not just one between black and white, but one held within the black community too. The novelist and critic Carl Van Vechten was a well-known figure in New York literary circles in the Twenties. He had a genuine interest in black folk culture, took handsome, much-reproduced photographs of leading figures in the Harlem Renaissance, and was a personal friend and supporter of many of them. He was also addicted to the bohemian night-life of Harlem's clubs and cabarets, a world which he attempted to evoke in his novel *Nigger Heaven* (1926).

Nigger Heaven provoked heated debate at the time of its publication because of its sexual suggestiveness. Du Bois, the incarnation (but for his feminism) of Victorian values within the black intellectual community, described the book as 'an affront to the hospitality of black folk and the intelligence of white', while several Harlem newspapers refused to advertise it. The younger black writers, on the other hand, sprang to Van Vechten's defence. For them the issue was one of artistic and sexual freedom, of presenting black popular culture as it was rather than how reformers would like it to be. Like the heroine of Nella Larsen's *Quicksand*, they wanted to break free from restricting bourgeois notions of racial uplift.

In Van Vechten's *Nigger Heaven*, and even more in Ronald Firbank's 'flapper' novel *Prancing Nigger* (1924), the black is made the totem for a camp aestheticism whose main aim is to affront respectable sensibilities. Negroes have become kings and queens of bohemia, figureheads of a late-flowering *fin de siècle* decadence, exotic blooms growing up amidst the ruins of nineteenth-century moral certainties. In Europe, too, black culture was used as a stick with which to beat conventional opinion – especially conventional opinion on sexual matters. Ernst Kirchner and other members of the Brücke school of painters expressed, in their canvases and their famous decorated studios, a generalised and eclectic primitivism that emphasised and celebrated the erotic. Kirchner's *Negro Couple* (1911) portrays his models in terms of their sexual potency – the man has an exaggeratedly long penis, the woman large buttocks and breasts – and places them against a backdrop (a hotch-potch of primitivist references, from an oriental rug to one of Kirchner's own murals) that emphasises the artificiality of the scene. 'Primitivism' is no longer the return to or recovery of any actually existing society, but a phenomenon that belongs entirely within and with reference to modernised urban society, a lifestyle that embodies certain reactions to conventional values.

This artificial quality of primitivism is the focus of Griselda Pollock's book on Gauguin – in which she shows how, for example, *Manao Tupapau* (1892), his famous picture of a Tahitian girl reclining on a bed, is locked in a complex dialogue with Manet's *Olympia*, painted some thirty years earlier. Gauguin clearly refers to the Manet (of which he made a copy before painting *Manao Tupapau*), and the projection of sexual availability on to the woman is the main theme of both pictures. But Gauguin also establishes a difference between himself and Manet, and the colour of the girl – with the shock that it brings to 'conventional' sensibilities – is a crucial part of the difference. Griselda Pollock shows how this dual strategy of establishing simultaneously a relation to and a self-conscious difference from the dominant canon was the basis for the formation of an avant-garde.

Negro art, by virtue of its 'primitivism', was in danger of becoming merely a style – a style of art, a lifestyle. The extent to which black artists should allow themselves to become appropriated by white tastes was debated at the time. When Claude McKay published *Home to Harlem* (1928), his colourful portrait of Harlem bohemian life, Du Bois was forthright in his condemnation, and linked its licentiousness directly to white influence:

> McKay has set out to cater for that prurient demand on the part of white folk for a portrayal in Negroes of that utter licentiousness which conventional civilization holds white folk from enjoying – if enjoyment it can be called . . . He has used every art and emphasis to paint drunkenness, fighting, lascivious sexual promiscuity and utter absence of restraint in as bold and as bright colors as he can.

Marcus Garvey and Du Bois didn't agree about much during the 1920s, but they did agree about McKay's best-selling novels. Garvey characteristically went further, accusing McKay of belonging to a group of 'literary prostitutes' who were working under the direction of white publishers to denigrate their own race.

White patronage did play an important part in the Harlem Renaissance, but Garvey's description of it as a form of literary prostitution didn't do justice to the ideological and personal complexities of the human relationships involved. Charlotte van der Veer Quick Mason, the wealthy widow of a prominent physician and psychologist, acted as patron to Alain Locke, Zora Neale Hurston and Langston Hughes. (They called her 'Godmother', while they, for her, became her 'Godchildren'.) With Alain Locke she conceived of the project of a museum of African art in New York, dreaming of

> little Negro children running in and out learning to respect themselves through the realization of those treasures. And . . . as the fire burned in me, I had the mystical vision of a great bridge reaching from Harlem to the heart of Africa, across which the Negro world, that our white United States had done everything to annihilate, should see the flaming pathway . . . and recover the

treasure their people had had in the beginning of African life on the earth.

Charlotte Mason's motivation was a passionate adherence to primitivism, to a belief that primitive peoples had access to an energy and intuition that had been lost to the overcivilised. She thought she could see in the young black writers she gathered around her the primitives she was looking for. 'You are a golden star', she wrote to Langston Hughes, 'in the Firmament of Primitive Peoples.'

'You may feel, Langston', she tells him another time, 'that I am pressing you forward very hard, but it is because I believe you have enough truth to dare to follow the urge in this late hour of the salvation of your people.' This was an extraordinary emotional investment to make in Hughes, a terrible pressure of expectation backed up by the very real financial indebtedness that Mason did not hesitate to point out to him when the going got rough between them. The correspondence between them during the final crisis, when Hughes inevitably failed to meet her demands, bears witness to a sad drama between an emotionally unstable and manipulative woman, driven by a peculiar obsession, and a young man who had got in way out of his depth. Hughes's self-flagellation, his blindness to the realisation that the failings may not all have been his, knows no bounds:

> I love you, Godmother. I need you. You can help me more than anyone on earth. Forgive me for the things I do not know, the things I cannot fight alone, the things I haven't understood. You know better than anyone else how stupid and unwise I am, how I must battle the darkness within my self. No one else would help me. No one else would care as you care. No one else would even try to understand. The door is never closed between us, Godmother. Only the ugly shadow of my self stands in the way now.

Hughes reassures Charlotte Mason that he will 'battle the darkness within my self', but one senses that the real issue is in fact the freedom for that darkness of his self to express itself. Hughes wanted to be himself.

For many African-American writers, artists and musicians, white patronage was unavoidable. This was particularly true for those working in the music industry, where recording and broadcasting were wholly in white hands. To take a famous example, the commercial context in which Duke Ellington launched his career was that of the Harlem nightclub, of which white patronage and the lure of exoticism were integral parts. Between 1927 and 1932, the Ellington band had a residency at perhaps the most famous nightclub in the world, the Cotton Club, the radio broadcasts from there by CBS and NBC making him a household name across the States. The club seated between seven and eight hundred, and the audience was entirely white apart from a few black celebrities and relatives of performers. The bandleader Cab Calloway described the club in his autobiography:

It was a huge room. The bandstand was a replica of a southern mansion, with large white columns and a backdrop painted with weeping willows and slave quarters. The band played on the veranda of the mansion, and in front of the veranda, down a few steps, was the dance floor, which was also used for the shows. The waiters were dressed in red tuxedos, like butlers in a southern mansion, and the tables were covered in red-and-white-checked gingham tablecloths ... the whole set was like the sleepy-time-down-South during slavery.[1]

Ellington's numbers, with titles like 'Arabian Lover', 'Harlem River Quiver' and 'Jungle Nights in Harlem', fostered this atmosphere of exoticism. There was a tradition of this in the stage presentation of African-Americans. Black-face performers of the nineteenth century (whether the performers themselves were black or white) were often known as 'Ethiopian delineators', and the term 'Ethiopian' was commonly applied to their material. This

[1] Quoted in Steven Lasker's liner notes to the album *Duke Ellington and his Cotton Club Orchestra: Jungle Nights in Harlem (1927–32)*, a fascinating compilation of material that Ellington performed at the club.

itself was a form of masking that, in fantasy, made things which were in reality familiar and intimate seem remote and exotic. If there were hints of the minstrel show in the Cotton Club set-up, Ellington's music transcended it – partly through its artistic originality, and partly through an ironic awareness of its own 'masking'. Professor Howard 'Stretch' Johnson, a dancer with the Cotton Club Boys in 1932, emphasised this aspect in recalling performances at the club:

> We didn't know at the time that the splendid sound of the Ellington organization was not jungle music but a creative form of irony which masked the commercial pandering to an upper-class white audience thrilled at the opportunity to hear and witness what it thought was genuine black exotica.

There were two ways in which black writers and artists overcame the stereotypes of a modish primitivism. There was realism. Hughes's own poetry and fiction were grounded in the details of poor black life. Novels by Nella Larsen, Jessie Redmon Fauset and Wallace Thurman picked apart the black bourgeoisie. Among the plays of the period, Ralf M. Coleman's *The Girl from Back Home* and Andrew M. Burris's *You Mus' Be Bo'n Ag'in* dealt directly and intimately with social issues such as the conflict of urban and rural values, and the authoritarianism of the church. Realism of this sort turned its back on white stereotypes and bent its attention to matters of immediate concern within the black community. But the second way of beating the white stereotype was by the 'creative form of irony' that Howard Johnson saw at work in the Duke Ellington band, a parodic self-reflection that enabled the music to transcend the imposed stereotype. It was a strategy that plugged straight into the strong tradition of 'masking' through parody in black American culture.

The use of parody in black culture is inseparable from the complex interaction, the hybridity, of white and black American cultures. Among historians of music, for example, a politically charged debate has been pursued on how far the distinctive characteristics of spirituals and the blues should be attributed to

African inheritances, and how far to adaptations of European influences. It is a difficult question to answer, because even where a connection of similarity is established between European-originated and African-American forms, there remains the issue of which influenced which – or indeed, whether there was some complex syncretic process at work, assisted perhaps by original parallels between African and European music. In addition, the nature of the relationship may have changed over time. The first white observers of slaves' music-making were certainly struck by its difference from white music and by the impossibility of capturing its peculiar characteristics in European notation. These differences were attributed to innate racial differences or African survivals. By the end of the nineteenth century, this initial reaction was being challenged by more scholarly students of folk song, who pointed out the similarities in terms of words, tunes and musical structures between the spirituals and white evangelical music. The ethnocentric assumptions of the time led them to assume that these similarities indicated an influence of white on black, cultural evolution carrying artistic expression upwards from the 'primitive' forms of savages to the more complex ones of the European. Then, with studies such as Du Bois's *Souls of Black Folk* and Melville Herskovits's *The Myth of the Negro Past*, the pendulum swung the other way and the 'African' element in spirituals was emphasised. More recently, historians have produced evidence of a complex cross-fertilisation, and also pointed out pre-existing shared characteristics (the diatonic scale) and parallels (between African 'call and response' and the 'lining-out' of Protestant hymnody, for example) that made such cross-fertilisation possible.[1]

Even more than slave spirituals, the blues have become iconic as representing a pure black authenticity. They were, so the story goes, the embryo of later black musics, the basic stalk from which later forms – jazz, rhythm and blues, rock and roll, even soul, funk and rap – branched off. There is in this popularly accepted picture of black music a strange repetition of nineteenth-century cultural

[1] For this historiography, see Lawrence W. Levine, *Black Culture and Black Consciousness: Afro-American Thought from Slavery to Freedom* (OUP, New York, 1977), pp. 19–30.

evolutionism: simple, primitive, rural forms were the direct antecedents of more complex, sophisticated, urban forms. During the folk and blues revival of the 1960s – overwhelmingly a middle-class white phenomenon – old blues musicians were discovered and put on festival stages with the same reverence as that with which a palaeontologist might unearth and examine the fossilised rudiment of living forms.

Recently, nearly all these assumptions have been challenged. Francis Davis's *The History of the Blues* (1995), in particular, questions the popular image of the early bluesman as raw, 'authentic' and amateur, a guitar-carrying sharecropper plucked from the fields and led into the studio to record the immemorial folk music of his people with barely time to wipe the dust from his overalls. Most bluesmen of the 1920s, Davis points out, described themselves as 'songsters', professional entertainers whose repertoire – which they largely shared with white songsters of the period – included not just blues but folk ballads, hymns, ragtime numbers, minstrel and 'coon' songs, dance numbers called 'reels' and popular tunes of the day. With the electrification of large areas of the Mississippi Delta and the spread of the phonograph from the 1920s, no hard-and-fast distinction can be drawn between 'rural' and 'urban' blues. And, as other commentators have noted, there are parallels between the basic verse structure of the blues and that of Irish and Scottish folk-song forms prevalent in the South. Davis's book may have swung the pendulum too far from the received view, but it is at least a necessary corrective to the sentimental view of the blues as a 'pure' and uncomplicated point of origin.

These historical debates need only affect one's view of the 'blackness' or otherwise of spirituals and the blues if one clings to the idea that it is origins that determine the significance of a cultural phenomenon. But one need not cling to that idea. As Lawrence Levine points out: 'It is not necessary for a people to originate or invent all or even most of the elements of their culture. It is necessary only that these components become their own, embedded in their traditions, expressive of their world view and life style.' Cultural forms can function like masks, borrowed and donned for their particular expressive possibilities. And in being borrowed and used in a different context, they change in character.

The history of American music provides many examples of such interactions between white and black. In the Fifties, white rock and roll commercialised black rhythm and blues, while the mid-Forties' bebop revolution in jazz provides an example of a different kind of interchange. Bebop was undoubtedly a black phenomenon, a self-conscious reaction against the sterilities of a swing idiom increasingly dominated by white big bands and by a formulaic use of standard 'riffs'. A group of younger black musicians, led by such figures as Dizzy Gillespie, Charlie Parker, Thelonius Monk and Kenny Clarke, enriched the music with polyrhythmic complexity, angular lines, extensions of conventional chord patterns, and, more generally, with a trenchant and self-assertive attitude towards their music-making. At the same time, all this was built, in terms of form, on an adherence not just to the twelve-bar blues structure, but also, and most prominently, to the thirty-two-bar song form enshrined in the classic numbers of white songwriters like George Gershwin, Cole Porter and Jerome Kern. Beneath some of Charlie Parker's most mould-breaking and daringly fantastical flights is the chord sequence for 'I Got Rhythm'.

Jazz is above all a music of style. Notoriously, just about any material can be 'jazzed up'. What struck Europeans who heard James Reese Europe's band in the 1910s was not the material that the band performed, which included light classics and marches, but the style. 'Jazz' was a verb rather than a noun, an approach rather than a canon. The closer one looks at the origins of jazz, the more miraculous becomes the process whereby such a characteristic and original musical style was crystallised from such a heterogeneous variety of sources. In his famous Library of Congress Recordings, Jelly Roll Morton recounts how he would visit the opera house in New Orleans, and demonstrates his ragtime versions of themes from Verdi. Sidney Bechet, another New Orleans musician, also had a lifelong love of Italian opera. That operatic influence can be heard in the soaring, impassioned *cantabile* of his soprano saxophone and clarinet playing, particularly on the famous ballad recordings such as 'Blue Horizon' and 'Summertime'. One friend recalled visiting him in his Harlem apartment in September 1940. Bechet stood in the middle of a bare room and gave what the friend, Bill Russell, described as 'probably the greatest performance I ever heard Sidney give', an unaccompanied version of the aria 'Vesti la giubba' from *I Pagliacci*. Russell added that it 'was done in the same grand manner which Caruso sang it'. The poet Philip Larkin, in his role as jazz critic, has described Bechet's performance on 'Blue Horizon' as 'soaring like [Dame Nellie] Melba in an extraordinary blend of lyricism and power'.

The hybridity of black and white American cultures was not a comfortable coexistence, as can be seen in the case of minstrel shows, the most popular form of theatre in nineteenth-century America. The vast majority of minstrels were white, but their source material was black. A well-known quotation from *Knicker-bocker Magazine* (1845) sums up the nature of the relationship between black and white embodied in minstrelsy:

> Let one of them [Negroes], in the swamps of Carolina, compose a new song, and it no sooner reaches the ear of a white amateur, than it is written down, amended (that is, almost spoilt), printed, and then put upon a course of rapid dissemination, to cease only with the utmost bounds of Anglo-Saxondom, perhaps with the world. Meanwhile, the poor author digs away with his hoe, utterly ignorant of his greatness.

Whites appropriated black artistic material. Not only that, but they watered down its emotional content and put the songs into the context of an openly insulting farce, with the white performers aping and exaggerating the supposed speech and mannerisms of blacks. Minstrel shows sustained white prejudice. The new segregation laws introduced in the South in the 1890s were popularly named after the minstrel show's stock plantation slave character: Jim Crow.[1]

[1] In 1958 'The Black and White Minstrel Show' was launched on British television. At the peak of its popularity, in the 1960s, it attracted an audience of 20 million. It was axed by the BBC in 1978, but in recent years there has been an attempt to bring back a stage version. See Giles Smith, 'Don't that old minstrel

But there were black minstrels too. William Henry Lane, stage name 'Master Juba', toured England with a white company in 1849 and was described by Charles Dickens in his *American Notes* (1842) as 'the greatest dancer known'. He has been credited with having pioneered black stage dance, especially the tap dance, but his jigs were also heavily influenced by the dances of his Irish neighbours in New York City where he began his career. After the Civil War, professional Negro minstrel companies like the Georgia Minstrels, Pringle Minstrels, McCabe and Young Minstrels were formed and became popular with black audiences. Minstrel songs passed into black hands, and thus, ironically, returned to the folk tradition from which they had come.

Even with black performers the minstrel show was based on masking through parody, so these first Negro minstrels wore traditional 'blackface' over their own real face. And there could be different levels of parody and imitation. One of the most famous dances taken up by the minstrels, the cakewalk, originated in a pastiche by plantation slaves of the manners of the whites in the big house. Negro minstrels performing this dance – heavily influenced by their white professional counterparts – were thus imitating whites who were parodying Negroes parodying whites.

Many of the early recorded singers of blues and jazz had connections with the 'tent show' and minstrel tradition, and there are echoes of the minstrel show in the 'hokum', the vocal and instrumental clowning, that one often hears on jazz recordings of the Twenties and Thirties. But the role of parody in jazz goes beyond its presentation to its very content. The writer who best captured this aspect of jazz – and argued for its wider relevance to black culture – was Ralph Ellison, and it is perhaps no coincidence that Ellison was a musician before he became a writer. An Ellison essay evoking Charlie Parker lights on the way Bird would ironically alter familiar melodic patterns and riffs by putting them in strange new contexts. His quicksilver, laconic wit encapsulated the tendency of jazz to carry on a dialogue with itself, to release and create tension by playing on the listeners' expectations.[1]

magic make you see red?', *Independent*, 28 August 1992.

[1] Jazz is often characterised – usually by those who have had little experience of it

The African-American critic Henry Louis Gates, an admirer of Ralph Ellison, has gone so far as to identify this parodic bent as being almost a defining characteristic of cultural 'blackness'. The folk culture of Africa and the African diaspora, he argues, is suffused with the idea of 'signifying', embodied in the trickster figure of the 'Signifying Monkey'. 'Signifying' is the practice of speaking by indirection, of insulting, needling or cajoling through the use of repetition and parody. It is the wearing of verbal masks. In post-structuralist mode, Gates points to the intertextuality of black literature, to the way that one text in the black literary canon will play riffs on another. His is a blackness constantly manufactured by the free play of signifiers.

Ellison and Gates belong to a tradition of African-American thought that argues that blacks should not define themselves in the white man's terms, in terms of their victimhood (a tendency both of white liberalism and of political correctness). Rather, blacks should celebrate the internal, self-generating qualities of black culture. This was the 'black nationalist' element to Ellison's cultural theory, but his deep suspicion of protest politics led him to steer clear of platforms during the radical Sixties. Whether one agrees with his analysis or not, the pressure he withstood and the accusations of Uncle Tomism that he endured make his stand a principled one.

But even Ellison recognised that in addition to this cultural 'inside' of blackness there was a political 'outside' in the form of white society. 'Blackness', for Ellison, lay somewhere in the dialogue between inside and outside, between tradition and the everyday encounter with white prejudice and persecution. It lay at the point of communication, the hinge, between these two worlds, which might be compared to the 'two souls' described by Du Bois in *The Souls of Black Folk*. So that while the hokum of early jazz may have been in part exuberant, it is also true that black musicians were often 'handed the burnt cork' by white employers and forced

– as a sheer emotional release. In fact the power of jazz lies in its inextricable combination of bodily appeal, felt through rhythmic propulsion, and a highly cerebral wit and irony. Its nakedly affective appeal is in fact considerably less than that of much 'classical' music.

into demeaning roles. Billie Holiday recalled that as late as 1936 the white female dancers who appeared alongside the Count Basie band were fitted out 'with special black masks and mammy dresses'. Holiday herself was ordered to apply 'special dark grease-paint' to her face to make her look blacker.

Ellison's originality lay in his ability to articulate the way in which black culture transformed the dross of these everyday encounters with the white world into the gold of art. He focused in particular on the way that racial stereotypes were stripped of their power by being rehearsed as comic catharsis, as tribal ritual. The ritualised insults of the 'Dozens' and black-to-black use of the word 'nigger' fell into this category. The stereotypes became masks, lacquered with irony. And the repetition of the stereotype as mask became an enactment and demonstration of the superficiality, the skin-deepness, of the stereotype.

It was here that the traditions of black culture – the traditions of cultural pluralism, flexibility, parody – fed into one of the principal concerns of early twentieth-century high culture: the slipperiness of identity. Whether in the ventriloquism of T. S. Eliot's *The Waste Land*, the parodic neo-classicism of Stravinsky or the theatrical alienation of Brecht and Pirandello, the donning of masks and the effects of illusion were all key ideas of high modernism. Ellison saw the aesthetics of the mask as being a characteristic not only of black culture, but also of white writers who had some understanding of America's racial politics. 'Change the Joke and Slip the Yoke' is a brilliant essay on the black trickster tradition, but in it he also notes the way in which, in *Huckleberry Finn*, Mark Twain relates Jim to the minstrel tradition. It is from behind the mask of this stereotype that Jim's dignity and human capacity – and Twain's complexity – emerge. 'Like the stage antics of Louis Armstrong,' Ellison writes, 'Jim's minstrelsy is the essential frame through (rather than despite) which we perceive his humanity.' Similarly, in his essay 'Twentieth-century Fiction and the Black Mask of Humanity' Ellison praises Faulkner, with respect to his treatment of the Negro, for being 'more willing perhaps than any other artist to start with the stereotype, accept it as true, and then seek out the human truth which it hides'.

Where Faulkner's use of the mask is tragic and dramatic, Ellison's is discursive and comic. *Invisible Man* (1952), his celebrated only novel, uses absurdity, exaggeration and parody to explore the symbolism of blackness. When he was asked about the book in a *Paris Review* interview, Ellison remarked that he was concerned with 'the meanings which blackness and light have long had in Western mythology: evil and goodness, ignorance and knowledge, and so on. In my novel, the narrator's development is one through blackness to light; that is, from ignorance to enlightenment: invisibility to visibility. He leaves the South and goes North; this, as you will notice in reading Negro folktales, is always the road to freedom – the movement upward. You have the same thing again when he leaves his underground cave for the open.'

Ellison plays on this nexus of Western mythopoeic images like a jazz musician improvising on an old standard. The 'underground cave' to which he refers in the interview is the basement of a New York apartment block where we find the narrator at the beginning of the novel and which he has rigged up with hundreds of light bulbs to combat his sense of his own invisibility. He is invisible because in the world above people don't see him, they see illusions, stereotypes, 'figments of their imagination'. At the beginning of the book he beats up a white man who calls him an insulting name. Standing over his victim, he achieves a comic catharsis:

> I was both disgusted and ashamed. I was like a drunken man myself, wavering about on weakened legs. Then I was amused. Something in this man's thick head had sprung out and beaten him within an inch of his life. I began to laugh at this strange discovery . . . The next day I saw his picture in the *Daily News*, beneath a caption stating that he had been 'mugged'. Poor fool, poor blind fool, I thought with sincere compassion, mugged by an invisible man!

Ellison's central image of a black man ensconced in a subterranean lair recalls Diderot's 'Eloge de Richardson', where the 'hideous Moor' guards the entrance to the cave of the subconscious, the place of secret and hidden motivation. Like Diderot's Moor, Ellison's narrator wears the ghostly drapery of dreams, reminding us of the role of illusion in the creation of race. 'You wonder', he muses, 'whether you aren't simply a phantom in other people's minds ... a figure in a nightmare.' Ellison may not have been aware of Diderot's essay, but he does draw on the common stock of ideas whereby the black is associated with what is hidden, buried, at the base of the brain. The difference in their treatment of this image, and all its associations, lies in the fact that while Diderot presents it directly and without reflection, Ellison renders it impotent by comic inflation – by, as Henry Louis Gates would say, signifying. His narrator sits in his lit-up basement smoking a reefer and listening to Louis Armstrong sing 'What Did I Do to Be So Black and Blue?' He descends into the music 'like Dante' and finds at its lowest level a Negro preacher preaching – in a wonderful parody of black revivalism (or perhaps more accurately, a parody of representations of black revivalism) on the 'Blackness of Blackness': 'Black will make you,' he intones, '... or black will un-make you.'

Ellison would have been the first to say that his darkly ironic humour and absurdity were not unique, but merely aspects of black popular culture transposed into a literary key. More recent black American artists – novelist Ishmael Reed, for example, and film-maker Spike Lee – have achieved the same mixture of populist exuberance and irony. Ellison's genius lay in his ability to articulate and amplify the central role played by illusion when it comes to matters of race. This interest in racial illusion – and the stylistic use of mask, alienation and parody that it entailed – was one of the two ways in which black culture informed modernism. The other was primitivism. The two tendencies overlapped sometimes, but nevertheless remained distinct. Ellison uses some of the same language and images as the primitivists (both black and white) of the Twenties, but does so by holding up to them an ironic mirror.

The same difference in conceptions of blackness can be seen in the literature of the French Caribbean and West Africa, on which the Harlem Renaissance had its most lasting and profound impact outside America. Langston Hughes, Claude McKay, Jean Toomer and other American Negro writers became important models and inspirations for a remarkable and talented generation of black students studying in Paris in the Thirties. The group – who, ironically, owed their existence to the French colonial policy of assimilation, which trained local administrators and taught them to be little Frenchmen – took the brave step of challenging white cultural patronage and denouncing assimilation as a sham.

The two most prominent members of the group, Léopold Senghor and Aimé Césaire, became significant international literary figures and also important politicians in their own countries. Senghor was a poet who became, for twenty years, president of the newly independent Senegal. Césaire was a poet and playwright who became mayor of Fort-de-France, capital of the French Caribbean colony of Martinique, as well as a representative at the National Assembly. As politicians, they have both been criticised for holding on to ties of assimilation with France, and thus fostering 'neocolonialism' in these former French colonies. But as writers, Senghor and Césaire are known as the originators of *négritude*, a concept and a movement that presaged the American black power movement in its celebration of blackness and its refusal to do obeisance to white cultural models.

Yet though they founded journals and worked together to promote black literature, their ideas of what blackness meant were very different. For Senghor, there was a black aesthetic which was the result of an African way of experiencing the world, an African awareness or consciousness that was essential to the culture both of the continent and of its diaspora. This consciousness was not irrational, but its rationality was of a different kind from that of the European mind. It was more fluid, less trapped in the dualism of subject and object:

The Negro's reason is synthetic rather than discursive. It is sympathetic rather than antagonistic. It is a different way of consciousness. The Negro's reason doesn't exhaust things, it doesn't force them into rigid schemes, destroying their essence and vitality; it flows in the arteries of things, testing all their contours in order to embed itself in the living heart of reality. *European reason is analytic through turning things to account, the Negro's reason intuitive by participating in them.*

This notion of a direct access to reality, unmediated by conventional Western logic or reason, recalls some theoretical formulations of surrealism. Senghor was aware of the possibility of such comparisons, but repudiated them. Surrealism, according to Senghor, was trapped in the realm of the material, whereas the African's direct, sensual apprehension of reality had a spiritual dimension. His reason was mystical. He intuited reality, apprehending it as part of a unified cosmos, a static hierarchy that moves concentrically outward from family, tribe, ancestors to the whole of creation.

The description of the African's mind as intuitive rather than analytical, as more predisposed to religious mysticism than that of the European, has a history that goes back at least to the eighteenth century. It was an aspect of the atavistic image of the African in imperial literature, and it lay behind the belief of Swedenborgian and other missionaries that Africa was ripe for religious revival. Indeed, in his essay 'Ce que l'homme noir apporte' ('What the Black Man Contributes'), Senghor cites as evidence of this fundamental difference between African and European ways of thinking the testimony of French Catholic missionaries. He was himself born into a Christian family in Senegal, and received his education at mission schools and seminaries before moving on to the Lycée Louis-le-Grand and the Sorbonne in Paris.

The main charge levelled by critics of the *négritude* movement has been precisely this, that it reproduced European stereotypes. By resorting to an essentialist black 'soul' or black 'way of looking at the world' it pandered to racism instead of challenging it. For Anglophone critics this has been mixed with hostility to a characteristically French intellectualisation of the issue. As Wole Soyinka succinctly put it: 'A tiger does not need to proclaim its tigritude.' These criticisms may hit their target with Senghor, but with Césaire the case is different. Where Senghor's theory of negritude is static and metaphysical, heavily influenced by Catholicism and leaning towards racialism, Césaire's literary and dramatic enactments of blackness are dynamic and existential.

Césaire's most celebrated work – it has become a canonic work of 'Third World' literature – is the *Cahier d'un retour au pays natal* (Notebook of a Return to My Native Land), the first version of which was published in 1939, the year Césaire returned to Martinique following his student days in Paris. In a whirlwind of voices and images, it describes the narrator/hero's return to his homeland, his memories of the poverty of his childhood, his identification with his degraded and insulted countrymen, and a final vision of liberation. Early issues of *Tropiques*, a journal that he helped with in Paris, show the influence on Césaire and those in his circle of Nietzsche. He was particularly interested in *The Birth of Tragedy* and its idea of the voluntary sacrifice of the Hero that gives the collectivity life. Césaire's poet-hero, clear-eyed in embracing his racial destiny in its most depraved, degrading and hateful forms, carries strong reverberations of Nietzsche's account in *The Birth of Tragedy* of the archetypal hero of Greek tragedy:

> Sophocles conceived doomed Oedipus, the greatest sufferer of the Greek stage, as a pattern of nobility, destined to error and misery despite his wisdom, yet exercising a beneficent influence on his environment in virtue of his boundless grief. The profound poet tells us that a man who is truly noble is incapable of sin; though every law, every natural order, indeed the very canon of ethics, perish by his actions, those very actions will create a circle of higher consequences able to found a new world on the ruins of the old.

The sacrifice of the poet-hero is therapeutic. And it is here that the poet's act of identification with his degraded fellow Martinicans is important. By embracing his blackness – not a noble blackness but the ignoble blackness, the niggerhood, that is forced on him by prejudice – he is transfigured.

Where *Invisible Man* dons the masks of race for the purpose of comic exorcism, Césaire does so with the goal of tragic catharsis.

As with the character of Jim in Eugene O'Neill's *All God's Chillun Got Wings*, the essence of the tragedy lies in the embracing by the tragic hero of his fate, his pain. The tragedy is the celebration of that sacrifice. The mask of race is imposed on the individual not so much in order to highlight the comic slipperiness of identity, as to signify the hero's wholesale commitment to authenticity, to being what he is in all its guises. This twentieth-century, tragic, Nietzschean view of the black – a successor to the sentimental image of the kneeling victim – has been particularly strong among writers influenced by existentialism. In America, as we shall see in the next chapter, it competes with survivals of Victorianism.

Although the jumble of voices and tones in Césaire's poem creates a deliberate sense of disjuncture and dissociation, there is also a clear structure: a journey that begins with stasis, a scene-setting, then moves on to arrival, then further into an interior journey, a return to the self, to 'blackness', ending in an explosion of those barriers between self and world and self and self that had earlier fractured the poem. Holding the whole poem together is the incantatory phrase 'At the brink of dawn...' ('Au bout du petit matin') that recurs throughout, but particularly in the desolate opening evocation of Fort-de-France itself, Césaire's home town:

At the brink of dawn, this flat town – staked out, stripped of its common-sense, inert, panting under the geometric burden of its forever renascent cross, unresigned to its fate, dumb, thwarted in every way, incapable of growing along the sap of this soil, burdened, clipped, diminished, alienated from its own flora and fauna.

The poem's lens focuses in on the poet's own home, 'another little foul-smelling house in a very narrow street' where as a boy he is 'awakened at night by [my mother's] tireless legs pedalling the night and by the Singer, bitterly biting into the soft flesh of the night as my mother pedals, pedals for our hunger every day, every night' (82–3). Then a second phase of the poem begins with the decision to leave Europe and return, a decision also to identify with the outcast and rejected:

To leave.
As there are hyena-men and panther-men, I shall be a Jew-man
a kaffir-man
a Hindu-from-Calcutta man
a man-from-Harlem-who-does-not-vote.

The decision to identify is, in the moment of decision, not so much
a recognition of something, a 'blackness', already given, but rather
an existential choice – an act of the imagination, of creativity.
Throughout the poem, the hero dons and strips off different levels
of deceit in order to gain a complete identification with the people.

The hero's identification with black people in *Cahier d'un retour
au pays natal* is very different from the sympathetic identification
with suffering of earlier literature. Wrongly expressed, Césaire's
tragic transfiguration could have looked like a Christian redemption through passive suffering – a martyrdom, even. Yet Césaire
avoids this. He keeps the ugliness before our eyes, dragging the
poetry back down to it when it is at its most exultant. And
corresponding to these changes of pitch, contributing to the sense
of dynamic struggle, is the kaleidoscopic variety of stylistic voices
used, from the lyrical to the surrealist, the prosaic to the parodic.
This is where Césaire and Ellison meet.

The poet-hero's identification is at first with the poverty of the
island, with the downtrodden citizens of Fort-de-France, but that
identification is expanded to take in the African diaspora. There are
references to places powerfully associated with the slave trade:
Bordeaux, Nantes, Liverpool, New York, Georgia, Alabama. And
there is identification, too, with Toussaint L'Ouverture, that great
symbol of black resistance, and with the alien place, the place of
exile, where he died:

What is mine too: a small cell in the Jura,
the snow lines it with white bars
the snow is the white gaoler who mounts guard in front of a
    prison.
What is mine
a man alone, imprisoned by whiteness

a man alone who defies the white screams of a white death.

It is at this point, the point where the poet's decision to return has been widened into an identification with the entire race, that the issue of language is raised:

> We would speak. Sing. Scream.
> Full voice, wide voice, you would be our right and our pointed
> spear.
> Words?
> Oh yes, words!
> Reason, I crown you wind of the evening.
> Mouth of order your name?
> To me it is the whip's corolla.

Western reason, the 'Mouth of order', is condemned as a velvet glove on the iron fist of white supremacy. 'Because we hate you, you and your reason, we invoke dementia praecox flamboyant madness tenacious cannibalism.'

This frustration with reason shares much with surrealism. Césaire's name is often linked to the movement, and especially to the patronage of André Breton. His poetry did become more surrealist later, but in the *Cahier* surrealism is introduced parodically, within world-weary quotation marks:

> And you know the rest
> That 2 and 2 make 5
> that the forest mews
> that the forest pulls the maroons out of the fire
> that the sky smooths its beard
> et cetera et cetera.[1]

There is a surrealist disordering of the senses here, a kind of

[1] 'Marrons' can refer either to chestnuts or to maroons (runaway slaves). It has been suggested that the line refers to runaway slaves seeking refuge from their pursuers in trees. See A. James Arnold, *Modernism and Negritude* (Harvard University Press, Cambridge, Mass., 1981), pp. 149–50.

madness, but it is interleaved with new depths of acidly humorous identification:

> I have worn parrot feathers and musk-cat skins
> I have tried the patience of missionaries
> insulted the benefactors of humankind.
> Defied Tyre. Defied Sidon.
> Adored the Zambezi.
> The extent of my perversity confounds me!

And when, in this process of identification, the language begins to soar, borne up by hope and by a vision of female beauty ('and may the time of promise come back / and the bird that knew my name / and the woman that had a thousand names / fountain sun and tears / and her alevin hair') it is pulled abruptly back to earth by the reminder that it was ugliness, the identification with poverty, that gave voice to that language:

> But who twists my voice? who scratches my voice? Stuffing a thousand bamboo fangs down my throat. A thousand sea-urchin stakes. It is you dirty old piece of world. Dirty old dawn. You dirty old hate. It is you the weight of insults and of a hundred years of whiplashes.

There follows a more directly political passage, which is prefaced by a call to revolution, to a complete overturning of the existing order of things. ('We do have to start. / Start what? / The only thing in the world worth starting: / The End of the world, for Heaven's sake.') Words are barely adequate to the occasion. ('In vain, twenty times over, in the tepid warmth of your throat do you ripen the same flimsy consolation that we are mutterers of words.') The poet ferociously attacks the tradition of French verse, represented by Saint-John Perse, that has treated the Caribbean as a romantically exotic backdrop, decorated with half-clad native women. Then he turns his fire on modern Negrophilia, on the febrile, jazz-age enthusiasm for what is seen as the primitive vitality of the Negro:

Or else they simply love us so much!
Gaily obscene, doudou about jazz in their excess of boredom,
I can do the tracking, the Lindy-hop and the tap-dance.
And as a last delicacy our muted complaints muffled in wah-wah
... Wait ...
Everything is in order. My good angel grazes on neon lights. I
swallow sticks.
My dignity wallows in puke.

The sense is of something being expelled, vomited out, something
that has stuck in the gorge. The mask has been tried on and thrown
off. This primitivism is not Césaire's negritude. Nor is Césaire's
negritude the racial flag-waving that lauds achievements of the past,
promoting 'African civilisation' as though on a league table:

No, we have never been amazons of the King of Dahomey, nor
princes of Ghana with eight hundred camels, nor doctors in
Timbuctoo under King Askia the Great, nor architects in
Djenne, nor Madhis, nor warriors. We do not feel the itch of
those used to hold the spear in our armpits. And since I have
sworn to suppress nothing in our history (I who admire nothing
so much as sheep grazing on their afternoon shadow), I will
admit that for as long as I can remember we have always been
quite pathetic dishwashers, shoeshiners with no ambition,
looking on the bright side, rather conscientious witch-doctors,
and the only undeniable record we ever broke was at endurance
under the whip ...

Césaire rejects all romanticisations of the Negro. His way is to
plunge into the degradation of the Negro's present condition – to
realise, appropriate and become it. And to do that he fixes on the
image of a black man on a tram, a figure in whom can be discerned
no nobility:

A nigger tall as a pongo who was trying to make himself small
on a tram seat. He was trying to relax his gigantic legs and his
starving boxer's shaking hands on that filthy tram seat ... He

was a gangling nigger with no rhythm or measure ... A shameless nigger and his toes were sniggering rather stinkingly deep in the lair of his shoes ... Overall it was a picture of a hideous nigger, a grumpy nigger, a gloomy nigger, a slumped nigger ... A nigger who was comical and ugly, and behind me women were looking at him and giggling.

In Césaire's revolution, victory belongs not to the conquerors but to 'Those who have invented neither gunpowder nor the compass / those who have never known how to subdue either steam or electricity'. Pity belongs not to the defeated but to the victors:

> Listen to the white world
> horribly weary from its immense effort
> its refractory joints cracking under the hard stars
> its stiffnesses of blue steel piercing mystic flesh
> listen to its proditorious victories trumpeting its defeats
> listen to its pathetic stumbling in its grandiose alibis
> Pity for our omniscient and naive conquerors!

There follows a powerfully expressed litany of acceptance of all the uglinesses, cowardices and betrayals in black life. It is the opposite of a paean of praise. And at the heart of this litany is an acceptance of race – not as a fact of biology, but as a fact of history:

> [I accept] the determination of my biology, not prisoner to a facial angle, to a type of hair, to a sufficiently flat nose, to a sufficiently melanous complexion, and negritude, not a cephalic index any more or a plasma or a soma but measured with the compass of suffering.

The final pages of the poem look to the future, to the 'mauvais nègre', the 'bad nigger', of the future who unlike the good nigger, the Uncle Tom, of the past will be set free by his negritude, his niggerhood. And the last lines articulate in a highly compressed, visionary form this dialectic whereby the allegiance, the binding, to a racial determination issues explosively in a new freedom:

bind my black vibration to the very navel of the world
bind me, bind me, bitter brotherhood
then strangling me with your lasso of stars,
rise, Dove
rise
rise
rise
I follow you, imprinted on my ancestral white cornea
rise sky-licker
and the great black hole where I wanted to drown a moon ago
this is where I now want to fish the night's malevolent tongue in
    its immobile
revolvolution!

It would be wrong to call this without qualification a release, because there is no letting go of the blackness. It is an aesthetic transformation, a shift to a different plane of existence. We find exactly the same movement – a sudden one upward, out of abasement – at the end of *All God's Chillun Got Wings*, when Jim, accepting the dreadful destiny of his marriage to Ella, 'suddenly throws himself on his knees and raises his shining eyes, his transfigured face'. He prays, 'Let this fire of burning suffering purify me,' and, 'still deeply exalted', promises Ella: 'Honey, Honey, I'll play right up to the gates of heaven with you!'

Within the context of Jim and Ella's horrific marriage, this is a bitterly ironic epiphany. Both O'Neill and Césaire were attempting to drive sentimentalism, the remnants of Christian piety, from their picture of the black man. Influenced by Nietzsche, they saw in pagan myth a way, in Frank Kermode's words, to 'short circuit the intellect and liberate the imagination which the scientism of the modern world suppresses'. The Negro could be seen mythically as the quintessence of alienated modernity, the person whose authentic self is stifled by the masks worn for others. This is the picture painted, in different ways, by Jean-Paul Sartre and Jean Genet.

Jazz was probably first heard in France during the First World War, when Jim Europe's famous band travelled with black troops, and in the interwar years it entered the mainstream of French culture along with American movies and literature. By the 1950s and 1960s Paris had become a Mecca for black American artists – writers like Richard Wright and James Baldwin, and jazz musicians attracted by French tolerance and enthusiasm for all things American. A leitmotif of *Nausea* (1938), Sartre's fictional exposition of existentialism, is the protagonist Antoine Roquentin's obsession with a particular jazz song, 'Some of these days'. Only when listening to the record of the black woman singing it does he feel free for a moment of his illness, his 'nausea', his sense of the vertigo of consciousness. In 1948 Sartre was asked by Senghor to contribute a preface to an anthology of black Francophone poetry. The anthology, a calling-card for the pioneering generation of Francophone black writers, included poetry by Senghor and a long extract from *Cahier d'un retour au pays natal*. Sartre's essay, 'Black Orpheus', has become the most famous exposition of *négritude*, though it is one very much geared to Sartre's own concerns. In trying to explain what he understands by *négritude*, Sartre recalls the myth of Orpheus and his descent into the underworld:

> It will be necessary . . . to smash the walls of the culture-prison, it will be necessary, one day, to return to Africa: thus negritude inextricably combines the theme of the return to the native land with that of the descent into the dazzling underworld of the black soul. This takes the form of a quest, of a systematic stripping-down and of an ascent accompanied by an unending striving for depth. I call this poetry 'Orphic' because this indefatigable descent by the negro into himself reminds me of Orpheus going to reclaim Eurydice from Pluto.

The idea of the Negro descending into the abyss of himself to claim his authenticity, his blackness, provided Sartre with a textbook example of the paradoxical notion of an existential choice, a choice that is made in absolute freedom but that issues in an objective, determined course of action. But the imagery he uses recalls older romanticisations of the Negro. The cluster of associations that links blackness with the underworld, the subconscious, the true, inner or natural self, has the force that comes with long cultural familiarity. Lurking in the shadow of Sartre's Black Orpheus is Diderot's Moor, standing guard at the cave of the subconscious – and behind him, the black devils of the medieval imagination. It is exactly that mythopoeic structure of thought that Ralph Ellison would parody in *Invisible Man*.

Sartre regards blacks as a special group. Unlike other victims of collective prejudice – Jews, for example – there is no possibility for the opportunistic individual to escape his condition:

> A Jew, white amongst whites, can deny that he is a Jew, can declare himself a man amongst men. The Negro can neither deny that he is a Negro nor claim for himself this colourless humanity: he is black. Thus is he driven toward authenticity: insulted, enslaved, he draws himself up, he gathers up the word 'nigger' that has been thrown at him like a stone, he asserts himself as black, in the face of the white, with pride. The final unity which will draw all the oppressed together in the same struggle must be preceded in the colonies by what I call this moment of separation or negativity: this anti-racist racism is the only road that can lead to the abolition of racial differences.

'Anti-racist racism' – the contradiction there is deliberate, of course, and deliberately provocative to tidy liberal minds. But there are other contradictions and weaknesses in the way that Sartre defines *négritude*. He describes blacks as forced to accept their blackness – as forced, in that sense, towards authenticity. Had he had wider experience of large-scale black communities, in America or the Caribbean, he would have been aware of the way colour prejudice can exist within the oppressed community as a kind of psychological collateral damage produced by the general prejudice in society at large. Not only is there the phenomenon of 'passing', but there is also the way in which the black may succumb to self-hatred on account of his blackness, producing the kind of psychological damage that the psychiatrist Frantz Fanon was to describe in *Black Skin, White Masks* (1952). (It is this self-hatred that Jim resigns himself to, out of his love for Ella, at the end of *All God's Chillun Got Wings*.) Thus the realisation of one's blackness is by no means an inevitability. It requires an act, a change in consciousness – which is surely the central point of negritude.

Another feature of Sartre's *négritude* is that it is political and utilitarian rather than aesthetic. He is able to take an Olympian view of its significance:

[N]egritude appears as the minor term of a dialectical progression: the theoretical and practical assertion of the supremacy of the white is the thesis; negritude's stance as an oppositional value is the moment of negativity. But this negative moment is insufficient by itself, and the Blacks who use it know this well; they know that it is intended to prepare for the synthesis, the realization of the human in a society without races. Thus negritude tends to its own destruction, it is a transition and not a conclusion, a means and not an ultimate end.

For Fanon, Sartre's detachment and paternalism – his lofty view of *négritude* as an idea whose time had come, but would pass – proved hard to stomach:

When I read that page, I felt that I had been robbed of my last chance. I said to my friends, 'The generation of the younger black poets has just suffered a blow that can never be forgiven.' Help had been sought from a friend of the coloured peoples, and that friend had found no better response than to point out the relativity of what they were doing. For once, that born Hegelian had forgotten that consciousness has to lose itself in the night of the absolute, the only condition to attain to consciousness of self ... Jean-Paul Sartre, in this work, has destroyed black zeal. In opposition to historical becoming, there had always been the unforeseeable. I needed to lose myself completely in negritude ... I *needed* not to know. This struggle, this new decline had to take on an aspect of completeness. Nothing is more unwelcome than the commonplace: 'You'll change, my boy; I was like that too when I was young ... you'll see, it will all pass.'

Orpheus's act in descending into the underworld, Fanon

reminds us, was an absolute one. He gave everything to reclaim Eurydice. He didn't have the luxury of Sartre's objective overview. This, according to Ovid, is what he says to Pluto:

> '... To you are owed
> Ourselves and all creation; a brief while
> We linger; then we hasten, late or soon,
> To one abode; here one road leads us all;
> Here in the end is home; over humankind
> Your kingdom keeps the longest sovereignty.
> She too, when ripening years reach their due term,
> Shall own your rule. The favour that I ask
> Is but to enjoy her love; and, if the Fates
> Will not reprieve her, my resolve is clear
> Not to return; may two deaths give you cheer.'

Orpheus's descent into darkness and re-emergence into light have the quality of an initiation. In pre-Homeric Orphic cults, there was an initiator whose power could transform and tame even the wildest creatures, animals and men who live in the wilderness. Such a figure would have been associated with the initiation of young men – in the wilds of nature, excluding women. 'There', according to Joseph Campbell, the great writer on myth and ritual, 'something significant was disclosed to them in music and song that delivered them from their blood-spilling savagery and gave a deep sense of the ceremonies of transit from immaturity to adulthood.' If Césaire plays the role of the Orphic initiator, singing his story of darkness and rebirth, then Sartre is like the anthropologist observing from the edge of the clearing, notebook in hand.

The novelist/playwright Jean Genet – of whom Sartre wrote a massive biography, *Saint Genet* – was also drawn to the idea of blacks embodying the alienated and dispossessed in modern society. (They play the same role as the criminals and prisoners of his autobiographical novels.) In the 1960s he became a prominent supporter of the Black Panthers, and his play *Les Nègres* (1958) goes further than Sartre in presenting *négritude* as a rite of passage leading the participants to a new state of consciousness. Instead of

Sartre's dry analysis, *Les Nègres* uses ritual, mask and parody to enact the appropriation and exorcism of prejudice. Blackness is no longer a political strategy, but an aesthetic act.

The stage is divided for the play into two levels. On the upper level sit actors representing white European authority – a colonial governor, the Queen, a missionary, etc. – while below them a group of Negroes have gathered round the coffin of a white woman in order to conduct a ritualistic re-enactment of her murder. All the actors are black, but those on the upper level – the 'Court' – wear white masks. At various points in the play, the masks are slipped off and the actors on both levels consult together on the progress of the performance. Similarly, the artificiality of the re-enactment of the white woman's murder is emphasised by interruptions as the Negroes stop to argue about how to present it.

To further emphasise the theatricality, one of the Negroes, Archibald, plays the role of compère, parodying the 'Mister Interlocutor' of minstrel shows. (The play is subtitled 'A Clown Show'.) In a preface, Genet specified that the play was written for, or at, a white audience, and that there should always be at least one token white present to witness it. At the beginning, Archibald addresses this white audience in terms that merely seem to be saying 'This is only a story', but that also have a sinister, unsettling undercurrent:

Archibald: When we leave this stage, we are involved in your life. I am a cook, this lady is a sewing-maid, this gentleman is a medical student, this gentleman is a curate at St Anne's, this lady ... skip it. Tonight our sole concern will be to entertain you. So we have killed a white woman.

One of the Negroes, Ville de Saint-Nazaire, seems to stand apart from the others. He goes barefoot and, unlike them, doesn't wear evening dress. He slips on and off stage during the play for furtive consultations with the actors. By the end it is clear that he is a participant in the true drama, which is taking place off stage. A militant black organisation is trying and executing one of its own number, a traitor. (As Ville de Saint-Nazaire comments: 'We'll have to get used to the responsibility of executing our own traitors.') Everything that has happened on the stage has been a diversion, something to distract the white audience while the blacks attend to this important business.

Genet uses these multiple layers of *mise-en-scène* – which bear some similarity to Pirandello's experiments, and to Artaud's Theatre of Cruelty – to draw the audience in, to highlight their complicity. The sense of ceremony is enhanced by the use of music and dance. The re-enactment of the white woman's murder is accompanied at one stage by the Dies Irae, reflecting Genet's lifelong obsession with Catholic ritual.

But for all the distractions, the clowning, the alienation effects, *Les Nègres* has a central idea that moves straight as an arrow to its final fulfilment. On the surface it is a play about hate. There is much talk among the Negroes on the lower level about hate, about the need to overcome or surpass the hatred of others. Hate is the reality of their lives, their starting-point. One of the Negro characters, Samba Graham Diouf, is a Christian, a humanist, a compromiser. He is mister half-and-half. But when he rambles, with his liberal, high-flown phrases, he is brutally interrupted by one of the others, bringing us back to one of the main motors of the drama:

Bobo: Who's asking you? What we need is hatred. Our ideas will spring from hatred.

Les Nègres is also, however, a play about love. Among the Negroes are a pair of lovers, Village and Virtue, but in a world where identity is defined by hatred (by blackness), to love is to betray, to go over to the other side. This is made brutally clear to Village by Archibald, the Master of Ceremonies:

Archibald: ... On this stage we're like the guilty who play at being guilty in prison.
Village: We don't want to be guilty of anything. Virtue is going to be my wife.
Archibald: Bugger off then! Get out of here! Go! Go to them.

239

(*He points at the audience.*) . . . if they'll have you. If they'll have you. And if you succeed in making yourself loved by them, come back and tell me. But get yourself bleached first. Go on, bugger off. Go and be spectators. Us, we're going to be saved by that. (*He indicates the coffin.*)

Village struggles to do what he must do: to hate Virtue, to become the hatred that is the reality of his life:

Village: I couldn't take the world's condemnation. And I began to hate you when everything about you made me glimpse love. Love made men's hatred of me unbearable, and their hatred made my love for you unbearable. So I hate you.

This is the psychic division that the Negroes must overcome. It is only through hatred that they can accomplish their rite of passage and become whole. 'Must we always only dream of murder?' Village asks Archibald, and the answer comes back: 'Always.' The rite, the descent into hatred, is a kind of death. Diouf states this explicitly when he is, appropriately, given the part of the white woman, the murderee, in the ceremony:

Diouf: (*Facing the public*) I, Samba Graham Diouf, born in the swamps of Oubangui Chari, sadly bid you farewell. I am not afraid. When you open the door, I shall enter. I shall descend into the death that you have prepared for me.

Through the ceremony, an integral love can be achieved. Death is followed by rebirth. The end is love. The play's final, touching words remind one of the scenes of homosexual tenderness among the prisoners of Genet's novel *Miracle of the Rose* (1951):

Village: (*To Virtue. They seem to be arguing.*) But if I held your hands in mine. If I put my arm round your shoulder – let me do it – if I took you in my arms?
Virtue: All men are like you: they imitate. Can't you invent something new?

Village: For you I could invent anything: fruits, brighter words, a two-wheeled wheelbarrow, oranges without pips, a bed for three, a needle that doesn't prick. But gestures of love, that's harder ... still, if you really want me to ...
Virtue: I'll help you.

The Negroes of *Les Nègres* have strong affinities with the prisoners of Genet's novels, just as his own life was, in his own eyes, that of a white 'nigger'. The confined yet fantastical lives of Genet's prisoners mix tender love and 'toughness' – to be a 'tough' is the highest accolade among them – in a miraculous way. The 'miracle' of *Miracle of the Rose* is the vision of a condemned man, the perpetrator of horrific murders, whose chains become a garland of roses. And the miracle of Genet's own life was that of the delinquent, institutionalised youth who became a great writer, a man who retained his poetic and idealistic nature despite the brutality that he lived out.

Genet's aesthetic is based on a sense of awe at the wisdom and beauty that can come through spiritual trials. (His suffering is not that of a victim, not that of the whipped slave of the sentimental imagination. It is the internal struggle of a protagonist, the result of internal struggle.) For all his fascination with the theatrical trappings of Catholicism, Genet's view of the human condition is existential rather than Christian. His prisoners are not redeemed, and nor are the Negroes in *Les Nègres*. They achieve authenticity through becoming wholly and excessively what they are – thieves, murderers, prisoners, the guilty, Negroes, 'niggers'.

This is how, for Genet, the black man is, as Sartre puts it, 'driven toward authenticity'. 'Insulted, enslaved,' Sartre continues, 'he draws himself up, he gathers up the word "nigger" that has been thrown at him like a stone, he asserts himself as black, in the face of the white, with pride.' Genet's *Nègres* achieve their pride by becoming, in a ritualised context, the fears and projections of the white audience. They wear the masks. A similar argument has been put forward by the critic Henry Louis Gates to defend the verbal obscenity and violence of some rap music. Rap, according to Gates, operates in a context of 'signifying', in which slurs, insults and stereotypes are rehearsed as parody, worn as masks. Other African-American commentators, such as Cornel West, take a less benign view of rap, seeing in it dangerous signs of a real 'black nihilism' produced by the social meltdown of America's inner cities.

Rap, with its huge audience among white youth, is big business, and West attributes much of the dehumanisation he finds in its lyrics to the pressures of corporate exploitation. This debate over the effects of patronage goes back to the Twenties, when Du Bois accused novelist Claude McKay of pandering to white prejudice by painting a lurid picture of Harlem. For McKay, what he was doing was bringing black culture out of the closet. But such exposure of black culture carries dangers of exploitation and misunderstanding. A good example of this is the use of the word 'nigger', a powerful word whose import can change explosively according to context and tone of voice. It has a long history in America as a term used by whites among themselves and against blacks as a term of racial abuse. But it also has a long history as a term used among blacks, a term whose emotional range runs from the faintly mocking endearment to downright contempt, but whose premise is a shared privacy of experience, a shared oppression, a shared 'niggerhood'. In the 1920s, with black artists as a group coming to general attention (and very consciously aware of that attention), this latter, private use of the term was coming out of its privacy into a public, interracial sphere. (Zora Neale Hurston famously coined the term 'Niggerati' for the group of younger writers who came to prominence in the 1920s.) This defiantly public, interracial use by blacks of the term 'nigger', a kind of verbal minstrelsy with attitude, was later taken up by black militant writers in the 1960s and 1970s, and then by rappers in the 1980s and 1990s. (The term *nègre* – as opposed to the more politically liberal *noir* – served a similar function for Francophone writers.) When Carl Van Vechten chose the title *Nigger Heaven* for his 1926 novel it was a provocation, a case of *épater les bourgeois*, of flying in the face of good, liberal 'race relations'. Only in the case of Carl Van Vechten, here was a white writer using it – a white writer thus donning a verbal mask at two removes. If the black artist appropriates the white racist's term 'nigger' in order to steal its power from the white oppressor, the white writer such as Van Vechten appropriates it in order to claim his solidarity with those blacks. Whether Van Vechten had a right to make such an appropriation is another matter, and while friends like Langston Hughes defended him, the feeling that he did not have such a right – that the same kinds of depictions of Negro life were qualitatively different and even less acceptable when presented by a white as against a black writer – lay behind the surface puritanism of the attacks on *Nigger Heaven*.

All the contemporary debates about multiculturalism and ethnic identity can be traced back to those crucial years after the First World War when African-American writers and musicians stepped out on to a national stage, at the same time as black peoples across the European colonies were beginning to assert their cultural identity against the European. Modern culture was influenced by this 'renaissance' in two ways. In the first place, an idea of the primitive was seized on that continued and amplified the exoticism that we find already in late nineteenth-century literature. There is no great distance – in substance certainly, if not in style – between the eroticisation of the Negro by modernist writers and artists of the 1920s and Gauguin's Tahitians or writers of the 1880s and 1890s such as Pierre Loti and Rider Haggard.[1] Indeed, the link between modernist primitivism and colonial exploitation was often a direct and practical one. Picasso and Kirchner both drew inspiration from displays of 'native life' at colonial expositions. Modernist primitivism was not so modern, drawing as it did on the nineteenth-century Darwinists' claims that black people were a substratum of human civilisation, a living rudiment that looked back at the European like a mirror, reflecting the white's own primitive, ancient *alter ego*.

[1] To be sure, Rider Haggard (and Conrad in *Heart of Darkness*) emphasise atavistic violence rather than atavistic sexuality, and violence is not such a prominent feature of modernist primitivism as sexuality. (Having said which, the two are combined powerfully in Stravinsky's *Rite of Spring*, one of the masterpieces of modernism.) But the saturating violence of Rider Haggard's novels is presented in such a vividly pornographic light as to become a kind of disturbing sensuality, a psychologically twisted sexuality – sadistic in *King Solomon's Mines*, sadistic and necrophiliac in *She*.

But this romantic primitivism was only one aspect of what happened when, in Langston Hughes's description of the Twenties, 'the Negro was in vogue'. The urbanisation of the African-Americans in the first half of the century coincided with the spectacular growth of the mass entertainment industries, and it was these media that projected black popular culture to a wider world – albeit sometimes in a distorted form, through a white lens. Jazz is the great example of this. And jazz – with its creative tension between individual freedom and collective tradition, its parodic play on standard 'riffs' – exemplifies a spirit and an aesthetic outlook that have pervaded modern popular culture, a spirit of irony, of exaggeration, of parodic play. Sanctified in recent years by the academic term 'postmodernism', this spirit was in at the inception of modernism, and one of its principal sources was black culture.

These two tendencies, the primitive and the parodic, were by no means mutually exclusive. Primitivist clichés could acquire by repetition a lacquer of irony, becoming self-parodic, while the ritualistic rehearsal and exorcism of racial stereotypes (either through tragic or comic catharsis) ran the risk of seeming to succumb to those stereotypes. And in post-war American writing we find these modernist tendencies competing with survivals in the liberal imagination of the sentimental ethos, the ethos of so much abolitionist literature. If modernist primitivism was anti-Christian or pagan in character, the survival of abolitionist attitudes testified to the pervasiveness of Christian culture in America.

Sources

Abrahams, Peter, *The View From Coyoba* (Faber, London, 1985).

Anderson, Sherwood, *Dark Laughter* (Jarrolds, London, 1926).

Arnold, A. James, *Modernism and Negritude: The Poetry and Poetics of Aimé Césaire* (Harvard University Press, Cambridge, Mass., 1981).

Bradbury, Malcolm, and James McFarlane (eds), *Modernism: A Guide to European Literature 1890–1930* (Penguin, London, 1991).

Campbell, Joseph, *The Masks of God: Occidental Mythology* (Penguin, New York, 1964).

Césaire, Aimé, *Cahier d'un retour au pays natal* [*Notebook of a Return to my Native Land*], transl. Mireille Rosello with Annie Pritchard (Bloodaxe, Newcastle upon Tyne, 1995). First published 1939.

Chilton, John, *Sidney Bechet: The Wizard of Jazz* (Macmillan, London, 1977).

Clarke, Donald, *The Rise and Fall of Popular Music* (Penguin, London, 1995).

Coulthard, G. R., *Race and Colour in Caribbean Literature* (Oxford University Press, 1962).

Cruse, Harold, *The Crisis of the Negro Intellectual* (W.H. Allen, London, 1969).

Davis, Francis, *The History of the Blues* (Secker & Warburg, London, 1995).

Douglas, Ann, *Terrible Honesty: Mongrel Manhattan in the 1920s* (Picador, London, 1996).

Ellison, Ralph, *Invisible Man* (Penguin, London, 1965). First published 1952.

— *Shadow and Act* (Secker & Warburg, London, 1967).

Fanon, Frantz, *Black Skin, White Masks* (Paladin, London, 1970). First published 1952.

Finn, Julio, *Voices of Negritude* (Quartet, London, 1988).

Firbank, Ronald, *Prancing Nigger* (Brentano, New York, 1924).

Gates, Henry Louis, *The Signifying Monkey: A Theory of Afro-American Literary Criticism* (Oxford University Press, New York, 1988).

Genet, Jean, *Miracle of the Rose* (Penguin, London, 1971). First published 1951.

— *Les Nègres*, in *Oeuvres complètes*, vol. 5 (Gallimard, Paris, 1979). First published 1958.

Haley, Alex, *Roots* (Vintage, London, 1991). First published 1976.

Hatch, James V., and Leo Hamalian (eds), *Lost Plays of the Harlem Renaissance 1920–40* (Wayne State University Press, Detroit, 1996).

Herskovits, Melville, *The Myth of the Negro Past* (Beacon Press, Boston, 1964). First published 1958.

Jones, LeRoi, *Blues People* (Payback Press, Edinburgh, 1995). First published 1963.

Larkin, Philip, *All What Jazz* (Faber, London, 1985).

Levine, Lawrence W., *Black Culture and Black Consciousness: Afro-American Thought from Slavery to Freedom* (Oxford University Press, New York, 1977).

Lewis, Wyndham, *Paleface: The Philosophy of the Melting-Pot* (Chatto & Windus, London, 1929).

McKay, Claude, *Home to Harlem* (Harper & Row, New York, 1928).

Nietzsche, Friedrich, *The Birth of Tragedy* (Doubleday, New York, 1956). First published 1872.

Ovid, *Metamorphoses*, transl. A. D. Melville (Oxford University Press, 1986).

Peretti, Burton W., *The Creation of Jazz: Music, Race and Culture in Urban America* (University of Illinois Press, Urbana, 1992).

Pollock, Griselda, *Avant-Garde Gambits, 1888–93: Gender and the Colour of Art History* (Thames & Hudson, London, 1992).

Rampersand, Arnold, *The Life of Langston Hughes, Volume 1, 1902–1941: I, Too, Sing America* (Oxford University Press, New York, 1986).

Rhodes, Colin, *Primitivism and Modern Art* (Thames & Hudson, London, 1994).

Sartre, Jean-Paul, 'Orphée noir', in Léopold Sédar Senghor, *La Nouvelle Poésie nègre et malgache de langue française* (Presses Universitaires de France, Paris, 1948).

Senghor, Léopold Sédar, *Négritude et humanisme* (Editions du Seuil, Paris, 1964).

Van Vechten, Carl, *Nigger Heaven* (Alfred A. Knopf, New York, 1926).

West, Cornel, *Race Matters* (Beacon Press, Boston, 1993).

White, Edmund, *Jean Genet* (Picador, London, 1994).

7

Black Apocalypse

When Genet's *Les Nègres* was produced in New York, Norman Mailer published a long criticism of the play in the *Village Voice*. The focus of his attack was what he saw as its abstraction, its lack of realism. While acknowledging that *Les Nègres* was 'the truest and most explosive play anyone has yet written about the turn of the tide, and the guilt and horror in the white man's heart as he turns to face his judge', Mailer argued that the conflict between black and white was too pressing and immediate a matter to become the subject of avant-garde, formalist experimentation. Liberalism, according to Mailer, was a cancer which had created a blindness to the reality and necessity of violence at the heart of Western society. Genet, by presenting the violence in a stylised form, was conniving with this blindness. The play would have been better, Mailer concluded, if, instead of presenting us with masks, it had shown real black in conflict with real white.

One answer to Mailer's attack is to point out that Genet's presentation of race as a series of disguises and gestures does rest, in the end, on a bedrock of reality, that reality being the trial and execution, offstage, of a black traitor. All the enactments of the white man's worst fears and fantasies have been a deliberate distraction from that. But the more pointed counter-argument is presented by Mailer himself in *The Man Who Studied Yoga*:

Marvin asks Sam if he has given up his novel, and Sam says, 'Temporarily.' He cannot find a form, he explains. He does not want to write a realistic novel, because reality is no longer realistic.

In the looking-glass world of race, where personal identity becomes absurd and impersonal, fantasy may be the best measure of reality.

More importantly, Mailer was wrong to claim that the liberal imagination is blind to violence. From the abolitionists onwards, violence and the threat of it have been intrinsic to how black and white liberals have depicted what used to be called 'race relations'. The image of the passively suffering slave (whose suffering was itself depicted in graphically violent terms) was always counterbalanced by the warning figure of the machete-wielding, vengeance-seeking slave rebel. The power of *Uncle Tom's Cabin* lies partly – as in scenes like Eliza's crossing of the Ohio River and the beating of Tom at Legree's plantation – in its sometimes painful physicality. Violence is essential to protest literature.

In the post-Second World War period, this fascination with violence has been given an apocalyptic edge. From J. G. Ballard's much-imitated science fictions to Doris Lessing's *Four-Gated City* and *Memoirs of a Survivor*, from *Apocalypse Now* to *Blade Runner*, countless examples could be produced from both sides of the Atlantic of novels and films captivated by the idea of civic and moral meltdown, of society destroyed by nuclear war, by rampant capitalism, by some inevitable process of entropy and exhaustion. It is a tradition that has acquired its own iconography – a visual symbolism of rubble and fires reproduced in films, TV dramas, stage productions, adverts. And the ethnic mix of these urban hellholes carries its own dark parody of liberalism's pluralist dream. Watts, Chicago's South Side, the Bronx – these are the models, and this is where the post-war apocalyptic tradition dovetails with older liberal traditions depicting racial violence. In Britain, 'race riots' in Brixton, Toxteth and other parts of the country in the early Eighties made inclusion of scenes of such urban apocalypse virtually *de rigueur* in novels, films and TV dramas for several years. Salman Rushdie's *The Satanic Verses* and Hanif Kureishi's film *Sammy and Rosie Get Laid* provide two well-known British examples. From America comes the hooded figure – dangerous but strangely attractive too – of the gangsta rapper, presiding over his kingdom of inner-city devastation.

To grasp the roots of these visions of racial apocalypse, in particular their roots in a Christian tradition – in what, in the title of his book on Judaeo-Christian linear narrative, Frank Kermode calls *The Sense of an Ending* – one has to go back to the Thirties, and to the most famous twentieth-century American protest novel, Richard Wright's *Native Son* (1940). Wright was born in 1908 in Mississippi and – as he recounts in *Black Boy*, his powerful and bitter memoir of childhood – grew up in terrible poverty. The two strongest influences on his early life, his mother and his maternal grandmother, were both very religious. His grandmother, a Seventh-day Adventist, fought a long and ultimately unsuccessful battle to get him to accept the church. But as he writes in *Black Boy*, while he may have broken free of conformity, his growing up in a religious culture did leave its traces:

> Many of the religious symbols appealed to my sensibilities and I responded to the dramatic vision of life held by the church, feeling that to live day by day with death as one's sole thought was to be so compassionately sensitive toward all life as to view all men as slowly dying, and the trembling sense of fate that welled up, sweet and melancholy, from the hymns blended with the sense of fate that I had already caught from life.

Like James Baldwin, whose stepfather was a preacher, Wright took from his upbringing an ability to turn the biblical rhetoric of black religion to secular ends. His first book, *Uncle Tom's Children* (1938), features a story in which this connection is dramatised. In 'Fire and Cloud', a black preacher, leader of his community in a Southern town, is faced with the greatest dilemma of his life. His people are starving, and the Communists are seeking his support for a demonstration they are organising for the following day. At the same time, the white authorities are looking to him to play the role he has played in the past, that of the 'responsible' Negro who will use his authority to stop trouble. They call on favours they have done him in the past. When the preacher refuses to commit himself, he is taken by some white men into the woods and whipped. The physical pain of the whipping is described repeatedly by Wright as being like a fire, a burning. But the fire is also metaphorical, an engine of transformation. The next morning, the preacher leads the demonstration and the white authorities, intimidated by the show of black solidarity, back down.

Black solidarity, for Wright, is forged in the crucible of shared suffering. As the preacher puts it in 'Fire and Cloud':

'Sistahs n Brothers, Ah *know* now! Ah done seen the sign! Wes gotta git together. Ah know what yo life is! Ah done felt it! Its *fire*! Its like the fire that burned me las night! Its sufferin! Its hell! Ah cant bear this fire erlone! Ah know now whut t do! Wes gotta git close t one ernother! Gawds done spoke! Gawds done sent His sign. Now its fer us t ack . . .'

The particular brutality and bleakness of Wright's upbringing undoubtedly influenced this grim view of what it was that blacks shared. As he writes in *Black Boy*:

After I had outlived the shocks of childhood, after the habit of reflection had been born in me, I used to mull over the strange absence of real kindness in Negroes, how unstable was our tenderness, how lacking in genuine passion we were, how void of great hope, how timid our joy, how bare our traditions, how hollow our memories, how lacking we were in those intangible sentiments that bind man to man and how shallow was even our despair . . . Whenever I thought of the essential bleakness of black life in America, I knew that Negroes had never been allowed to catch the full spirit of Western civilization, that they lived somehow in it but not of it. And when I brooded upon the cultural barrenness of black life, I wondered if clean, positive tenderness, love, honor, loyalty and the capacity to remember were native with man.

Wright's view contrasts strongly with that of Ralph Ellison, who in an interview affirmed his aim as being 'to commemorate in fiction . . . those human qualities which the American Negro has developed despite and in rejection of the obstacles and meannesses imposed on us [and to preserve] in art those human values which can endure by confronting change'. Wright's world is one of unremitting violent conflict between black and white. Even where there is a hint of racial conflict being transcended at the end of *Native Son*, it is transcended not by blacks as a group but by Bigger Thomas alone in his condemned cell. Wright makes his a deeply personal and spiritual redemption.

The dominant theme of the stories in *Uncle Tom's Children* is that of the lone black male confronting white racism. Their names – Big Boy, Mann – demonstrate their representative character. Violence and injustice are everywhere. In 'Down by the Riverside', a Southern town is flooded, and Mann, in trying to save his family, steals a boat and is forced to kill a white man, Heartfield, in self-defence. Mann's pregnant wife dies, but Mann throws himself into the collective effort to save the town's population. He rescues Heartfield's family, even though he knows that they will identify him as the killer. He is shot trying to escape from the white mob. His body 'rolled heavily down the wet slope and stopped about a foot from the water's edge; one black palm sprawled limply outward and upward, trailing in the brown current...' In 'Long Black Song', Silas's wife is raped by a white gramophone salesman. When the white man returns next day with a friend, Silas shoots one of them, and the other goes off to fetch the mob. Sending his wife away, Silas dies in the house, taking as many as possible of the white mob with him. And in the first story, 'Big Boy Leaves Home', four Negro boys go skinny-dipping in a swimming hole on a white man's land. A white woman comes upon them and starts screaming. She is joined by her fiancé, the son of the landowner, who shoots two of the boys. The remaining two boys, Big Boy and Bobo, grapple with the white man and Big Boy is forced to shoot him with his own gun. They flee, but Bobo is caught and from his hideaway Big Boy witnesses his friend's torture and murder. The black community rallies round to smuggle Big Boy out of town on a truck bound for the North.

The moral choices in *Uncle Tom's Children* are thus stark and clear, black and white, delineated by graphic physical action. It was this quality in Wright's work that both James Baldwin and Ralph Ellison were to criticise so eloquently, accusing him of bypassing the complex human realities of black life in order to deliver a simple message of protest to a white audience. Wright himself seemed to recognise that fault in *Uncle Tom's Children*. In 'How "Bigger" Was Born', an essay on the writing of *Native Son*, he recalls how one of the spurs to beginning that work was the realisation of what had gone wrong with his stories:

> When the reviews [of *Uncle Tom's Children*] began to appear, I realised that I had made an awfully naive mistake. I found that I had written a book which even bankers' daughters could read and weep over and feel good about. I swore to myself that if I ever wrote another book, no one would weep over it; that it would be so hard and deep that they would have to face it without the consolation of tears. It was this that made me get to work in dead earnest.

The image of bankers' daughters weeping over *Native Son* reminds one of the observations made about sentimental literature 150 years earlier – that the works were written to elicit an immediate emotional response, and that their readership was predominantly female. The stories in *Uncle Tom's Children* – despite, or perhaps because of, their directness and violence – share that sentimentalism of anti-slavery propagandist literature. The black protagonists are ciphers, shallowly characterised actors who share some simple moral virtues – loyalty, courage, fortitude. They are noble in the same way that the noble slaves of abolitionist literature are noble. It is this that allows them to be wept over by bankers' daughters, and this that is the flaw that Richard Wright came to see in the collection. When he came to write *Native Son*, he created a protagonist, Bigger Thomas, whose actions were increasingly ignoble, and whom it would be difficult – though perhaps not impossible – to weep over.

Native Son is divided into three parts, titled 'Fear', 'Flight' and 'Fate'. They are as sharply delineated as the acts of a play or film. (The novel was later to be made into a movie, with Wright himself playing the part of Bigger Thomas.) In the first part Thomas, a delinquent youth from the Black Belt of Chicago, is given a job as chauffeur to the family of a white philanthropist. Mary, the philanthropist's daughter, tries to befriend him. She persuades him to come out for the evening with her and her left-wing boyfriend, Jan. When Bigger takes Mary home she is in a drunken stupor, and he has to carry her up to her bedroom. He has got her on to the bed when Mary's blind mother enters the room. Terrified that he will be discovered in this compromising position, he puts a pillow over Mary's face to stop her crying out, and suffocates her. Then, to cover up his crime, he drags the body down to the boiler room, decapitates it, and incinerates it in the furnace.

Book Two, 'Flight', deals with the aftermath of the killing. At first Bigger seems to be in control; his answers to questions successfully distance him from any knowledge of Mary's disappearance, and he even tests his power by sending her parents a ransom note. But when the police gets interested in the furnace he panics. They discover some unburnt bones and Bigger flees, thereby admitting his guilt. The end of Book Two forms the climax of the book's physical action, as Bigger, now the object of a city-wide manhunt, first rapes and murders his black girlfriend and is then, eventually, cornered, like a caged animal.

We have seen how, in *Black Boy*, Wright identified a 'trembling sense of fate' as being one of the legacies bequeathed to him by black Christianity. If Bigger's capture is the physical climax of the narrative, his trial and condemnation to death are its moral climax. Central to this last part of the book, titled 'Fate', is the relationship between Bigger and his Communist lawyer, Max. Max's long, eloquent speech to the court in defence of Bigger carries the explicit political burden of the novel. Bigger's character and actions, he argues, are the product of his environment, his poverty and degraded upbringing.

Wright's putting this speech into the mouth of a white man, addressing other white men, has been controversial. In his essay 'Many Thousands Gone', James Baldwin described it as 'one of the most desperate performances in American fiction'. For Max, Bigger Thomas is a mirror image of white society, the human price of capitalist oppression. He is a warning, a projection of the (white) readership's darkest fears. He is, in Baldwin's words, 'a monster created by the American republic'. And this is the essence of

Baldwin's and Ellison's strictures concerning the novel – that in creating Bigger, Wright was creating not a whole human being but a puppet of white neuroses. In Baldwin's words:

> Bigger has no discernible relationship to himself, to his own life, to his own people, nor to any other people ... and his force comes ... from his significance as the incarnation of a myth.

And Ellison surely gets to the heart of the matter when he writes: 'Wright could imagine Bigger, but Bigger could not possibly imagine Richard Wright. Wright saw to that.'

The criticism that Bigger Thomas is merely an automaton, a thing without a life of its own, is clearly true of the first part of *Native Son*. Indeed, the main point of the picture that Wright paints of Bigger's life is to show how much he is the victim of impulse, of forces that come from outside himself. All he can do is react, which he does with ever-increasing violence. He is hemmed in physically and economically by the ghetto. (An image that is used repeatedly is that of Bigger and his friends gazing up at an aeroplane and dreaming of becoming pilots. But they know that they never will, for only white boys become pilots.) And at a deep psychological level he is subject, too, to outside forces:

> These were the rhythms of his life: indifference and violence; periods of abstract brooding and periods of intense desire; moments of silence and moments of anger – like water ebbing and flowing from the tug of a far-away, invisible force.

'That was the way he lived,' Wright concludes. 'He passed his days trying to defeat or gratify powerful impulses in a world he feared.'

The image of Bigger as a compulsive automaton recalls the tradition of seeing the Negro as a creature of instinctual response, an *homme machine*. In its late nineteenth- and early twentieth-century manifestations, in Conrad and in the O'Neill of *The Hairy Ape*, this tradition acquires a modernist gloss. The Negro becomes the prime denizen of the urban jungle, a symbol of the link between our primitive origins and the atavism that seems to well to the surface of our increasingly fractured modern world. Bigger is part of that tradition, and the fact that the final summation of who he is seems to be put into the mouth of a white man can only increase the sense felt by Baldwin and Ellison that Wright was appealing to a white readership and reflecting back white psychological projections: in Wright's grim dialectic, Bigger is the antithesis to the white man, the shadow cast by the thesis of white racial purity. For Baldwin, Wright's making Bigger a monster falls into the trap of admitting 'that Negro life is in fact as debased and impoverished as our theology claims'.

'Many Thousands Gone', Baldwin's essay on *Native Son*, doesn't do justice to the last few pages of the book, in which, for the first time, Bigger takes responsibility for his actions and appears as a human being rather than simply a monster. Why was Baldwin so unfair to Wright? It is impossible to understand Baldwin's critical battle with Wright without understanding how intensely personal it was. Baldwin identified with the older man, to the extent of seeing him as his father. He dreamed of the day when the battle between them would end:

> One day, Richard would turn to me, with the light of sudden understanding on his face, and say, 'Oh, *that's* what you mean.' ... [I]t would have been nothing less than that so universally desired, so rarely achieved reconciliation between spiritual father and spiritual son.

The essay from which this is taken, one of two obituaries of Wright he published in the early Sixties, is a remarkable document in the way it reveals the depth of Baldwin's identification with Wright. It was, as Baldwin freely admits ('he had never really been a human being for me, he had been an idol'), an identification based not on who Wright was as a person, but on what he represented as a projection of what Baldwin felt himself to be and also of what he feared he might become. He saw him as someone who had come from the same background and who had the same vocation:

> I had identified with him long before we met: in a sense by no means metaphysical, his example had helped me to survive. He

was black, he was young, he had come out of the Mississippi nightmare and the Chicago slums, and he was a writer.

But as Baldwin adds when he describes Wright as being an idol to him: '[I]dols are created to be destroyed.' 'Alas, Poor Richard' turns into a pretty comprehensive demolition of Wright's character and later achievements, especially of the way (as Baldwin saw it) he had retreated into a cocoon of literary celebrity and lost touch with the realities of black life. But the violence of the attack is blurred by a prophetic identification: 'I could not help feeling: *Be careful. Time is passing for you, too, and this may be happening to you one day.*'[1]

When Baldwin writes about Richard Wright, he is essentially writing about himself, specifically an aspect of himself that he is reluctant to acknowledge and so projects on to the older man. This can be seen not just in the personal, but also in the political accusations that Baldwin makes against Wright. Wright, according to Baldwin, has fallen into the trap of believing in the liberal dream. He has written in fulfilment of white expectations. Max's speech, which for Baldwin carries the burden of *Native Son*,

> is addressed to those among us of good will and it seems to say that, though there are white and blacks among us who hate each other, we will not; there are those who are betrayed by greed, by guilt, by blood lust, but not we; we will set our faces against them and join hands and walk together into that dazzling future when there will be no white or black. This is the dream of all liberal men, a dream not at all dishonourable, but, nevertheless, a dream.

But this, in fact, is Baldwin's dream, not Wright's. Bigger Thomas redeems himself, in the last few pages of the book, not through love or through a liberal dream – not by turning his back on reality – but by becoming fully what he is, by internalising that which has hitherto been turned outward in violent, reactive gestures. And this is what frightens the liberal Max. In Baldwin's

[1] According to at least one observer, this was indeed a prophetic identification, for it was what actually happened to Baldwin himself. See Peter Dailey's essay 'Jimmy' (*The American Scholar*, Winter 1994).

fiction, by contrast, we hear again and again the theme of love as a kind of redemption, a blotting out of those binary oppositions of black and white, innocence and guilt, that divide up reality. Baldwin shared with Wright a religious upbringing, and his outlook remained essentially Christian in a way that went beyond the oft-noted biblical cadences of his prose. Near the beginning of his first novel, *Go Tell It on the Mountain* (1953), the young protagonist John Grimes goes to the top of a hill in Central Park and looks down on New York:

> [W]hen he reached the summit he paused; he stood on the crest of the hill, hands clasped beneath his chin, looking down. Then he, John, felt like a giant who might crumble this city beneath his heel; he felt like a long-awaited conqueror at whose feet flowers would be strewn, and before whom multitudes cried, Hosanna! He could be, of all, the mightiest, the most beloved, the Lord's anointed; and he would live in this shining city which his ancestors had seen with longing from far away. For it was his; the inhabitants of the city had told him it was his; he had but to run down, crying, and they would take him to their hearts and show him wonders his eyes had never seen.

John's Bigger-like moment of anger, when he thinks he might crush the city, is short-lived. He enters into a dream, a dream in which he does not just walk hand in hand with the (white) inhabitants of the city, but is embraced by them and taken into their hearts.

Race was fundamental to Baldwin's writings, as it was to Wright's. The age-old antithesis of black and white was, for Baldwin, a social product, a creature of the imagination. He never – even at his most angry and rhetorically extreme – flirted with biological or essentialist definitions of 'blackness'. But at the same time, race was a living reality in the contemporary world, and to ignore that fact was to be an accomplice to it. Baldwin saw his own role as prophetic, as bearing witness to the collective suffering of African-Americans. This romantic identification was purposefully dramatic and sometimes abandoned literal truth altogether, as in this speech to the Cambridge Union in 1965: 'I am speaking very seriously, and this is not an overstatement: I picked cotton, I carried it to the market, I built the railroads under someone else's whip . . .' Reactions to such statements varied. Many fell under the spell of his extraordinary personality, others did not. For the younger African-American novelist Ishmael Reed, Baldwin was 'a hustler who comes on like Job'.

One scene is played out again and again in Baldwin's novels, stories, essays and – as one of his biographers, James Campbell, testifies at first hand – in his life: the confrontation between the 'well-meaning' white liberal and the African-American for whom the white liberal's bland and easy 'colour blindness' is also a blindness to the terrible burden of history. Often in the fiction, to add to the drama of the confrontation, the pair are lovers. In *Another Country* (1962), the role of witness, of tormentor of the white liberal conscience, is given to Ida Scott, a jazz singer. And the history to which she is continually recalling attention is both collective and personal. The first fifth of the book tells the story of her musician brother Rufus – of his abusive, mutually destructive relationship with a Southern white woman, and of how his sensitivity, in a racist society, leads him to throw himself off the George Washington Bridge. The rest of the book describes the emotional and sexual couplings and decouplings of Ida and of Rufus's white friends, and although these machinations are disconnected from Rufus's suicide, that event casts a pall of guilt over these people. Perhaps they could have saved him, could have understood him more, could have loved him more. But they couldn't, according to Ida, because of the abyss of colour separating them. The way in which Ida harks back to this is repetitive, almost ritualistic:

> [Vivaldo] was silent for a moment. Then, 'You're never going to forgive me, are you? for your brother's death.'
> Then she, too, was silent. He said, 'I loved your brother, too, Ida. You don't believe that, I know, but I did. But he was just a man, baby. He wasn't a saint.'
> 'I never said he was a saint. But I'm black, too, and I know

how white people treat black boys and girls. They think you're
something for them to wipe their pricks on.' ...
　'After all this time we've been together,' he said, at last, 'you
still think that?'
　'Our being together doesn't change the world, Vivaldo.'
　'It does,' he said, 'for me.'
　'That,' she said, 'is because you're white.' ...
　'You stop that. You stop trying to kill me. It's not my fault
I'm white. It's not my fault you're black. It's not my fault he's
dead.'

And again:

Ida leaned forward and lit a cigarette with trembling hands, then
gestured out the window. 'I bet you think we're in a goddam
park. You don't know we're in one of the world's great jungles.
You don't know that behind all them damn dainty trees and
shit, people are screwing and fixing and dying ... And you
don't know it, even when you're told; you don't know it, even
when you see it.'
　[Cass] felt very far from Ida, and very small and cold. 'How
can we know it, Ida? How can you blame us if we don't know?
... There were hardly any coloured people in the town I grew
up in – how am I to know?'

One formulation of this was, according to those who knew him, a
favourite of Baldwin's in conversation:

'What you people don't know,' [Ida] said, 'is that life is a *bitch*,
baby. It's the biggest hype going. You don't have any experience
in paying your dues and it's going to be rough on you, baby,
when the deal goes down. There're lots of back dues to be
collected, and I know damn well you haven't got a penny saved.'

Baldwin had come up from the streets of Harlem. He had paid
his dues, and this gave him the moral authority to bear witness.
Whites had not paid their dues. All his life, Baldwin was caught
between his desire for a colour-blind society (he was, in that sense,
a liberal) and his knowledge that white liberals, who professed to

want the same thing, had not gone through the painful process of confrontation with their own history that was necessary for such a society to be achieved. This was the great dilemma with which Baldwin wrestled: race was everything, and it was nothing.

But how were black and white to confront and overcome their history? Was it even possible? History – the history that lives on in the colour of people's skin – is the ghost at Baldwin's feast, the spectre that haunts his interracial 'welcome table'. But Baldwin's sense of history was in a way profoundly unhistorical. During the last twenty years of his life he often talked about a novel he was planning that would be set during the time of slavery. But like a number of other projects he discussed at that time, it never got written. Since the 1960s, many African-American writers have drawn strength and inspiration from a rediscovered black literary and cultural tradition. Baldwin, by contrast, was strangely uninterested in these precursors. In the address to Cambridge students quoted above, Baldwin recalls being 'taught in American history books that Africa had no history and that neither had I'. 'Of course,' he continues, 'I believed it. I didn't have much choice. These were the only books there were.' But those weren't in fact the only books. There were books by W. E. B. Du Bois and others that affirmed the positive value of African diasporic cultural traditions. About these Baldwin is largely silent. Music and the black church were important to him, of course – particularly to the style of his rhetoric – but as far as black Christianity is concerned, it is portrayed in *Go Tell It on the Mountain* and elsewhere as more curse than blessing.

Black history was not, for Baldwin, a 'heritage', a place you went to feel good about yourself; it was, rather, a place of unremitting hostility and struggle, a wasteland of slavery, lynchings and oppression. In this respect he is with Wright. And Baldwin's conception of history was also essentially static. In his essay 'White Man's Guilt', he writes that 'the great force of history comes from the fact that we carry it within us . . . History is literally present in all that we do.' The past is not a process, a flux of external social movements, but something internalised, a devil inside us with which we all – black and white – must struggle. It was in this sense that Baldwin's view of history was metaphysical and religious rather than truly historical. In the tradition of the nineteenth-century radical abolitionists – and sharing their evangelical background – Baldwin saw America's only possible salvation from its racial sickness as lying primarily not in political campaigns or economic pressures but in the individual, in a personal agony of confession and expiation. The white man's guilt was Baldwin's instrument, and he played it with all the passionate eloquence at his command.

Baldwin failed to move convincingly beyond the racial dilemma he presented with such fire and brilliance in *Go Tell It on the Mountain*, *Going to Meet the Man* and the early essays. Reading the later Baldwin, one gets the impression that our fallen nature is stained into our skins by the weight of our fathers' misdeeds, and that nothing in this world can remove them. Racial prejudice becomes a kind of original sin. *Another Country*, it is true, has a feel-good ending, with intimations that love is something stronger and more enduring than hatred and guilt. But it also has to be said that Baldwin's writing is at its most crassly romantic in the latter parts of this novel, with 'love' reduced to an unlovely mixture of sex and sentiment. He was better at portraying the problem than its solution.

Towards the end of his life, according to at least one observer, the religious bent that was always there in his outlook and writing came to the fore, acquiring as it did so an apocalyptic hue. It would indeed be 'the fire next time', and that reckoning was something to be looked forward to. 'If I'm to be honest,' he told an interviewer, '– one can't but feel, no matter how deeply one distrusts the feeling, that the holocaust, the total levelling, salvation by fire, "no remission of sins save by the shedding of blood," may be the only hope.'

In 1957, Normal Mailer published an – at the time – notorious essay titled 'The White Negro'. The White Negro was the hipster, a man (in all Mailer's language and assumptions it has to be a man) whose commitment to spontaneity, to the exigencies of the eternal present moment, has overcome all societal restrictions. This man, according to Mailer, is the American existentialist. Courage and nerve are cool, and life is a never-ending, restless journey. The hipster is 'a frontiersman in the Wild West of American night life'. Mailer presents two paradigms for this new, peculiarly modern, psychological type. One is the psychopath, and the other is the Negro. They are interlinked, because 'psychopathy is most prevalent with the Negro'. Psychopathy brings to hipsterism a lack of inhibition and an insatiable hunger for immediate orgasmic experience. The Negro fleshes this out, as it were, with history and culture:

> Knowing in the cells of his existence that life was war, nothing but war, the Negro (all exceptions admitted) could rarely afford the sophisticated inhibitions of civilization, and so he kept for his survival the art of the primitive, he lived in the enormous present, he subsisted for his Saturday night kicks, relinquishing the pleasures of the mind for the more obligatory pleasures of the body, and in his music he gave voice to the character and quality of his existence, to his rage and the infinite variations of joy, lust, languor, growl, cramp, pinch, scream and despair of his orgasm.

For Mailer, 'The White Negro' was 'one of the best things I have done', and it is certainly compelling in the way that it articulates without embarrassment or inhibition a major myth of our time. The black as urban outlaw, as sexual outlaw – this was the image uppermost in the minds of those who read *Nigger Heaven* or *Home to Harlem* in the 1920s, and in the minds of the post-war Beats. It is an image projected by many black artists themselves, with various degrees of connivance, from the 'blaxploitation' films of the 1970s to the gangsta rappers of the present day. In 'The Black Boy Looks at the White Boy', a highly personal essay on Mailer by Baldwin, Baldwin expresses his 'fury that so antique a vision of the blacks should, at this late hour, and in so many borrowed heirlooms, be stepping off the A-train'. And most devastatingly, he remarks that '[Mailer's] glorification of the orgasm was but a way of avoiding all the terrors of life and love'. But although Baldwin may reject the way Mailer deals in stereotypes, the two writers do have something fundamental in common. They share an apocalyptic vision of the world, and a belief that blacks have a special part to play in that apocalypse. Baldwin's apocalypse is moral, a day of reckoning when unpaid dues will have to be paid. Mailer's apocalypse involves a massive release of previously repressed or restricted energy, primarily sexual. Here we hear him sounding – not a million miles away from Baldwin – like an Old Testament prophet:

> With this possible emergence of the Negro, Hip may erupt as a psychically armed rebellion whose sexual impetus may rebound against the antisexual foundation of every organized power in America, and bring into the air such animosities, antipathies, and new conflicts of interest that the mean empty hypocrisies of mass conformity will no longer work. A time of violence, new hysteria, confusion and rebellion will then be likely to replace the time of conformity.

Both Baldwin and Mailer address their jeremiads to white liberals, identifying their past sins and warning of retribution. And both call on imaginative conceptions of the Negro that are part of that liberal tradition and that date back to the anti-slavery culture of the eighteenth century. Baldwin's Negro is the redemptive figure, the figure whose suffering – now actively psychological and spiritual rather than merely passively physical – bears witness to the moral failings of society. Although Baldwin published a damning criticism of the particular way in which Harriet Beecher Stowe presents Negro characters in her novel, it is equally clear that *Uncle Tom's Cabin* was an important book to him, and that he shared with Stowe a view of human history and of the Negro's place in it that drew heavily on the evangelical tradition. Mailer's Negro is the obverse of this. His is the vengeful, violent Negro, the Negro of brute physical reaction that was always an important part of the abolitionists' warnings about slavery. Mailer identifies himself as a 'radical' rather than a liberal, and berates liberalism for ignoring the violence in society. But liberal writers have always been obsessed with violent, apocalyptic imagery, with warnings as to what will flow from the dissolution of society. (And some writers come to fall in love with the imagery, to treat it as an end in itself, just as de Sade revelled in the pain that was part of the imaginative equipment of sentimentalism.) Mailer's placing himself outside the liberal tradition in 'The White Negro' is essentially a rhetorical device, a means by which to give his warnings greater weight.

An important attribute of the Negro-Hipster, for Mailer, is the way his consciousness is plugged into immediate experience. Again one is reminded of eighteenth-century formulations, of the idea that the slave is a creature without cultural or personal memory, a creature of instinct and reaction. Whether one sees this as a good thing or a bad will depend on whether one sees Nature, in the sense of human nature untrammelled by social convention, as benevolent or threatening. For the eighteenth-century sentimentalists it is benevolent – as it is, ultimately, for Mailer:

> [The Negro-Hipster] exists in the present, in that enormous present which is without past or future, memory or planned intention, the life where a man must go until he is beat, where he must gamble with his energies through all those small or large crises of courage and unforeseen situations which beset his day, where he must be with it or doomed not to swing.

Mailer reproduces, too, the sentimental notion that the Negro is 'more in touch' with his feelings than the white, making it the basis of his naturalised version of existentialism. 'To be an existentialist,' he writes, 'one must be able to feel oneself – one must know one's desires, one's rages, one's anguish, one must be aware of the character of one's frustration and know what would satisfy it.' This is indeed a power-crazed version of existentialism. Existentialism in its purer versions is concerned with discovering what one is *not* rather than what one is.

Hipsterism, for Mailer, is about power, about the power to identify who one is and to manipulate the world in order to allow that natural self its fullest and most extreme expression. It is about victory rather than defeat, success rather than failure:

> The unstated essence of Hip, its psychopathic brilliance, quivers with the knowledge that new kinds of victories increase one's

power for new kinds of perception; and defeats, the wrong kinds of defeats, attack the body and imprison one's energy until one is jailed in the prison air of other people's habits, other people's defeats, boredom, quiet desperation, and muted icy self-destroying rage.

This contrasts strongly with Césaire and Genet, for whom 'new kinds of perception' emerge from failure and defeat, a defeat that is re-enacted as ritual. And this defeat consists precisely in the failure to transcend the mask and discover a 'true self'. In place of Mailer's narcissistic vision of a self in love with itself (Mailer's 'good orgasm' is essentially onanistic, since its external circumstances are mere material to be manipulated to that end), Césaire and Genet portray a loss of the self, a realisation of the void that lies behind the mask. And in O'Neill's *All God's Chillun Got Wings*, Jim achieves a kind of tragic victory by committing himself to the mask, by becoming it, in the form of his marriage to Ella. '[T]he prison air of other people's habits, other people's defeats, boredom, quiet desperation, and muted icy self-destroying rage' – these words that Mailer uses to describe a Hipster's defeat could be used to describe Jim's triumph.

In an astute reply to Mailer's essay, Ned Polsky – as well as making the simple point that by Mailer's definitions of 'squares' and 'Hipsters' 'most Negroes are also squares' – identifies what is really wrong with Mailer's hipsterism as regards race:

> Even in the world of the hipster the Negro remains essentially what Ralph Ellison called him – an invisible man. The white Negro accepts the real Negro not as a human being in his totality, but as the bringer of a highly specified and restricted 'cultural dowry' ... In so doing he creates an inverted form of keeping the nigger in his place.

This 'cultural dowry' – made up of spontaneity, emotional warmth and directness, physicality, sex, drugs, violence – was to become increasingly important in the general cultural climate of the Sixties. In *The Confessions of Nat Turner* (1967), possibly the most publicly controversial American novel of that decade, William

Styron portrayed the leader of the 1831 slave revolt as a man of extremes, an existential anti-hero, even a psychotic. The journalistic storm that the novel prompted – Styron was bitterly attacked by a group of younger African-American intellectuals, though defended by older ones such as Baldwin and John Hope Franklin – was in part over the mere fact that a well-known white Southern author had taken on the voice of an iconic figure of black resistance. But there were also well-directed criticisms of Styron's use of historical fact, and in particular of the way he cranks up the themes of religious mania and sexual obsession (with a young white woman) in his portrayal of Turner. Whether consciously or not, in putting together the ingredients for an intelligent, high-brow potboiler Styron had drawn on old images that, in the volatile atmosphere of Sixties America, were finding new imaginative power.

In addition to these transgressive versions of the Negro's 'cultural dowry' it was also still possible to draw on the old sentimental and abolitionist idea that the Negro embodied moral redemptiveness. Rufus in *Another Country* is one such black-as-Christ-figure, as is the protagonist of John Clellon Holmes's characteristic novel of the Beat period, *The Horn* (1958). (Holmes's first novel, *Go* (1952), had established him as a chronicler of the times, including as it did fictionalised portraits of his friends Jack Kerouac and Allen Ginsberg.) In *The Horn*, an alcohol- and drug-riddled saxophone player stumbles to his martyrdom, the whole weight of the failed American Dream around his neck, and dies in a nightclub, still clutching his horn.

Baldwin, Mailer, Styron and Holmes all write from within the notion of this cultural dowry – emphasising certain elements of it, giving it imaginative force and complication, but at bottom taking it on its own terms. They stand four-square within the liberal tradition. By the end of the Sixties, however, we find two of America's leading novelists adopting a more self-conscious, postmodern attitude towards racial imagery. John Updike's *Rabbit Redux* and Bernard Malamud's *The Tenants* (both 1971) are, in very different ways, reports on the American *Zeitgeist* that focus on how whites and blacks perceive each other. They unearth the subconscious, the subtext, of white liberalism, holding it up for ironic scrutiny, even ridicule. The change of direction, which is never completed in Updike's novel, is aesthetic as much as political, a turn towards that tricksterism and ironic trying-on of masks that, as we saw in the last chapter, has been the true 'cultural dowry' of blacks to modern culture.

'When the century closes in a few years,' the British novelist Ian McEwan has written, 'and we consider who has best captured America in its second half, I think it will be seen to have been Updike.' Another critic has described Updike's work as an 'index to the fears and dreams of middle-America during the last thirty years'. The picture painted here is of Updike the realist, the chronicler of American life. In his autobiography, he writes of 'I whose stock in trade as an American author included an intuition into the mass consciousness and an identification with our national fortunes'. In the four 'Rabbit' novels, the passage of Harry 'Rabbit' Angstrom's life is indeed pinned to a backdrop of national events, national preoccupations. Written a decade apart – at the end of the Fifties, the Sixties, the Seventies and the Eighties – they consciously create in Rabbit a lens through which the big picture can be seen. In *Rabbit Is Rich* (1981), for example, Rabbit's ownership of a Toyota dealership is a way into two of the 'big themes' of Seventies America – the oil crisis and the collapse of the smokestack industries. In *Rabbit Redux*, Updike's summary of the Sixties, technological change features, through Rabbit's losing his job as an old-style printer. And Vietnam is there, especially through Rabbit's acerbic exchanges with the peacenik Charlie Stavros, who is screwing his wife. The 1969 moon landing, and a screening of Stanley Kubrick's *2001: A Space Odyssey*, recur also as sublime counterpoints to the small goings-on down below. And there is one public topic that predominates: race.

But language, of course, is never a clean window on the world. Updike's richly textured prose, full of whorls and graces, is more like a net, catching with artful ease the smallest inclination of life – a smell, a feel, a slippage of emotion. There is no transparency here. Updike's net has a substance and density itself, made up of an essentially elegiac vision of life. This is his characteristic tone, his characteristic thought. The immediate world around us, the domestic, ordinary world, is an Eden from which we are exiled even as we move in the midst of it. We are exiled by time, and by the depthless, dark motions of nature within us. These motions bring us brushing against the bright roughness of the world – a quality captured particularly brilliantly in Updike's epiphanic prose – then take us away again. The moon can stand for these dark undercurrents, or sex, or death. Updike's prose oscillates constantly between enchantment and disenchantment, between Eden and the Fall.

Like Baldwin and Mailer, Updike's imagination in *Rabbit Redux* is apocalyptic. The apocalypse is personal and domestic, but no less apocalyptic for that. Rabbit discovers that Janice, his wife, is being unfaithful. Janice moves out, and Rabbit is left alone with his son, Nelson. His life begins to go into a nose dive, to spin out of control. He is approached one day at work by Buchanan, a Negro, who commiserates with him ('Gettin' any tail? . . . Man has to have tail.') and invites him for a drink at a local bar. There Rabbit is presented with the Negroes' 'cultural dowry' – drugs, sex and the threat of violence. He has begun his Fall. He meets Babe, an old singer, and Skeeter, a goateed young man who has a line in laconic black argot. He also meets Jill, a young white drop-out for whom, it is hinted, Babe or Skeeter may be pimping. He takes her home to bed. She stays. And then one day she brings Skeeter back to Rabbit's house, Skeeter who has jumped bail and is on the run from the police. The strange domestic community thus formed – the white man; the black man; the available white girl between them; Nelson, the kid, observing with wonder and horror from his position of innocence – has an archetypal quality, plugging into old, basic scenarios of interracial sexual competition. Updike is aware of these echoes, and amplifies them.

Part of the humour and surrealism of the set-up arises from Rabbit's primitive attitude towards black people. Rabbit is not an intellectual, he is Everyman, or at least Everywhiteman – a mixture of exquisite individuality of experience and lumpen generality of thought. And Rabbit's view of African-Americans is introduced early, when the scene is still being set. Getting close to his thoughts gives Updike the chance to shock – perhaps even to give his white middle-class readership an illicit shock of recognition:

> The bus has too many Negroes. Rabbit notices them more and more. They've been here all along, as a tiny kid he remembers streets in Brewer you held your breath walking through, though they never hurt you, just looked; but now they're noisier. Instead of bald-looking heads they're bushy. That's O.K., it's more Nature, Nature is what we're running out of . . . They are a strange race. Not only their skins but the way they're put together, loose-jointed like lions, strange about the head, as if their thoughts are a different shape and come out twisted even when they mean no menace. It's as if all these Afro hair bushes and gold earrings and hoopy noise on buses, seeds of some tropical plant sneaked in by the birds were taking over the garden. His garden.

Rabbit's views – on Vietnam, on blacks – are shocking, deliberately shocking, to the liberal readership of John Updike's novels. There is a sense of something dark and unspoken being dragged into the glare of public print. There is also a dimension of class to it, since Updike's readership (his mode of irony makes the assumption itself) is more likely to be composed of educated professionals than obsolescent printworkers like Rabbit. One recalls the strain in anti-slavery fiction and poetry of the late eighteenth and early nineteenth centuries – Anna Maria Mackenzie's *Slavery* was a stark example, and, at a popular level, *Inkle and Yarico* – that associated sensibility with social refinement, and prejudice with social debasement. Updike oscillates between an intimate identification with Rabbit's consciousness and an awareness of his context.[1]

---

[1] Lest this sociological reading of what Rabbit is about be thought too concerned, in a characteristically English way, with nuances of class, there is the testimony of 'On Not Being a Dove', the section of Updike's memoirs dealing with his own Rabbitish political inclinations: 'There was a small, scarcely noticed difference . . . between the Harvard-Radcliffe Democrats and me that was to emerge in the Vietnam years: they, Unitarian or Episcopalian or Jewish, supported Roosevelt and Truman and Stevenson out of enlightenment, *de haut en bas*, whereas in my heart of hearts, I, however veneered with an education and button-down shirts, was *de bas*. They, secure in the upper-middle class, were Democrats out of human

The central section of *Rabbit Redux*, titled 'Skeeter', has such a sense of surrealism that even time seems to have taken on a different dimension, the members of the menage engaging in all-night political discussions, arguments and role-playing games that spin off into sex and drug-taking. In an Introduction to a recent complete edition of the Rabbit tetralogy, Updike draws attention to two characteristically Sixties motifs operating here. The first is the moon trip, happening on the TV all the while. It is there, available, as a metaphor for the 'trip', the strange inner journey or escape, that Rabbit, Jill and Skeeter are on. The second is the 'teach-in'. On a shelf Skeeter has lined up his books – *The Selected Writings of W. E. B. Du Bois, The Wretched of the Earth, Soul on Ice, The Life and Times of Frederick Douglass*. His whizz through black American history, for Rabbit's benefit, is pure vaudeville. ('Down South, one big nigger barbecue ... Some nigger didn't hop off the sidewalk and lick up the tobacco juice whenever the town trash spit, he was tucked into a chain gang and peddled to the sheriff's brother-in-law cheaper than an alligator egg.') He gets Rabbit to read out extracts from Civil War speeches, passages from Frederick Douglass. The books themselves are like masks, props, and the staginess – the role-playing, the role-swapping – is continually brought back to the reader's attention. ('You're just gorgeous, right? You're gone to be our big nigger tonight. As a white man, Chuck, you don't amount to much, but niggerwise you groove.') The theatricality becomes Grand Guignol; while Rabbit reads from Frederick Douglass, Skeeter masturbates and almost rapes Jill. Things are truly falling apart. Rabbit's learning-curve is getting steep. The trip has become a bad one.

The teach-in reaches its final lesson with a staged sex scene. 'You want to be a good nigger, right?' Skeeter asks Rabbit. He strips off, strips Jill too:

> 'Okay,' Skeeter says. 'Now here's you. You is a big black man sittin' right there. You is chained to that chair. And I, I is white

sympathy and humanitarian largesse, because this was the party that helped the poor. Our family had simply *been* poor, and voted Democrat out of crude self-interest' (*Self-Consciousness* (Penguin, London, 1990), p. 113).

as snow. Be-hold.' . . . 'And this little girl here,' he calls, 'is black as coal. An ebony virgin torn from the valley of the river Niger, right? Stand up, honey, show us your teeth. Turn clean around.'

What Rabbit sees, dreamlike through the shadows, is filled with primal imagery. 'The black shadows of his hands glide into the white blur Jill is . . . A soft slap gilds the darkness, the whiteness revolves. Rabbit's eyes, enlarged, can sift out shades of light and dark . . .' He turns on the light and sees, starkly, Skeeter being fellated by Jill.

This is the end, the beginning of the apocalypse, for it isn't just Rabbit who has been watching. His white neighbours have been keeping an eye on Rabbit's new domestic arrangements, and they don't like what they see. One night, when Skeeter and Jill are alone, a couple of the local crackers fire-bomb the house. Skeeter escapes, but Jill burns. 'Redux' means 'brought back', and in a specific medical sense 'restored to health after a disease'. Rabbit is brought or led back from his trip; in the charred ruins of their house, he and his wife Janice are reconciled. The novel ends in resignation and sleep.

Though all the Rabbit novels – especially after the first, *Rabbit, Run* (1960) – are abreast of the wider world, in none of them does the *Zeitgeist* penetrate Rabbit's life with the violence that it does in *Rabbit Redux*. The intrusion of blackness, in the form of Skeeter, introduces a turn to melodrama, to the gothic, that marks the novel out from the elegiac realism, flecked with comedy, of the others in the series. The comedy of Skeeter's orations is brilliant but broader, much broader, than anything else in the tetralogy. Rabbit's 'trip' is a detour, not part of the main journey. As Updike himself comments, writing of the overall scheme of the Rabbit series: 'Skeeter, who takes over *Redux*, dwindles to a news item and a troubling memory; what later novel could hold him?' We have already seen, in the 'passing' novels of the early part of the century, how the theme of racial identity lends itself to melodrama, to a tragicomic sense of playing preassigned roles. Playing a role is what Skeeter does, with the difference that he knows it. As he tells it to Rabbit: 'Some white man see a black man he don't see a man he sees a *symbol*, right? All these people around here are walking around inside their own *heads . . .*'

The last thing that Updike is is a perpetrator of protest fiction. The interest of *Rabbit Redux* lies in the fact that it represents an attempt by a white author to write about race without buying into any of the available racial mythologies. Both Norman Mailer and James Baldwin articulate racial myths, hanging around the neck of blackness a baggage of significance, just as the saxophonist in John Clellon Holmes's *The Horn* has to carry around his neck not just his saxophone but the whole dead weight of the failed American Dream. Updike doesn't buy any of the myths, he merely notates their display in the person of the quick, chameleon-like Skeeter. If they are held up for anything, it is ridicule.

From the moment that Rabbit first encounters Skeeter, in the bar, he sees surfaces ('Some white man see a black man he don't see a man he sees a *symbol*, right?') rather than a whole, depthless individual:

> Rabbit wonders if this is how the young Negro really talks, wonders if there is a real way.

To some extent, because the narrative for the most part is so close to Rabbit's consciousness, these flatnesses represent Rabbit's own projections. But they are also how Skeeter, obsessed with varieties of racial language, with racial jokes, presents himself. In an essay on the Rabbit series, Updike has described Skeeter as 'a black rhetorician'. His blackness lies in his use of black language, and thus anticipates the postmodern 'blackness' of literary theorists such as Henry Louis Gates. Skeeter plays the 'dozens' to the hilt.

All Updike's characters have mystery. He has that knack, common to great novelists, of suggesting a penumbra of reality, an unarticulated depth of presence, around and behind the words. But Skeeter is different. He is a mystery only in the sense of a puzzle. What, if anything, is behind the rhetoric, the verbal mask? Is there 'a real way'? It appears not. At times, in *Rabbit Redux*, Updike seems to be following the same path as Césaire and Genet, to be treating the racial mask non-naturalistically, as something not to be cast aside but to be entered into and plumbed through ritual. The exchanges between Rabbit, Skeeter and Jill have that ritualism, and in this section of the book, with its darkly comic intensity, Updike seems to be veering towards a different story, a different kind of novel.

But it doesn't go that way. In the first place, Updike wobbles badly in presenting us once, just once, with Skeeter's inner life, his 'real way', when he tells Rabbit and Jill about his experiences in Vietnam. 'Skeeter tells them about Vietnam. He tilts his head back as if the ceiling is a movie screen. He wants to do it justice but is scared to let it back in ... He knows he can never make it intelligible to these three ofays that worlds do exist beyond these paper walls.' Reading this, being given a peek behind the mask, the reader wants more. But all one gets is the wobble, the slippage.

More seriously, Rabbit comes back to earth. The trip is an outing, not a journey. Rabbit's encounter with Skeeter and all he represents is circumscribed not just by the errant husband's trajectory, but also by the way in which Skeeter himself is framed within a number of roles (black revolutionary, 'panther', pimp, drug pusher). Everything he does and says is loaded with cultural, historical significance. Even at the end, when Rabbit helps him to escape from the local police, the white man makes a joke about the Underground Railway. Updike gives Skeeter life, of course – he is too good a writer not to – but the life lies in the force and liveliness with which he acts out his roles, rather than in the background resonance we find with other Updike characters. With Skeeter everything is on the surface, including his blackness.

The appearance of Skeeter in *Rabbit Redux* marks a detour from the elegiac into the gothic and schematic, just as racial melodrama tips Harriet Beecher Stowe from sentimentalism to the gothic in the Legree plantation scenes of *Uncle Tom's Cabin*. Bernard Malamud's *The Tenants*, first published in 1971, has many parallels with *Rabbit Redux* in the way the main black character is presented as a conscious, ironic composite of stereotypes – some of them very old, but given new and vivid forms by the end of the Sixties. As in Updike, the injection of blackness is also an injection of the gothic, but the overall trajectory of *The Tenants* is quite different from that of *Rabbit Redux*. Where Updike returns to realism and the elegiac (it is not just Rabbit who is 'brought back to health', but the narrative itself), Malamud uses the assumption of racial masks to spin the narrative further away from realism in the limitless direction of postmodernist doubt. For *The Tenants* is not only a novel about racial insult and racial stereotype, it is also a book about writing.

Lesser is a Jewish writer in his mid-thirties who has spent the last nine years struggling with his third novel. His first novel was a success, his second wasn't. He is the sole remaining tenant of a derelict New York apartment block, his life a lonely mortification before the typewriter. Apart from his writing career, we learn virtually nothing about his past. His existence is ruled by his single-minded, mildly insane devotion to his novel – titled, ironically, *The Promised End*. He is his book. 'He tests his fate: He lives to write, writes to live.' And, more radically: 'Lesser writes the book and the book writes Lesser.' His novel is about love, but he begins to suspect that he is only writing about love because he has never experienced it. His landlord, Levenspiel, visits him regularly to beg and bribe him to move out so that the building can be demolished and the site developed. But Lesser refuses. It would interrupt work on his book.

One day, making the grim journey up the stairwell to his room, Lesser hears the familiar sound of a typewriter coming from one of the abandoned apartments. ('[F]or an odd minute [he] played with the thought he had left himself hard at work somewhere around while he was out getting his groceries.') The man at the typewriter is black, his name is Willie Spearmint, and he is pursuing the Holy Grail of a completed novel with the same zeal, if not the same pedantic doggedness, as Lesser. Fellow writers, at once competitors and comrades, the two men strike up a wary friendship.[1]

---

[1] Lesser's first encounter with Spearmint carries strong echoes of *Rabbit Redux*: 'No handshake though Harry was willing, in fact had stuck out his white paw. There it remained – extended. He was, in embarrassment, tempted to play for comedy: Charlie Chaplin, with his moth-eaten mustache, examining his sensitive mitt to see if it was a hand and not a fish held forth in greeting before he told it to come back home; but in the end Lesser withdrew it, no criticism of anyone intended or implied. Who said anybody had to shake somebody else's hand? That wasn't in the Fourteenth Amendment. He was tempted then to explain that he

The white writer and the black writer, alone in the apocalyptic landscape of the derelict apartment block: already the novel is far from realism, far into a world of fable. Like Skeeter, Willie Spearmint brings with him the blacks' cultural dowry of sex, drugs and the threat of violence. Lesser has a party in his apartment at which the only guests are those that Willie has invited – a black couple, Sam and Mary, and Willie's own girlfriend, the white (and Jewish) Irene. They smoke hash and Lesser makes passes at both the women, unsuccessfully. Later in the book there is another get-together, at which Lesser does succeed in bedding Mary. The black men at this party gather round Lesser threateningly and Willie tries to entice him into a game of the 'dozens', a trading of (racial) insults. Lesser backs down and slinks away, humbled and humiliated.

Lesser may be the lesser of the two in the transgression department, but when it comes to writing he has, as the published author, the upper hand. Willie brings the white man his novel to be read and criticised. Titled variously *A Nigger Ain't Shit*, *Missing Life* and *Black Writer*, it is an ur-African-American 'Life', a quintessence of what one might stereotypically expect from a black American (autobiographical) novel. ('. . . from "Downsouth Boy" to "Black Writer"; via progression "Upsouth," "Harlem Nights," "Prison Education". The short last chapter was entitled, "I Write for Black Freedom." The book was naturalistic confessional . . .') Lesser's conclusion is that the same thing has 'been written before,

had, as a boy, for years lived at the edge of a teeming black neighbourhood in South Chicago, had had a friend there; but in the end skipped it. Who cares?' (*The Tenants*, pp. 31–2)

'Jill rises, quick as smoke, from the chair with the silver threads. "You remember Skeeter?"
"How could I forget him?" [Rabbit] goes forward a step, his hand lifted ready to be shaken, the palm tingling with fear; but since Skeeter makes no move to rise, he lets it drop back to his side, unsullied.
Skeeter studies the dropped white hand, exhaling smoke from a cigarette . . . "I like it," Skeeter says. "I like your hostility, Chuck. As we used to say in Nam, it is my meat." ' (*A Rabbit Omnibus*, p. 298)
The refused handshake is a primal scene, analogous to the exasperation and hurt, on a larger scale, of Baldwin's lovers. What can a white liberal do?

and better, by Richard Wright, Claude Brown, Malcolm X, and in his way, Eldridge Cleaver'.

And so there is set up in *The Tenants* a debate on art, a debate between form and content, reason and passion. It is also a debate on the limits of empathy, on that sympathetic identification with the experience of suffering that was the basis of the sentimental aesthetic:

> Lesser asks Willie to grant him good will. 'I know how you feel, I put myself in your place.'
>
> In cold and haughty anger the black replies. 'No ofay motherfucker can put himself in *my* place. This is a *black* book we talkin about that you don't understand at all. White fiction ain't the same as *black*. It *can't* be.'
>
> 'You can't turn black experience into literature just by writing it down.'

To immediate experience are opposed the demands of form, of language. But in Lesser's position there is something defensive and contradictory. Through form, the universal in art, he can, he claims, put himself inside Willie's skin, inside his experience. Yet faced with the irate black man, he sets the two in opposition. The argument, Malamud implies, is a sterile one, the positions entrenched. The two writers, black and white, are dependent upon one another, like an object and its image in a mirror:

> 'If we're talking about art, form demands its rights, or there's no order and maybe no meaning . . .'
>
> 'Art can kiss my juicy ass. You want to know what's really art? *I* am art. Willie Spearman, *black man*. My form is *myself*.'
>
> They faced each other, their eyes reflecting their images . . .

In fact the confrontation between Willie and Lesser is less an argument than a ritual, something that is to be played out in action. Willie is hurt and made angry by Lesser's criticisms of his novel, but swallows his pride and comes back for further advice because he wants to use the technique that Lesser can teach him to further his black revolutionary ends, to articulate his radical blackness. Cleverly, Willie turns against him the sharp distinction that Lesser has drawn between form and content. Form is fickle. White form can be used to express black content:

'... I think this is the main way the blacks have to head along – to kill whites till those who are alive vomit with pain at the thought of what wrongs they have done us ... Now all I want you to do for me, Lesser, and I wouldn't be asking if we both wasn't writers, is not to spend any time criticizing the subject of any stuff I might show you, but to tell me the best way how I can write the same thing, with the same ideas, better. Only the form of it, in other words, dig?'

Lesser ... beheld in his dark thoughts Bill Spear, potential executioner, requesting him to midwife his bloody fable.

Hand in hand with the conflict between white and black over representation (who should represent whom? can white enter the skin of black?) goes sexual competition. As in *Rabbit Redux*, there is a triangle. Willie, absorbed by his writing, neglects his girlfriend Irene, and Lesser begins an affair with her. (Though even here the issues of empathy and identification are not absent. 'One thing about loving a black man,' Irene comments, 'there are times you feel black yourself.') After months of secret meetings, Lesser tells Willie about the affair. In his fury, Willie destroys Lesser's manuscript. Lesser retaliates by smashing Willie's typewriter with an axe. Willie disappears, and Lesser, laboriously, begins once again to assemble his novel. (Irene, now twice a writer's widow, moves to San Francisco in disgust.) Then, one day, Lesser discovers some familiar-looking discarded pages in the trash. Willie is back. Now the narrative spins even further from reality. There are dream sequences, in one of which Lesser dreams of a double wedding in which he will marry Mary and Willie will marry Irene. Willie's manuscript, retrieved from the trash by Lesser, become increasingly strange, increasingly driven (in a way that for Mailer in 'The White Negro' characterises the modern, apocalyptic age) towards the statement of polar extremes. One of them is titled 'Manifested Destiny':

black, white, black, white, black, white, black, white

(go to bottom of page),
black, whit, black, whit, black, whit, black, whit, black
(go to bottom of page)
black, whi, black, whi, black, whi, black, whi, black
(go to bottom of page)
black, wh, black, wh, black, wh, black, wh, black, wh
(go to bottom of page)
black, w, black, w, black, w, black, w, black
(go to bottom of page)
black black black black black black black black black
black black black black black black black black black
(make two pages)
BLACKBLACKBLACKBLACKBLACKBLACKBLACK
BLACKBLACKBLACKBLACKBLACKBLACKBLACK
BLACKBLACKBLACKBLACKBLACKBLACKBLACK
BLACKBLACKBLACKBLACKBLACKBLACKBLACK
(make five pages of this)
BLACKNESSBLACKNESSBLACKNESSBLACKNESS
BLACKNESSBLACKNESSBLACKNESSBLACKNESS
BLACKNESSBLACKNESSBLACKNESSBLACKNESS
BLACKNESSBLACKNESSBLACKNESSBLACKNESS
(This is the rest of the book).

The apartment block itself, too, has begun to metamorphose, to luxuriate, to grow vegetation within its walls. And then they meet. This is the end of the ritual, to which is added a bitterly ironic comment on their craft, on its ability to enter another's experience:

One night Willie and Lesser met in a grassy clearing in the bush. The night was moonless above the moss-dripping, rope-entwined trees. Neither of them could see the other but sensed where he stood. Each heard himself scarcely breathing.

'Bloodsuckin Jew Niggerhater.'

'Anti-Semitic Ape.'

Their metal glinted in hidden light, perhaps starlight filtering greenly through dense trees. Willie's eyeglass frames momentarily gleamed. They aimed each other accurate blows. Lesser felt his jagged ax sink through bone and brain as the groaning

black's razor-sharp saber, in a single boiling stabbing slash, cut
the white's balls from the rest of him.

Each, thought the writer, feels the anguish of the other.

THE END

The Tenants is a novel saturated in cultural significance. The
white man strikes the black in the brain, the faculty in which he
sees himself as superior. The black strikes the white in the genitals,
that lower, more atavistic area which Western culture has seen as
the domain of the black. 'Each, thought the writer, feels the
anguish of the other.' Willie and Lesser operate within a closed
system, reflecting each other, creating each other's significance.
And in this novel their significance is their whole being. There is
not the sense, the sense one gets in John Updike, that another
world – in Updike's case the lost Eden of American innocence – is
being suggested beyond the world of the book. Following 'The
End' of Willie and Lesser's mutual murder, the landlord Levenspiel
intones the word 'mercy' over and over again. This, to be sure, is
suggestive of something beyond the world of Willie and Lesser's
book(s), something behind the literary mask of cultural significance. But it is purely religious, an invocation of some higher
being's redeeming power over us humans. Willie and Lesser, the
two humans, destroy each other. They do not change, they do not
learn, they do not grow. It is all bleakly comic, of course, because
Willie and Lesser are novelists, are attempting to create through the
imagination other (fictional) people, and in particular their sufferings. All they succeed in creating is projections of their own
psyches. The very act of attempting to reach out beyond
themselves that is implied in the imaginative act results only in
their more profound isolation, both physical and psychic. This is
Malamud's irony, his black comedy.

Malamud's novel is not just about writing, of course, but also
about race as a mode of representation. The problem is how to be
both inside race and outside it at the same time, to experience and
not deny the existential reality of race as a shaping significance of
life, and at the same time to transcend it (and hence, in a sense,
deny it) in favour of some spiritual unity. This is the true liberal

dilemma. Updike's *Rabbit Redux* and Malamud's *The Tenants*, both written at the end of the Sixties, provide examples of American artists attempting this by a reinvention of racial stereotype as farce and absurdity. Malamud's is the more complete exorcism, with its postmodern questioning of all forms of representation, while Updike's narrative returns home to realism. But for both writers, the apocalyptic is the key to racial stereotype.

From Joseph Conrad's *Heart of Darkness*, reinterpreted by Francis Ford Coppola as *Apocalypse Now*, to contemporary images of social meltdown in the inner city, blacks have been associated in the white liberal mind with such an apocalypse, with the disappearance of order and reason down a vortex of violence and primitive instinct. It is an association in which key strands of the liberal imagination – the dire warnings of 'protest' literature; the fear, engendered by guilt, of black backlash – mesh with the Judaeo-Christian conception of time as linear and as leading to a once-and-for-all event: the Last Judgement. This – the opposition of time and the end of time – is perhaps Christianity's greatest dualism, and marks it out from those Eastern religions and philosophies for which time is cyclical or open-ended. It is in this context that blackness has spoken, to the Western imagination, of the beginning and end of things.

Sources

Baldwin, James, *Go Tell It on the Mountain* (Penguin, London, 1991). First published 1953.
— *Another Country* (Penguin, London, 1990). First published 1962.
— *The Price of the Ticket: Collected Nonfiction 1948–85* (Michael Joseph, London, 1985).
Campbell, James, *Talking at the Gates* (Faber, London, 1991).
Ellison, Ralph, *Shadow and Act* (Secker & Warburg, London, 1967).
Mailer, Norman, 'The White Negro', in *Advertisements for Myself* (Panther, London, 1968).
Malamud, Bernard, *The Tenants* (Eyre Methuen, London, 1972).
Updike, John, *Self-Consciousness: Memoirs* (Penguin, London, 1989).
— *Rabbit Redux*, in *A Rabbit Omnibus* (Penguin, London, 1991).
— *Rabbit Angstrom: A Tetralogy* (Everyman, London, 1995).
Wright, Richard, *Black Boy* (Harborough Publishing, London, 1959). First published 1945.
— *Uncle Tom's Children* (Harper Perennial, New York, 1993). First published 1938.
— *Native Son* (Harper Perennial, New York, 1993). First published 1940.

Epilogue

Beyond Race?

It was in the early part of this century that American writers like Horace Kallen and Randolph Bourne first put forward the idea of 'cultural pluralism'. They did so in opposition to the nativism embodied in a resurgent Ku Klux Klan and in the halting of mass immigration into the United States in 1924. This was also the period when writers of the Harlem Renaissance, partly influenced by the relativist anthropology of Franz Boas, were turning from the racialist formulations of black identity that one finds in the writings of nineteenth-century black nationalists (traces of them survive, as we have seen, in Du Bois's *Souls of Black Folk*) to what one might call a cultural black nationalism. And, crucially, this was also the era of modernism. Modernisms, one might more accurately say, because perhaps the only thing they had in common was a reaction to the universalism and complacency of Victorian culture. The cultural pluralism of the Harlem Renaissance and its white allies was a part of this reaction, a response to Anglo-Saxon cultural arrogance.

This sense of pluralism was essential to the modern movement. It is there in the ventriloquism and fractured layering of *The Waste Land* and *Ulysses*. It can be seen in the fractured montage style of Eisenstein and some French and German film-makers of the period. (Albert Cavalcanti's *Rien que les heures* (1926–7) and Walther Ruttmann's *Berlin: Symphony of a City* (1927) are the best-known examples, documentaries whose montage technique is aimed at conveying the complexity and vastness of modern city life.) It can be heard in the diversity and self-consciousness of concert music in the 1920s, with styles such as neoclassicism, jazz and various forms of the exotic adopted like masks, all with the effect of producing music that was cooler and more detached than the emotionally saturated, self-absorbed world of nineteenth-century romanticism.

The eruption of black culture into the mainstream of American life (and thereby, through the power of the media, European life) played an important part in the formation of this pluralism. Not only did black speech, music and dance provide a style to feed the polyglot appetite of modern culture, but the ambiguities and illusions involved in relations between black and white provided a model for the alienation and role-playing of contemporary life. We have seen in the case of 'passing' novels how the subject matter of race pushed writers towards absurdity even when they wanted to stay within the conventions of Victorian fiction. It was only in *Invisible Man* that that absurdity was to find full expression. But for a whole series of twentieth-century writers, blackness has been expressive of the sense that one must wear a mask before the world. In O'Neill the alienation has pessimistic, tragic dimensions, while for Césaire it is a heroic opportunity to choose and thereby transcend one's destiny. By Genet the motif of the mask is pushed further artistically, transformed almost into a hall of mirrors, while for Sartre the mask is less a mask than a weapon, something to be hurled at the opposition.

The raw material of this modern, ironic twist on racial identity was the existing European mythology of race. There were two aspects to this. There was the pseudo-scientific ordering of a hierarchy of races, an idea born in the eighteenth century and adapting itself in the Darwinian intellectual climate of the late nineteenth century into a more virulent and aggressive form.[1] But the language and emotional appeal of these pseudo-scientific formulations also drew on older, Christian ideas linking blackness

[1] For a profound evocation of the depths of European violence against Africa in the late nineteenth century see Sven Lindqvist, *'Exterminate All the Brutes'* (Granta, London, 1997). Lindqvist's book lends powerful support to Hannah Arendt's argument in *The Origins of Totalitarianism* that the precursors of fascism and the Holocaust are to be found in European imperialism.

with sin and defilement. These ideas not only fed aggressive racism, but seeped into the language and attitudes of those who saw themselves as friends of the Negro. Just as, for example, the story of the suppression of the African slave trade by the British cannot be told in terms of unalloyed benevolence, so the cultural history of race cannot be written in terms of a clearcut distinction between 'liberals' and 'racists'. Even somebody as independent-minded as Darwin could swing both ways, swayed by the force of Europe's deepest prejudices.

The liberal mythology of race developed its own character, influenced by the evangelical religion that played such an important role in the abolition movement, and by the ideas of Rousseau and others. Blacks represented a primitive naturalness, an authenticity, a democracy – they represented, in fact, all those things valued by liberals seeking to divest themselves of an old political order at home in Europe. Blackness was established as an emblem of projected desire. But the enthusiasm for these supposed positive traits proved short-lived. The writing was on the wall for 'nigger philanthropists', and by the late ninteenth century the European dehumanisation of the Negro had proceeded far enough for popular opinion to swallow the massacre at the Battle of Omdurman in 1898 (eleven thousand Sudanese killed, as against forty-eight British) and the sustained campaign of atrocity under Leopold II in the Belgian Congo. The gunboat, the automatic rifle and the dumdum bullet had provided Europeans with the modern means of mass killing. Staring into the moral abyss of Europe's actions in Africa, writers like Conrad and Rider Haggard became confused. The imperial progress began to look less like a process of rational and benevolent improvement, and more like a symptom of psychic disturbance or philosophical nihilism.

In an age of radical scepticism we have learned to pay attention to the historical context of liberalism. That John Locke was a shareholder in the Royal African Company, that Thomas Jefferson was a slave-owner, no longer look like incidental details. In a process that began in the early part of this century, the universal pretensions of liberalism – which drew historically on the universal claims of Christianity – have been challenged. The tradition of

European liberalism has been questioned and its claims to a grand overview challenged. Liberals have become multiculturalists, advocates of identity politics.

For the first multiculturalists, those who in the early part of this century welcomed the cosmopolitanism of the Harlem Renaissance, the issue of cultural identity was quite simple. It could be defined by a limited number of hyphenated categories. Now, however, the situation is more complex. Ethnicity no longer has the field to itself. It must be cross-referenced by gender, sexual orientation, age cohort, region and so on. In the end, perhaps, one identifies with no one but oneself.

One response to this conundrum is David Hollinger's idea of 'postethnicity'. Where multiculturalism emphasises an individual's fixed identity as a member of a minority group, promoting that individual's right *as a member of that group*, postethnicity treats identity as more problematic and fluid. Citing the increasing complexity of ethnic and racial affiliation – to be seen, for example, in the sense of distinctiveness felt by many mixed-race Americans – Hollinger describes a sense of ethnic affiliation that is both voluntary and revocable. Where the old model of pluralism respected inherited boundaries between groups, placing individuals within a limited series of racial or ethnic groups that are preserved and protected, the new cosmopolitanism 'promotes multiple identities, emphasizes the dynamic and changing character of many groups, and is responsive to the potential for creating new cultural combinations'.[1] Like religious affiliation, postethnicity is rooted in history – and, often, genealogy – yet is voluntary, and also flexible in the degree of identification with the group.

The idea of postethnicity accords with the modern tendency to see ethnicity as performative rather than essentialist. Blackness becomes a cultural style, a signifier that has floated free of its moorings in pigmentation. Stripped of any deterministic associations, its gift is the freedom (or, negatively, the alienation) of the mask. In his 'The Concept of Race as Applied to Social Culture' (1924) the leading philosopher of the Harlem Renaissance, Alain

[1] David A. Hollinger, *Postethnic America: Beyond Multiculturalism* (Basic Books, New York, 1995), pp. 3–4.

Locke, argued that increasing ethnicisation and assimilation could go hand-in-hand. The increasing black consciousness of the New Negro, in other words, was not necessarily a sign that African-Americans were ceasing to be American. Indeed, it was necessary for the establishment of a new, multicultural nation. Following on from Alain Locke, it is possible to see extreme expressions of 'blackness' not as a sign that divisions are growing greater, but rather as a healthy indication that divisions of the past are being exorcised. This lies at the heart of the contemporary debate on rap. For some commentators, such as Cornel West, rap is indicative of a corrosive nihilism in the black community. Others, like Henry Louis Gates, are inclined to take the violence and racism of some rap lyrics less at face value, and to place them instead in a performative and parodic tradition of black cultural expression. The difference between the two views is epistemological and aesthetic – to do with how we think we know the world and how we propose to celebrate it. To celebrate rap in the way that Gates or Spike Lee celebrates it is – to use a term that everybody understands but none can define – postmodern. It represents a new way of looking at the world and at the ways in which we define ourselves, but at the same time a way that is rooted in history through an awareness of the importance of image and representation. The racial past cannot be erased, but it can be rendered impotent.

Index